Classic
AMERICAN HERO STORIES

Classic

AMERICAN HERO STORIES

*Twelve Inspirational Tales
of American Heroism*

EDITED BY
STEPHEN VINCENT
BRENNAN

THE LYONS PRESS
GUILFORD, CONNECTICUT
AN IMPRINT OF THE GLOBE PEQUOT PRESS

The Lyons Press is an imprint of The Globe Pequot Press.

10 9 8 7 6 5 4 3 2 1

Printed in the United States of America

Library of Congress Cataloging-in-Publication Data

Classic American hero stories: eleven inspirational tales of
American heroism / edited by
    Stephen Brennan.
        p. cm.
    ISBN 1-59228-738-7 (trade pbk.)
1. Heroes—United States—Biography. 2. Courage—United
States. I. Brennan,
Stephen Vincent.

CT215.C57 2005
920.0073—dc22
[B]

                              20055044253

For Jen

Contents

CONTENTS

Introduction

No! let me taste the whole of it, fare like my peers
  The heros of old,
Bear the brunt, in a minute pay glad life's arrears
  Of pain, darkness and cold.

—Robt. Browning

It's night, and except within the circle of our fire, the darkness is all around us. Sure, there are long stretches of silence, when each of us is lost in his or her own private dream of their life. But then the wind stirs the embers and makes them redden and glow and something pops, and sparks arc up into the night (they seem to burn brightest just before they die—not a good omen) and we come to ourselves with a gentle start or shudder, and we remember one and other, and then one of us begins to speak. The old adage has it that "talk is cheap," but not tonight. On this night, dark as it is, and with just the merest scent of danger in the wind, our speaker begins a tale of one who is fearless and strong and determined.

And as we hear the story told, a kind of miracle occurs, not only do all of us within the sound of that voice become as one with the storyteller, but more strange still, we all imagine or discover ourselves to be the hero.

We've done this since the very beginning.

In antiquity the hero was most often child of the union of the human and the divine. He was a doer of mighty deeds, like Prometheus, who dared to steal the fire of the gods so that humankind might have heat and light—and paid the price. Or like Achilles, that great runner, free to choose his path, but finally, fated to his end. Hercules is a hero's hero. Like Beowulf—in a later time, he's a man of huge strength. He undertakes twelve nearly impossible labors, and wins through each of them, attaining much fame and honor. The story goes he dies tragically, poisoned by the very robes of honor that are the symbol of his heroism. In his life, Hercules does much good, but also wreaks much havoc; he does much harm. We sense that there is something unstable about a hero. Most often, he's a loner. He doesn't play well with others. He may well be too driven, too fierce, too on-task, or just plain too mighty for his own good, or for ours. We take this as a caution, and instead of giant killers, we tend to look for balance and judgement in our civic leaders. Perhaps this is why, in our own age, our elected leaders are rarely our heros. Of course, George Washington certainly was a hero, but John Adams certainly was not. In fact, it is not until Andrew Jackson is elected the seventh president that the country again chooses an honest-to-goodness hero as Head of State. We can count the genuine hero-presidents on the fingers of one hand. It may be that ultimately, we feel we can't afford to take the chance. One man's hero, may be another man's berserker.

Nowadays we recognize all kinds of heros. They may be comic or tragic. They may be folk-heros or sports-heros or war-heros. They may even be mere celebrities. And just as each age chooses or names its own heros, each of us has his/her own personal candidate. I may know someone of strength and ability and a mighty heart who has faced down one of life's great challenges, and thus I regard her as my hero. A father may be, and often is, a hero to his son. Generally though, we appreciate a hero best at some distance. You don't want to get too close, you may be disappointed. The great, up close, are mostly normal size. At home, even so great a man as Jesus (though we can't quite call him a hero) got no respect. Saint Mark tells us that when he went back to his hometown to preach the good news, the locals—all the people he'd known growing up—weren't buying it. They knew him too well. "From whence hath this man these things?" they complained, "Is this not the carpenter, the son of Mary?" Prompting Jesus to remark that "A prophet is not without honor, but in his own country, and among his own kin, and in his own house. And he could do there no mighty works." So too the hero at home. It's well said that no man is a hero to his valet, just as no one is ever really a hero to their spouse. Their very intimacy makes this impossible. The distance between them is all wrong, and celebrity, up close, is likely to wear a little thin.

And yet fame and celebrity are vital components in the making of a hero; celebrity in the lifetime of the hero, and fame for the ages to come. Ask yourself: if a hero falls in the forest, and nobody hears, does he make a sound? Or put another way: if a hero goes unrecognized, can he still be said to truly be a hero? I say—Yes. If a hero goes to her grave, and her mighty deeds go unrecalled by coming generations, is she also truly a hero? Yes, again. But the *classic heros* are the ones we remember and still tell stories on.

I offer you eleven stories, each of them based upon the life or deeds of a classic American hero. Each hero, in his or her own time, knew more celebrity than any reasonable person would dream of. Each of them is remembered still. Some are remembered differently than before. General Custer, at the time of the firefight at the Little Bighorn, was a national hero. Not so much today, let us say that we have reassessed. However, it is important to remember that in his day, he was a very big chief.

In this anthology I've chosen hero stories that are as different (in their telling) one from the other, as I could manage. In "Pocahontas" we have a careful and meticulous history (herstory) of the famous Indian princess, while the "Washington" story is mostly bull. Bull yes, but important bull. The purported biography from which this tale is excerpted was written by the famous Parson Weems, who fixed our general idea of George Washington for generations. Remember the apple tree and the lie that could not be told? He invented them both. The Nathan Hale story is almost abrupt in its brevity, as befits a hero we know almost nothing about. "Eddie Rickenbacker" is a true memoir of war in the skies above the Western Front, while "Buffalo Bill" is excerpted from a work billed as memoir, but was most probably written by someone else. My particular favorites are "David Crockett" from a wonderful popular history by John Abbott, and "Harriet Tubman," the bulk of which is rendered almost as a gospel opera.

The sky has gone from black to blue, and it is late now and the story has ended. As the children are asleep, there are no questions asked. We heave a collective shiver and we wrap ourselves more tightly in our skins and look for sleep. Out beyond the firelight's reach shadows move and flicker, there are noises off. But we are not afraid, we are heartened, and the campfire fairly blazes.

—*Stephen Vincent Brennan*
Thanksgiving 2004

Pocahontas

[CHARLES DUDLEY WARNER]

The simple story of the life of Pocahontas is sufficiently romantic without the embellishments which have been wrought on it either by the vanity of Captain Smith or the natural pride of the descendants of this dusky princess who have been ennobled by the smallest rivulet of her red blood.

That she was a child of remarkable intelligence, and that she early showed a tender regard for the whites and rendered them willing and unwilling service, is the concurrent evidence of all contemporary testimony. That as a child she was well-favored, sprightly, and prepossessing above all her copper-colored companions, we can believe, and that as a woman her manners were attractive. If the portrait taken of her in London—the best engraving of which is by Simon de Passe—in 1616, when she is said to have been twenty-one years old, does her justice, she had marked Indian features.

The first mention of her is in "The True Relation," written by Captain Smith in Virginia in 1608. In this narrative, as our readers have seen, she is not referred to until after Smith's return from the captivity in which Powhatan used him "with all the kindness he could devise." Her name first appears, toward the close of the relation, in the following sentence:

"Powhatan understanding we detained certain salvages, sent his daughter, a child of tenne yeares old, which not only for feature, countenance, and proportion, much exceedeth any of the rest of his people, but for wit and spirit the only nonpareil of his country: this hee sent by his most trusty messenger, called Rawhunt, as much exceeding in deformitie of person, but of a subtill wit and crafty understanding, he with a long circumstance told mee how well Powhatan loved and respected mee, and in that I should not doubt any way of his kindness, he had sent his child, which he most esteemed, to see mee, a Deere, and bread, besides for a present: desiring mee that the Boy [Thomas Savage, the boy given by Newport to Powhatan] might come again, which he loved exceedingly, his little Daughter he had taught this lesson also: not taking notice at all of the Indians that had been prisoners three daies, till that morning that she saw their fathers and friends come quietly, and in good termes to entreate their libertie.

"In the afternoon they (the friends of the prisoners) being gone, we guarded them (the prisoners) as before to the church, and after prayer, gave them to Pocahuntas the King's Daughter, in regard of her father's kindness in sending her: after having well fed them, as all the time of their imprisonment, we gave them their bows, arrowes, or what else they had, and with much content, sent them packing: Pocahuntas, also we requited with such trifles as contented her, to tel that we had used the Paspaheyans very kindly in so releasing them."

The next allusion to her is in the fourth chapter of the narratives which are appended to the "Map of Virginia," etc. This was sent home by Smith, with a description of Virginia, in the late autumn of 1608. It was published at Oxford in 1612, from two to three years after Smith's return to England. The appendix contains the narratives of several of Smith's companions in Virginia, edited by Dr. Symonds and overlooked by Smith. In one of these is a brief reference to the above-quoted incident.

This Oxford tract, it is scarcely necessary to repeat, contains no reference to the saving of Smith's life by Pocahontas from the clubs of Powhatan.

The next published mention of Pocahontas, in point of time, is in Chapter X and the last of the appendix to the "Map of Virginia," and is Smith's denial, already quoted, of his intention to marry Pocahontas. In this passage he speaks of her as "at most not past 13 or 14 years of age." If she was thirteen or fourteen in 1609, when Smith left Virginia, she must have been more than ten when he wrote his "True Relation," composed in the winter of 1608, which in all probability was carried to England by Captain Nelson, who left Jamestown June 2d.

The next contemporary authority to be consulted in regard to Pocahontas is William Strachey, who, as we have seen, went with the expedition of Gates and Somers, was shipwrecked on the Bermudas, and reached Jamestown May 23 or 24, 1610, and was made Secretary and Recorder of the colony under Lord Delaware. Of the origin and life of Strachey, who was a person of importance in Virginia, little is known. The better impression is that he was the William Strachey of Saffron Walden, who was married in 1588 and was living in 1620, and that it was his grandson of the same name who was subsequently connected with the Virginia colony. He was, judged by his writings, a man of considerable education, a good deal of a pedant, and shared the credulity and fondness for embellishment of the writers of his time. His connection with Lord Delaware, and his part in framing the code of laws in Virginia, which may be inferred from the fact that he first published them, show that he was a trusted and capable man.

Our own inference is, from all the circumstances, that Strachey began his manuscript in Virginia or shortly after his return, and added to it and corrected it from time to time up to 1616.

We are now in a position to consider Strachey's allusions to Pocahontas. The first occurs in his description of the apparel of Indian women:

"The better sort of women cover themselves (for the most part) all over with skin mantells, finely drest, shagged and fringed at the skyrt, carved and coloured with some pretty work, or the proportion of beasts, fowle, tortayses, or other such like imagry, as shall best please or express the fancy of the wearer; their younger women goe not shadowed amongst their owne companie, until they be nigh eleven or twelve returnes of the leafe old (for soe they accompt and bring about the yeare, calling the fall of the leaf tagnitock); nor are they much ashamed thereof, and therefore would the before remembered Pocahontas, a well featured, but wanton yong girle, Powhatan's daughter, sometymes resorting to our fort, of the age then of eleven or twelve yeares, get the boyes forth with her into the markett place, and make them wheele, falling on their hands, turning up their heeles upwards, whome she would followe and wheele so herself, naked as she was, all the fort over; but being once twelve yeares, they put on a kind of semecinctum lethern apron (as do our artificers or handycrafts men) before their bellies, and are very shamefac't to be seene bare. We have seene some use mantells made both of Turkey feathers, and other fowle, so prettily wrought and woven with threeds, that nothing could be discerned but the feathers, which were exceedingly warme and very handsome."

Strachey did not see Pocahontas. She did not resort to the camp after the departure of Smith in September, 1609, until she was kidnapped by Governor Dale in April, 1613. He repeats what he heard of her. The time mentioned by him of her resorting to the fort, "of the age then of eleven or twelve yeares," must have been the time referred to by Smith when he might have married her, namely, in 1608-9, when he calls her "not past 13 or 14 years of age." The description of her as a "yong girle" tumbling about the fort, "naked as she was," would seem to preclude the idea that she was married at that time.

The use of the word "wanton" is not necessarily disparaging, for "wanton" in that age was frequently synonymous with "playful" and "sportive"; but it is singular that she should be spoken of as "well featured, but wanton." Strachey, however, gives in another place what is no doubt the real significance of the Indian name "Pocahontas." He says:

"Both men, women, and children have their severall names; at first according to the severall humor of their parents; and for the men children, at first, when they are young, their mothers give them a name, calling them by some affectionate title, or perhaps observing their promising inclination give it accordingly; and so the great King Powhatan called a young daughter of his, whom he loved well, Pocahontas, which may signify a little wanton; howbeyt she was rightly called Amonata at more ripe years."

The Indian girls married very young. The polygamous Powhatan had a large number of wives, but of all his women, his favorites were a dozen "for the most part very young women," the names of whom Strachey obtained from one Kemps, an Indian a good deal about camp, whom Smith certifies was a great villain. Strachey gives a list of the names of twelve of them, at the head of which is Winganuske. This list was no doubt written down by the author in Virginia, and it is followed by a sentence, quoted below, giving also the number of Powhatan's children. The "great darling" in this list was Winganuske, a sister of Machumps, who, according to Smith, murdered his comrade in the Bermudas. Strachey writes:

"He [Powhatan] was reported by the said Kemps, as also by the Indian Machumps, who was sometyme in England, and comes to and fro amongst us as he dares, and as Powhatan gives him leave, for it is not otherwise safe for him, no more than it was for one Amarice, who had his braynes knockt out for selling but a baskett of corne, and lying in the English fort two or three days without Powhatan's leave; I say they often reported unto us that Powhatan had then lyving twenty sonnes and ten daughters, besyde a young one by Winganuske, Machumps his sister, and a great darling of the King's; and besides, younge Pocohunta, a daughter of his, using sometyme to our fort in tymes past, nowe married to a private Captaine, called Kocoum, some two years since."

This passage is a great puzzle. Does Strachey intend to say that Pocahontas was married to an Indian named Kocoum? She might have been during the time after Smith's departure in 1609, and her kidnapping in 1613, when she was of marriageable age. We shall see hereafter that Powhatan, in 1614, said he had sold another favorite daughter of his, whom Sir Thomas Dale desired, and who was not twelve years of age, to be wife to a great chief. The term "private Captain" might perhaps be applied to an Indian chief. Smith, in his "General Historie," says the Indians have "but few occasions to use any officers more than one commander, which commonly they call Werowance, or Caucorouse, which is Captaine." It is probably not possible, with the best intentions, to twist Kocoum into Caucorouse, or to suppose that Strachey intended to say that a private captain was called in Indian a Kocoum. Werowance and Caucorouse are not synonymous terms. Werowance means "chief," and Caucorouse means "talker" or "orator," and is the original of our word "caucus."

Either Strachey was uninformed, or Pocahontas was married to an Indian—a not violent presumption considering her age and the fact that war between Powhatan and the whites for some time had cut off intercourse between them—or Strachey referred to her marriage with Rolfe, whom he calls by mistake Kocoum. If this is to be accepted, then this paragraph must have been written in England in 1616, and have referred to the marriage to Rolfe it "some two years since," in 1614.

That Pocahontas was a gentle-hearted and pleasing girl, and, through her acquaintance with Smith, friendly to the whites, there is no doubt; that she was not different in her habits and mode of life from other Indian girls, before the time of her kidnapping, there is every reason to suppose. It was the English who magnified the imperialism of her father, and exaggerated her own station as princess. She certainly put on no airs of royalty when she was "cart-wheeling" about the fort. Nor does this detract anything from the native dignity of the mature, and converted, and partially civilized woman.

We should expect there would be the discrepancies which have been noticed in the estimates of her age. Powhatan is not said to have kept a private secretary to register births in his family. If Pocahontas gave her age correctly, as it appears upon her London portrait in 1616, aged twenty-one, she must have been eighteen years of age when she was captured in 1613. This would make her about twelve at the time of Smith's captivity in 1607-8. There is certainly room for difference of opinion as to whether so precocious a woman, as her intelligent apprehension of affairs shows her to have been, should have remained unmarried till the age of eighteen. In marrying at least as early as that she would have followed the custom of her tribe. It is possible that her intercourse with the whites had raised her above such an alliance as would be offered her at the court of Werowocomoco.

We are without any record of the life of Pocahontas for some years. The occasional mentions of her name in the "General Historie" are so evidently interpolated at a late date, that they do not aid us. When and where she took the name of Matoaka, which appears upon her London portrait, we are not told, nor when she was called Amonata, as Strachey says she was "at more ripe yeares." How she was occupied from the departure of Smith to her abduction, we can only guess. To follow her authentic history we must take up the account of Captain Argall and of Ralph Hamor, Jr., secretary of the colony under Governor Dale.

Captain Argall, who seems to have been as bold as he was unscrupulous in the execution of any plan intrusted to him, arrived in Virginia in September, 1612, and early in the spring of 1613 he was sent on an expedition up the Patowomek to trade for corn and to effect a capture that would bring Powhatan to terms. The Emperor, from being a friend, had become the most implacable enemy of the English. Captain Argall says: "I was told by certain Indians, my friends, that the great Powhatan's daughter Pokahuntis was with the great King Potowomek, whither I presently repaired, resolved to possess myself of her by any stratagem that I could use, for the ransoming of so many Englishmen as were prisoners with Powhatan, as also to get such armes and tooles as he and other Indians had got by murther and stealing some others of our nation, with some quantity of corn for the colonies relief."

By the aid of Japazeus, King of Pasptancy, an old acquaintance and friend of Argall's, and the connivance of the King of Potowomek, Pocahontas was enticed on board Argall's ship and secured. Word was sent to Powhatan of the capture and the terms on which his daughter would be released; namely, the return of the white men he held in slavery, the tools and arms he had gotten and stolen, and a great quantity of corn. Powhatan, "much grieved," replied that if Argall would use his daughter well, and bring the ship into his river and release her, he would accede to all his demands. Therefore, on the 13th of April, Argall repaired to Governor Gates at Jamestown, and delivered his prisoner, and a few days after the King sent home some of the white captives, three pieces, one broad-axe, a long whip-saw, and a canoe of corn. Pocahontas, however, was kept at Jamestown.

Why Pocahontas had left Werowocomoco and gone to stay with Patowomek we can only conjecture. It is possible that Powhatan suspected her friendliness to the whites, and was weary of her importunity, and it may be that she wanted to escape the sight of continual fighting, ambushes, and murders. More likely she was only making a common friendly visit, though Hamor says she went to trade at an Indian fair.

The story of her capture is enlarged and more minutely related by Ralph Hamor, Jr., who was one of the colony shipwrecked on the Bermudas in 1609, and returned to England in 1614, where he published (London, 1615) "A True Discourse of Virginia, and the Success of the Affairs there till the 18th of June, 1614." Hamor was the son of a merchant tailor in London who was a member of the Virginia company. Hamor writes:

"It chanced Powhatan's delight and darling, his daughter Pocahuntas (whose fame has even been spread in England by the title of Nonparella of Firginia) in her princely progresse if I may so terme it, tooke some pleasure (in the absence of Captaine Argall) to be among her friends at Pataomecke (as it seemeth by the relation I had), implored thither as shopkeeper to a Fare, to exchange some of her father's commodities for theirs, where residing some three months or longer, it fortuned upon occasion either of promise or profit, Captaine Argall to arrive there, whom Pocahuntas, desirous to renew her familiaritie with the English, and delighting to see them as unknown, fearefull perhaps to be surprised, would gladly visit as she did, of whom no sooner had Captaine Argall intelligence, but he delt with an old friend Iapazeus, how and by what meanes he might procure her caption, assuring him that now or never, was the time to pleasure him, if he intended indeede that love which he had made profession of, that in ransome of hir he might redeeme some of our English men and armes, now in the possession of her father, promising to use her withall faire and gentle entreaty; Iapazeus well assured that his brother, as he promised, would use her courteously, promised his best endeavors and service to accomplish his desire, and thus wrought it, making his wife an instrument (which sex have ever been most powerful in beguiling inticements) to effect his plot which hee had thus laid, he agreed that himself, his wife and Pocahuntas, would accompanie his brother to the water side, whither come, his wife should faine a great and longing desire to goe aboorde, and see the shippe, which being there three or four times before she had never seene, and should be earnest with her husband to permit her—he seemed angry with her, making as he pretended so unnecessary request, especially being without the company of women, which denial she taking unkindly, must faine to weepe (as who knows not that women can command teares) whereupon her husband seeming to pitty those counterfeit teares, gave her leave to goe aboord, so that it would pleese Pocahuntas to accompany her; now was the greatest labour to win her, guilty perhaps of her father's wrongs, though not knowne as she supposed, to goe with her, yet by her earnest persuasions, she assented: so forthwith aboord they went, the best cheere that could be made was seasonably provided, to supper they went, merry on all hands, especially Iapazeus and his wife, who to expres their joy would ere be treading upon Captaine Argall's foot, as who should say tis don, she is your own. Supper ended Pocahuntas was lodged in the gunner's roome, but Iapazeus and his wife desired to have some conference with their brother, which was onely to acquaint him by what stratagem they had betraied his prisoner as I have already related: after which discourse to sleepe they went, Pocahuntas nothing mistrusting this policy, who nevertheless being most possessed with feere, and desire of returne, was first up, and hastened Iapazeus to be gon. Capt. Argall having secretly well rewarded him, with a small Copper kittle, and some other les valuable toies so highly by him esteemed, that doubtlesse he would have betraied his own father for them, permitted both him and his wife to returne, but told him that for divers considerations, as for that his father had then eigh [8] of our Englishe men, many swords, peeces, and other tooles, which he hid at severall times by trecherous murdering our men, taken from them which though of no use to him, he would not redeliver, he would reserve Pocahuntas, whereat she began to be exceeding pensive, and discontented, yet ignorant of the dealing of Japazeus who in outward appearance was no les discontented that he should be the meanes of her captivity, much adoe there was to pursuade her to be patient, which with extraordinary curteous usage, by little and little was wrought in her, and so to Jamestowne she was brought."

Smith, who condenses this account in his "General Historie," expresses his contempt of this Indian treachery by saying: "The old Jew and his wife began to howle and crie as fast as Pocahuntas." It will be noted that the account of the visit (apparently alone) of Pocahontas and her capture is strong evidence that she was not at this time married to "Kocoum" or anybody else.

Word was dispatched to Powhatan of his daughter's duress, with a demand made for the restitution of goods; but although this savage is represented as dearly loving Pocahontas, his "delight and darling," it was, according to Hamor, three months before they heard anything from him. His anxiety about his daughter could not have been intense. He retained a part of his plunder, and a message was sent to him that Pocahontas would be kept till he restored all the arms.

This answer pleased Powhatan so little that they heard nothing from him till the following March. Then Sir Thomas Dale and Captain Argall, with several vessels and one hundred and fifty men, went up to Powhatan's chief seat, taking his daughter with them, offering the Indians a chance to fight for her or to take her in peace on surrender of the stolen goods. The Indians received this with bravado and flights of arrows, reminding them of the fate of Captain Ratcliffe. The whites landed, killed some Indians, burnt forty houses, pillaged the village, and went on up the river and came to anchor in front of Matchcot, the Emperor's chief town. Here were assembled four hundred armed men, with bows and arrows, who dared them to come ashore. Ashore they went, and a palaver was held. The Indians wanted a day to consult their King, after which they would fight, if nothing but blood would satisfy the whites.

Two of Powhatan's sons who were present expressed a desire to see their sister, who had been taken on shore. When they had sight of her, and saw how well she was cared for, they greatly rejoiced and promised to persuade their father to redeem her and conclude a lasting peace. The two brothers were taken on board ship, and Master John Rolfe and Master Sparkes were sent to negotiate with the King. Powhatan did not show himself, but his brother Apachamo, his successor, promised to use his best efforts to bring about a peace, and the expedition returned to Jamestown.

"Long before this time," Hamor relates, "a gentleman of approved behaviour and honest carriage, Master John Rolfe, had been in love with Pocahuntas and she with him, which thing at the instant that we were in parlee with them, myselfe made known to Sir Thomas Dale, by a letter from him [Rolfe] whereby he entreated his advice and furtherance to his love, if so it seemed fit to him for the good of the Plantation, and Pocahuntas herself acquainted her brethren therewith." Governor Dale approved this, and consequently was willing to retire without other conditions. "The bruite of this pretended marriage [Hamor continues] came soon to Powhatan's knowledge, a thing acceptable to him, as appeared by his sudden consent thereunto, who some ten daies after sent an old uncle of hirs, named Opachisco, to give her as his deputy in the church, and two of his sonnes to see the mariage solemnized which was accordingly done about the fifth of April [1614], and ever since we have had friendly commerce and trade, not only with Powhatan himself, but also with his subjects round about us; so as now I see no reason why the collonie should not thrive a pace."

This marriage was justly celebrated as the means and beginning of a firm peace which long continued, so that Pocahontas was again entitled to the grateful remembrance of the Virginia settlers. Already, in 1612, a plan had been mooted in Virginia of marrying the English with the natives, and of obtaining the recognition of Powhatan and those allied to him as members of a fifth kingdom, with certain privileges. Cunega, the Spanish ambassador at London, on September 22, 1612, writes: "Although some suppose the plantation to decrease, he is credibly informed that there is a determination to marry some of the people that go over to Virginia; forty or fifty are already so married, and English women intermingle and are received kindly by the natives. A zealous minister hath been wounded for reprehending it."

Mr. John Rolfe was a man of industry, and apparently devoted to the welfare of the colony. He probably brought with him in 1610 his wife, who gave birth to his daughter Bermuda, born on the Somers Islands at the time of the shipwreck. We find no notice of her death. Hamor gives him the distinction of being the first in the colony to try, in 1612, the planting and raising of tobacco. "No man [he adds] hath labored to his power, by good example there and worthy encouragement into England by his letters, than he hath done, witness his marriage with Powhatan's daughter, one of rude education, manners barbarous and cursed generation, meerely for the good and honor of the plantation: and least any man should conceive that some sinister respects allured him hereunto, I have made bold, contrary to his knowledge, in the end of my treatise to insert the true coppie of his letter written to Sir Thomas Dale."

The letter is a long, labored, and curious document, and comes nearer to a theological treatise than any love-letter we have on record. It reeks with unction. Why Rolfe did not speak to Dale, whom he saw every day, instead of inflicting upon him this painful document, in which the flutterings of a too susceptible widower's heart are hidden under a great resolve of self-sacrifice, is not plain.

The letter protests in a tedious preamble that the writer is moved entirely by the Spirit of God, and continues:

"Let therefore this my well advised protestation, which here I make between God and my own conscience, be a sufficient witness, at the dreadful day of judgment (when the secrets of all men's hearts shall be opened) to con-demne me herein, if my chiefest interest and purpose be not to strive with all my power of body and mind, in the undertaking of so weighty a matter, no way led (so far forth as man's weakness may permit) with the unbridled desire of carnall affection; but for the good of this plan-tation, for the honour of our countrie, for the glory of God, for my owne salvation, and for the converting to the true knowledge of God and Jesus Christ, an unbe-lieving creature, namely Pokahuntas. To whom my heartie and best thoughts are, and have a long time bin so entangled, and inthralled in so intricate a laborinth, that I was even awearied to unwinde myself thereout."

Master Rolfe goes on to describe the mighty war in his meditations on this subject, in which he had set before his eyes the frailty of mankind and his proneness to evil and wicked thoughts. He is aware of God's displeasure against the sons of Levi and Israel for marrying strange wives, and this has caused him to look about warily and with good circumspection "into the grounds and principall agitations which should thus provoke me to be in love with one, whose education hath bin rude, her manners barbarous, her generation accursed, and so discrepant in all nurtriture from myselfe, that oftentimes with feare and trembling, I have ended my private controversie with this: surely these are wicked instigations, fetched by him who seeketh and delighteth in man's distruction; and so with fervent prayers to be ever preserved from such diabolical assaults (as I looke those to be) I have taken some rest."

The good man was desperately in love and wanted to marry the Indian, and consequently he got no peace; and still being tormented with her image, whether she was absent or present, he set out to produce an ingenious reason (to show the world) for marrying her. He continues:

"Thus when I thought I had obtained my peace and quietnesse, beholde another, but more gracious tentation hath made breaches into my holiest and strongest meditations; with which I have been put to a new triall, in a straighter manner than the former; for besides the weary passions and sufferings which I have dailey, hourely, yea and in my sleepe indured, even awaking me to astonishment, taxing me with remissnesse, and carelessnesse, refusing and neglecting to perform the duteie of a good Christian, pulling me by the eare, and crying: Why dost thou not indeavor to make her a Christian? And these have happened to my greater wonder, even when she hath been furthest seperated from me, which in common reason (were it not an undoubted work of God) might breede forgetfulnesse of a far more worthie creature."

He accurately describes the symptoms and appears to understand the remedy, but he is after a large-sized motive:

"Besides, I say the holy Spirit of God hath often demanded of me, why I was created? If not for transitory pleasures and worldly vanities, but to labour in the Lord's vineyard, there to sow and plant, to nourish and increase the fruites thereof, daily adding with the good husband in the gospell, somewhat to the tallent, that in the ends the fruites may be reaped, to the comfort of the labourer in this life, and his salvation in the world to come.... Likewise, adding hereunto her great appearance of love to me, her desire to be taught and instructed in the knowledge of God, her capablenesse of understanding, her aptnesse and willingness to receive anie good impression, and also the spirituall, besides her owne incitements stirring me up hereunto."

The "incitements" gave him courage, so that he exclaims: "Shall I be of so untoward a disposition, as to refuse to lead the blind into the right way? Shall I be so unnatural, as not to give bread to the hungrie, or uncharitable, as not to cover the naked?"

It wasn't to be thought of, such wickedness; and so Master Rolfe screwed up his courage to marry the glorious Princess, from whom thousands of people were afterwards so anxious to be descended. But he made the sacrifice for the glory of the country, the benefit of the plantation, and the conversion of the unregenerate, and other and lower motive he vigorously repels: "Now, if the vulgar sort, who square all men's actions by the base rule of their own filthinesse, shall tax or taunt mee in this my godly labour: let them know it is not hungry appetite, to gorge myselfe with incontinency; sure (if I would and were so sensually inclined) I might satisfy such desire, though not wiihout a seared conscience, yet with Christians more pleasing to the eie, and less fearefull in the offense unlawfully committed. Nor am I in so desperate an estate, that I regard not what becometh of me; nor am I out of hope but one day to see my country, nor so void of friends, nor mean in birth, but there to obtain a mach to my great con'tent…. But shall it please God thus to dispose of me (which I earnestly desire to fulfill my ends before set down) I will heartily accept of it as a godly taxe appointed me, and I will never cease (God assisting me) untill I have accomplished, and brought to perfection so holy a worke, in which I will daily pray God to bless me, to mine and her eternal happiness."

It is to be hoped that if sanctimonious John wrote any love letters to Amonata they had less cant in them than this. But it was pleasing to Sir Thomas Dale, who was a man to appreciate the high motives of Mr. Rolfe. In a letter which he despatched from Jamestown, June 18, 1614, to a reverend friend in London, he describes the expedition when Pocahontas was carried up the river, and adds the information that when she went on shore, "she would not talk to any of them, scarcely to them of the best sort, and to them only, that if her father had loved her, he would not value her less than old swords, pieces, or axes; wherefore she would still dwell with the Englishmen who loved her."

"Powhatan's daughter [the letter continues] I caused to be carefully instructed in Christian Religion, who after she had made some good progress therein, renounced publically her countrey idolatry, openly confessed her Christian faith, was, as she desired, baptized, and is since married to an English Gentleman of good understanding (as by his letter unto me, containing the reasons for his marriage of her you may perceive), an other knot to bind this peace the stronger. Her father and friends gave approbation to it, and her uncle gave her to him in the church; she lives civilly and lovingly with him, and I trust will increase in goodness, as the knowledge of God increaseth in her. She will goe into England with me, and were it but the gayning of this one soule, I will think my time, toile, and present stay well spent."

Hamor also appends to his narration a short letter, of the same date with the above, from the minister Alexander Whittaker, the genuineness of which is questioned. In speaking of the good deeds of Sir Thomas Dale it says: "But that which is best, one Pocahuntas or Matoa, the daughter of Powhatan, is married to an honest and discreet English Gentleman—Master Rolfe, and that after she had openly renounced her countrey Idolatry, and confessed the faith of Jesus Christ, and was baptized, which thing Sir Thomas Dale had laboured a long time to ground her in." If, as this proclaims, she was married after her conversion, then Rolfe's tender conscience must have given him another twist for wedding her, when the reason for marrying her (her conversion) had ceased with her baptism. His marriage, according to this, was a pure work of super-erogation. It took place about the 5th of April, 1614. It is not known who performed the ceremony.

How Pocahontas passed her time in Jamestown during the period of her detention, we are not told. Conjectures are made that she was an inmate of the house of Sir Thomas Dale, or of that of the Rev. Mr. Whittaker, both of whom labored zealously to enlighten her mind on religious subjects. She must also have been learning English and civilized ways, for it is sure that she spoke our language very well when she went to London. Mr. John Rolfe was also laboring for her conversion, and we may suppose that with all these ministrations, mingled with her love of Mr. Rolfe, which that ingenious widower had discovered, and her desire to convert him into a husband, she was not an unwilling captive. Whatever may have been her barbarous instincts, we have the testimony of Governor Dale that she lived "civilly and lovingly" with her husband.

★   ★   ★

Sir Thomas Dale was on the whole the most efficient and discreet Governor the colony had had. One element of his success was no doubt the change in the charter of 1609. By the first charter everything had been held in common by the company, and there had been no division of property or allotment of land among the colonists. Under the new regime land was held in severalty, and the spur of individual interest began at once to improve the condition of the settlement. The character of the colonists was also gradually improving. They had not been of a sort to fulfill the earnest desire of the London promoter's to spread vital piety in the New World. A zealous defense of Virginia and Maryland, against "scandalous imputation," entitled "Leah and Rachel; or, The Two Fruitful Sisters," by Mr. John Hammond, London,

1656, considers the charges that Virginia "is an unhealthy place, a nest of rogues, abandoned women, dissolut and rookery persons; a place of intolerable labour, bad usage and hard diet"; and admits that "at the first settling, and for many years after, it deserved most of these aspersions, nor were they then aspersions but truths.... There were jails supplied, youth seduced, infamous women drilled in, the provision all brought out of England, and that embezzled by the Trustees."

Governor Dale was a soldier; entering the army in the Netherlands as a private he had risen to high position, and received knighthood in 1606. Shortly after he was with Sir Thomas Gates in South Holland. The States General in 1611 granted him three years' term of absence in Virginia. Upon his arrival he began to put in force that system of industry and frugality he had observed in Holland. He had all the imperiousness of a soldier, and in an altercation with Captain Newport, occasioned by some injurious remarks the latter made about Sir Thomas Smith, the treasurer, he pulled his beard and threatened to hang him. Active operations for settling new plantations were at once begun, and Dale wrote to Cecil, the Earl of Salisbury, for 2,000 good colonists to be sent out, for the three hundred that came were "so profane, so riotous, so full of mutiny, that not many are Christians but in name, their bodies so diseased and crazed that not sixty of them may be employed." He served afterwards with credit in Holland, was made commander of the East Indian fleet in 1618, had a naval engagement with the Dutch near Bantam in 1619, and died in 1620 from the effects of the climate. He was twice married, and his second wife, Lady Fanny, the cousin of his first wife, survived him and received a patent for a Virginia plantation.

Governor Dale kept steadily in view the conversion of the Indians to Christianity, and the success of John Rolfe with Matoaka inspired him with a desire to convert another daughter of Powhatan, of whose exquisite perfections he had heard. He therefore despatched Ralph Hamor, with the English boy, Thomas Savage, as interpreter, on a mission to the court of Powhatan, "upon a message unto him, which was to deale with him, if by any means I might procure a daughter of his, who (Pocahuntas being already in our possession) is generally reported to be his delight and darling, and surely he esteemed her as his owne Soule, for surer pledge of peace." This visit Hamor relates with great naivete.

At his town of Matchcot, near the head of York River, Powhatan himself received his visitors when they landed, with great cordiality, expressing much pleasure at seeing again the boy who had been presented to him by Captain Newport, and whom he had not seen since he gave him leave to go and see his friends at Jamestown four years before; he also inquired anxiously after Namontack, whom he had sent to King James's land to see him and his country and report thereon, and then led the way to his house, where he sat down on his bedstead side. "On each hand of him was placed a comely and personable young woman, which they called his Queenes, the howse within round about beset with them, the outside guarded with a hundred bowmen."

The first thing offered was a pipe of tobacco, which Powhatan "first drank," and then passed to Hamor, who "drank" what he pleased and then returned it. The

Emperor then inquired how his brother Sir Thomas Dale fared, "and after that of his daughter's welfare, her marriage, his unknown son, and how they liked, lived and loved together." Hamor replied "that his brother was very well, and his daughter so well content that she would not change her life to return and live with him, whereat he laughed heartily, and said he was very glad of it."

Powhatan then desired to know the cause of his unexpected coming, and Mr. Hamor said his message was private, to be delivered to him without the presence of any except one of his councilors, and one of the guides, who already knew it.

Therefore the house was cleared of all except the two Queens, who may never sequester themselves, and Mr. Hamor began his palaver. First there was a message of love and inviolable peace, the production of presents of coffee, beads, combs, fish-hooks, and knives, and the promise of a grindstone when it pleased the Emperor to send for it. Hamor then proceeded:

"The bruite of the exquesite perfection of your youngest daughter, being famous through all your territories, hath come to the hearing of your brother, Sir Thomas Dale, who for this purpose hath addressed me hither, to intreate you by that brotherly friendship you make profession of, to permit her (with me) to returne unto him, partly for the desire which himselfe hath, and partly for the desire her sister hath to see her of whom, if fame hath not been prodigall, as like enough it hath not, your brother (by your favour) would gladly make his nearest companion, wife and bed fellow [many times he would have interrupted my speech, which I entreated him to heare out, and then if he pleased to returne me answer], and the reason hereof is, because being now friendly and firmly united together, and made one people [as he supposeth and believes] in the bond of love, he would make a natural union between us, principally because himself hath taken resolution to dwel in your country so long as he liveth, and would not only therefore have the firmest assurance hee may, of perpetuall friendship from you, but also hereby binde himselfe thereunto."

Powhatan replied with dignity that he gladly accepted the salute of love and peace, which he and his subjects would exactly maintain. But as to the other matter he said: "My daughter, whom my brother desireth, I sold within these three days to be wife to a great Weroance for two bushels of Roanoke [a small kind of beads made of oyster shells], and it is true she is already gone with him, three days' journey from me."

Hamor persisted that this marriage need not stand in the way; "that if he pleased herein to gratify his Brother he might, restoring the Roanoke without the imputation of injustice, take home his daughter again, the rather because she was not full twelve years old, and therefore not marriageable; assuring him besides the bond of peace, so much the firmer, he should have treble the price of his daughter in beads, copper, hatchets, and many other things more useful for him."

The reply of the noble old savage to this infamous demand ought to have brought a blush to the cheeks of those who made it. He said he loved his daughter as dearly as his life; he had many children, but he delighted in none so much as in her; he could not live if he did not see her often, as he would not if she were living with the whites, and he was determined not to put himself in their hands. He desired no other assurance of friendship than his brother had given him, who had already one of his daughters as a pledge, which was sufficient while she lived; "when she dieth he shall have another child of mine." And then he broke forth in pathetic eloquence: "I hold it not a brotherly part of your King, to desire to bereave me of two of my children at once; further give him to understand, that if he had no pledge at all, he should not need to distrust any injury from me, or any under my subjection; there have been too many of his and my men killed, and by my occasion there shall never be more; I which have power to perform it have said it; no not though I should have just occasion offered, for I am now old and would gladly end my days in peace; so as if the English offer me any injury, my country is large enough, I will remove myself farther from you."

The old man hospitably entertained his guests for a day or two, loaded them with presents, among which were two dressed buckskins, white as snow, for his son and daughter, and, requesting some articles sent him in return, bade them farewell with this message to Governor Dale: "I hope this will give him good satisfaction, if it do not I will go three days' journey farther from him, and never see Englishmen more." It speaks well for the temperate habits of this savage that after he had feasted his guests, "he caused to be fetched a great glass of sack, some three quarts or better, which Captain Newport had given him six or seven years since, carefully preserved by him, not much above a pint in all this time spent, and gave each of us in a great oyster shell some three spoonfuls."

We trust that Sir Thomas Dale gave a faithful account of all this to his wife in England.

Sir Thomas Gates left Virginia in the spring of 1614 and never returned. After his departure scarcity and severity developed a mutiny, and six of the settlers were executed. Rolfe was planting tobacco (he has the credit of being the first white planter of it), and his wife was getting an inside view of Christian civilization.

In 1616 Sir Thomas Dale returned to England with his company and John Rolfe and Pocahontas, and several other Indians. They reached Plymouth early in June, and on the 20th Lord Carew made this note: "Sir Thomas Dale returned from Virginia; he hath brought divers men and women of thatt countrye to be educated here, and one Rolfe who married a daughter of Pohetan (the barbarous prince) called Pocahuntas, hath brought his wife with him into England." On the 22d Sir John Chamberlain wrote to Sir Dudley Carlton that there were ten or twelve, old and young, of that country.

The Indian girls who came with Pocahontas appear to have been a great care to the London company. In May, 1620, is a record that the company had to pay for physic and cordials for one of them who had been living as a servant in Cheapside, and was very weak of a consumption. The same year two other of the maids were shipped off to the Bermudas, after being long a charge to the company, in the hope that they might there get husbands, "that after they were converted and had children, they might be sent to their country and kindred to civilize them." One of them was there married. The attempt to educate them in England was not very successful, and a proposal to bring over Indian boys obtained this comment from Sir Edwin Sandys:

"Now to send for them into England, and to have them educated here, he found upon experience of those brought by Sir Thomas Dale, might be far from the Christian work intended." One Nanamack, a lad brought over by Lord Delaware, lived some years in houses where "he heard not much of religion but sins, had many times examples of drinking, swearing and like evils, ran as he was a mere Pagan," till he fell in with a devout family and changed his life, but died before he was baptized. Accompanying Pocahontas was a councilor of Powhatan, one Tomocomo, the husband of one of her sisters, of whom Purchas says in his "Pilgrimes": "With this savage I have often conversed with my good friend Master Doctor Goldstone where he was a frequent guest, and where I have seen him sing and dance his diabolical measures, and heard him discourse of his country and religion.... Master Rolfe lent me a discourse which I have in my Pilgrimage delivered. And his wife did not only accustom herself to civility, but still carried herself as the daughter of a king, and was accordingly respected, not only by the Company which allowed provision for herself and her son, but of divers particular persons of honor, in their hopeful zeal by her to advance Christianity. I was present when my honorable and reverend patron, the Lord Bishop of London, Doctor King, entertained her with festival state and pomp beyond what I had seen in his great hospitality offered to other ladies. At her return towards Virginia she came at Gravesend to her end and grave, having given great demonstration of her Christian sincerity, as the first fruits of Virginia conversion, leaving here a goodly memory, and the hopes of her resurrection, her soul aspiring to see and enjoy permanently in heaven what here she had joyed to hear and believe of her blessed Saviour. Not such was Tomocomo, but a blasphemer of what he knew not and preferring his God to ours because he taught them (by his own so appearing) to wear their Devil-lock at the left ear; he acquainted me with the manner of that his appearance, and believed that their Okee or Devil had taught them their husbandry."

Upon news of her arrival, Captain Smith, either to increase his own importance or because Pocahontas was neglected, addressed a letter or "little booke" to Queen Anne, the consort of King James. This letter is found in Smith's "General Historie" (1624), where it is introduced as having been sent to Queen Anne in 1616. Probably he sent her such a letter. We find no mention of its receipt or of any acknowledgment of it. Whether the "abstract" in the "General Historie" is exactly like the original we have no means of knowing. We have no more confidence in Smith's memory than we have in his dates. The letter is as follows:

"To the most high and vertuous Princesse Queene Anne of Great Brittaine.

Most ADMIRED QUEENE.

"The love I beare my God, my King and Countrie hath so oft emboldened me in the worst of extreme dangers, that now honestie doth constraine mee presume thus farre beyond my selfe, to present your Majestie this short discourse: if ingratitude be a deadly poyson to all honest vertues, I must be guiltie of that crime if I should omit any meanes to bee thankful. So it is.

"That some ten yeeres agoe being in Virginia, and taken prisoner by the power of Powhaten, their chiefe

King, I received from this great Savage exceeding great courtesie, especially from his sonne Nantaquaus, the most manliest, comeliest, boldest spirit, I ever saw in a Savage and his sister Pocahontas, the Kings most deare and wel-beloved daughter, being but a childe of twelve or thirteen yeeres of age, whose compassionate pitifull heart, of desperate estate, gave me much cause to respect her: I being the first Christian this proud King and his grim attendants ever saw, and thus enthralled in their barbarous power, I cannot say I felt the least occasion of want that was in the power of those my mortall foes to prevent notwithstanding al their threats. After some six weeks fatting amongst those Salvage Courtiers, at the minute of my execution, she hazarded the beating out of her owne braines to save mine, and not onely that, but so prevailed with her father, that I was safely conducted to Jamestowne, where I found about eight and thirty miserable poore and sicke creatures, to keepe possession of all those large territories of Virginia, such was the weaknesse of this poore Commonwealth, as had the Salvages not fed us, we directly had starved.

"And this reliefe, most gracious Queene, was commonly brought us by this Lady Pocahontas, notwithstanding all these passages when inconstant Fortune turned our Peace to warre, this tender Virgin would still not spare to dare to visit us, and by her our jarres have been oft appeased, and our wants still supplyed; were it the policie of her father thus to imploy her, or the ordinance of God thus to make her his instrument, or her extraordinarie affection to our Nation, I know not: but of this I am sure: when her father with the utmost of his policie and power, sought to surprize mee, having but eighteene with mee, the dark night could not affright her from comming through the irksome woods, and with watered eies gave me intilligence, with her best advice to escape his furie: which had hee known hee had surely slaine her. Jamestowne with her wild traine she as freely frequented, as her father's habitation: and during the time of two or three yeares, she next under God, was still the instrument to preserve this Colonie from death, famine and utter confusion, which if in those times had once beene dissolved, Virginia might have laine as it was at our first arrivall to this day. Since then, this buisinesse having been turned and varied by many accidents from that I left it at: it is most certaine, after a long and troublesome warre after my departure, betwixt her father and our Colonie, all which time shee was not heard of, about two yeeres longer, the Colonie by that meanes was releived, peace concluded, and at last rejecting her barbarous condition, was maried to an English Gentleman, with whom at this present she is in England; the first Christian ever of that Nation, the first Virginian ever spake English, or had a childe in mariage by an Englishman, a matter surely, if my meaning bee truly considered and well understood, worthy a Princes understanding.

"Thus most gracious Lady, I have related to your Majestic, what at your best leasure our approved Histories will account you at large, and done in the time of your Majesties life, and however this might bee presented you from a more worthy pen, it cannot from a more honest heart, as yet I never begged anything of the State, or any, and it is my want of abilitie and her exceeding desert, your birth, meanes, and authoritie, her birth, vertue, want and simplicitie, doth make mee thus bold, humbly to beseech your Majestic: to take this knowledge of her though it be from one so unworthy to be the reporter, as myselfe, her husband's estate not being able to make her fit to attend your Majestic: the most and least I can doe, is to tell you this, because none so oft hath tried it as myselfe: and the rather being of so great a spirit, however her station: if she should not be well received, seeing this Kingdome may rightly have a Kingdome by her meanes: her present love to us and Christianitie, might turne to such scorne and furie, as to divert all this good to the worst of evill, when finding so great a Queene should doe her some honour more than she can imagine, for being so kinde to your servants and subjects, would so ravish her with content, as endeare her dearest bloud to effect that, your Majestic and all the Kings honest subjects most earnestly desire: and so I humbly kisse your gracious hands."

The passage in this letter, "She hazarded the beating out of her owne braines to save mine," is inconsistent with the preceding portion of the paragraph which speaks of "the exceeding great courtesie" of Powhatan; and Smith was quite capable of inserting it afterwards when he made up his "General Historie."

Smith represents himself at this time—the last half of 1616 and the first three months of 1617—as preparing to attempt a third voyage to New England (which he did not make), and too busy to do Pocahontas the service she desired. She was staying at Branford, either from neglect of the company or because the London smoke disagreed with her, and there Smith went to see her. His account of his intercourse with her, the only one we have, must be given for what it is worth. According to this she had supposed Smith dead, and took umbrage at his neglect of her. He writes:

"After a modest salutation, without any word, she turned about, obscured her face, as not seeming well contented; and in that humour, her husband with divers others, we all left her two or three hours repenting myself to have writ she could speak English. But not long after she began to talke, remembering me well what courtesies she had done: saying, 'You did promise Powhatan what was yours should be his, and he the like to you; you called him father, being in his land a stranger, and by the same reason so must I do you:' which though I would have excused, I durst not allow of that title, because she was a king's daughter. With a well set countenance she said: 'Were you not afraid to come into my father's country and cause fear in him and all his people (but me), and fear you have I should call you father; I tell you then I will, and you shall call me childe, and so I will be forever and ever, your contrieman. They did tell me alwaies you were dead, and I knew no other till I came to Plymouth, yet Powhatan did command Uttamatomakkin to seek you, and know the truth, because your countriemen will lie much.'"

This savage was the Tomocomo spoken of above, who had been sent by Powhatan to take a census of the people of England, and report what they and their state were. At Plymouth he got a long stick and began to make notches in it for the people he saw. But he was quickly weary of that task. He told Smith that Powhatan bade him seek him out, and get him to show him his God, and the King, Queen, and Prince, of whom Smith had told so much. Smith put him off about showing his

God, but said he had heard that he had seen the King. This the Indian denied, James probably not coming up to his idea of a king, till by circumstances he was convinced he had seen him. Then he replied very sadly: "You gave Powhatan a white dog, which Powhatan fed as himself, but your king gave me nothing, and I am better than your white dog."

Smith adds that he took several courtiers to see Pocahontas, and "they did think God had a great hand in her conversion, and they have seen many English ladies worse favoured, proportioned, and behavioured;" and he heard that it had pleased the King and Queen greatly to esteem her, as also Lord and Lady Delaware, and other persons of good quality, both at the masques and otherwise.

Much has been said about the reception of Pocahontas in London, but the contemporary notices of her are scant. The Indians were objects of curiosity for a time in London, as odd Americans have often been since, and the rank of Pocahontas procured her special attention. She was presented at court. She was entertained by Dr. King, Bishop of London. At the playing of Ben Jonson's "Christmas his Mask" at court, January 6, 1616-17, Pocahontas and Tomocomo were both present, and Chamberlain writes to Carleton: "The Virginian woman Pocahuntas with her father counsellor have been with the King and graciously used, and both she and her assistant were pleased at the Masque. She is upon her return though sore against her will, if the wind would about to send her away."

Mr. Neill says that "after the first weeks of her residence in England she does not appear to be spoken of as the wife of Rolfe by the letter writers," and the Rev.

Peter Fontaine says that "when they heard that Rolfe had married Pocahontas, it was deliberated in council whether he had not committed high treason by so doing, that is marrying an Indian princesse."

It was like James to think so. His interest in the colony was never the most intelligent, and apt to be in things trivial. Lord Southampton (Dec. 15, 1609) writes to Lord Salisbury that he had told the King of the Virginia squirrels brought into England, which are said to fly. The King very earnestly asked if none were provided for him, and said he was sure Salisbury would get him one. Would not have troubled him, "but that you know so well how he is affected to these toys."

There has been recently found in the British Museum a print of a portrait of Pocahontas, with a legend round it in Latin, which is translated: "Matoaka, alias Rebecka, Daughter of Prince Powhatan, Emperor of Virginia; converted to Christianity, married Mr. Rolff; died on shipboard at Gravesend 1617."

Camden in his "History of Gravesend" says that everybody paid this young lady all imaginable respect, and it was believed she would have sufficiently acknowledged those favors, had she lived to return to her own country, by bringing the Indians to a kinder disposition toward the English; and that she died, "giving testimony all the time she lay sick, of her being a very good Christian."

The Lady Rebecka, as she was called in London, died on shipboard at Gravesend after a brief illness, said to be of only three days, probably on the 21st of March, 1617. I have seen somewhere a statement, which I cannot confirm, that her disease was smallpox. St. George's

Church, where she was buried, was destroyed by fire in 1727. The register of that church has this record:

"1616, May 21 Rebecca Wrothe Wyff of Thomas Wroth gent A Virginia lady borne, here was buried in ye chaunncle."

Yet there is no doubt, according to a record in the Calendar of State Papers, dated "1617 29 March, London," that her death occurred March 21, 1617.

John Rolfe was made Secretary of Virginia when Captain Argall became Governor, and seems to have been associated in the schemes of that unscrupulous person and to have forfeited the good opinion of the company. August 23, 1618, the company wrote to Argall: "We cannot imagine why you should give us warning that Opechankano and the natives have given the country to Mr. Rolfe's child, and that they reserve it from all others till he comes of years except as we suppose as some do here report it be a device of your own, to some special purpose for yourself." It appears also by the minutes of the company in 1621 that Lady Delaware had trouble to recover goods of hers left in Rolfe's hands in Virginia, and desired a commission directed to Sir Thomas Wyatt and Mr. George Sandys to examine what goods of the late "Lord Deleware had come into Rolfe's possession and get satisfaction of him." This George Sandys is the famous traveler who made a journey through the Turkish Empire in 1610, and who wrote, while living in Virginia, the first book written in the New World, the completion of his translation of Ovid's "Metamorphosis."

John Rolfe died in Virginia in 1622, leaving a wife and children. This is supposed to be his third wife, though there is no note of his marriage to her nor of

the death of his first. October 7, 1622, his brother
Henry Rolfe petitioned that the estate of John should
be converted to the support of his relict wife and children and to his own indemnity for having brought up
John's child by Powhatan's daughter.

This child, named Thomas Rolfe, was given after the
death of Pocahontas to the keeping of Sir Lewis
Stukely of Plymouth, who fell into evil practices, and
the boy was transferred to the guardianship of his uncle
Henry Rolfe, and educated in London. When he was
grown up he returned to Virginia, and was probably
there married. There is on record his application to the
Virginia authorities in 1641 for leave to go into the
Indian country and visit Cleopatra, his mother's sister.

In 1618 died the great Powhatan, full of years and
satiated with fighting and the savage delights of life. He
had many names and titles; his own people sometimes
called him Ottaniack, sometimes Mamauatonick, and
usually in his presence Wahunsenasawk. He ruled, by
inheritance and conquest, with many chiefs under him,
over a large territory with not defined borders, lying on
the James, the York, the Rappahannock, the Potomac,
and the Pawtuxet Rivers. He had several seats, at which
he alternately lived with his many wives and guard of
bowmen, the chief of which at the arrival of the English
was Werowomocomo, on the Pamunkey (York) River.
His state has been sufficiently described. He is said to
have had a hundred wives, and generally a dozen—the
youngest—personally attending him. When he had a
mind to add to his harem he seems to have had the
ancient oriental custom of sending into all his dominions for the fairest maidens to be brought from whom

to select. And he gave the wives of whom he was tired to his favorites.

Strachey makes a striking description of him as he appeared about 1610: "He is a goodly old man not yet shrincking, though well beaten with cold and stormeye winters, in which he hath been patient of many necessityes and attempts of his fortune to make his name and famely great. He is supposed to be little lesse than eighty yeares old, I dare not saye how much more; others saye he is of a tall stature and cleane lymbes, of a sad aspect, rownd fatt visaged, with graie haires, but plaine and thin, hanging upon his broad showlders; some few haires upon his chin, and so on his upper lippe: he hath been a strong and able salvadge, synowye, vigilant, ambitious, subtile to enlarge his dominions...cruell he hath been, and quarellous as well with his own wercowances for trifles, and that to strike a terrour and awe into them of his power and condicion, as also with his neighbors in his younger days, though now delighted in security and pleasure, and therefore stands upon reasonable conditions of peace with all the great and absolute werowances about him, and is likewise more quietly settled amongst his own."

Powhatan is a very large figure in early Virginia history, and deserves his prominence. He was an able and crafty savage, and made a good fight against the encroachments of the whites, but he was no match for the crafty Smith, nor the double-dealing of the Christians. There is something pathetic about the close of his life, his sorrow for the death of his daughter in a strange land, when he saw his territories overrun by the invaders, from whom he only asked peace, and the poor privilege of moving further away from them into the wilderness if they denied him peace.

In the midst of this savagery Pocahontas blooms like a sweet, wild rose. She was, like the Douglas, "tender and true." Wanting apparently the cruel nature of her race generally, her heroic qualities were all of the heart. No one of all the contemporary writers has anything but gentle words for her. Barbarous and untaught she was like her comrades, but of a gentle nature. Stripped of all the fictions which Captain Smith has woven into her story, and all the romantic suggestions which later writers have indulged in, she appears, in the light of the few facts that industry is able to gather concerning her, as a pleasing and unrestrained Indian girl, probably not different from her savage sisters in her habits, but bright and gentle; struck with admiration at the appearance of the white men, and easily moved to pity them, and so inclined to a growing and lasting friendship for them; tractable and apt to learn refinements; accepting the new religion through love for those who taught it, and finally becoming in her maturity a well-balanced, sensible, dignified Christian woman.

According to the long-accepted story of Pocahontas, she did something more than interfere to save from barbarous torture and death a stranger and a captive, who had forfeited his life by shooting those who opposed his invasion. In all times, among the most savage tribes and in civilized society, women have been moved to heavenly pity by the sight of a prisoner, and risked life to save him—the impulse was as natural to a Highland lass as to an African maid. Pocahontas went further than efforts to make peace between the superior race and her own. When the whites forced the Indians to contribute from their scanty stores to the support of the invaders, and burned their dwellings and shot them on sight if they refused, the Indian maid sympathized with the exposed whites and warned them of stratagems against them; captured herself by a base violation of the laws of hospitality, she was easily reconciled to her situation, adopted the habits of the foreigners, married one of her captors, and in peace and in war cast in her lot with the strangers. History has not preserved for us the Indian view of her conduct.

It was no doubt fortunate for her, though perhaps not for the colony, that her romantic career ended by an early death, so that she always remains in history in the bloom of youth. She did not live to be pained by the contrast, to which her eyes were opened, between her own and her adopted people, nor to learn what things could be done in the Christian name she loved, nor to see her husband in a less honorable light than she left him, nor to be involved in any way in the frightful massacre of 1622. If she had remained in England after the novelty was over, she might have been subject to slights and mortifying neglect. The struggles of the fighting colony could have brought her little but pain. Dying when she did, she rounded out one of the prettiest romances of all history, and secured for her name the affection of a great nation, whose empire has spared little that belonged to her childhood and race, except the remembrance of her friendship for those who destroyed her people.

Washington

[M. L. WEEMS]

OH! As along the stream of time thy name
Expanded flies, and gathers all its fame;
May then these lines to future days descend, And
prove thy COUNTRY'S good thine only end!

A h, gentlemen!"—exclaimed Bonaparte— 'twas just as he was about to embark for Egypt—some young Americans happening at Toulon, and anxious to see the mighty Corsican, had obtained the honour of an introduction to him. Scarcely were past the customary salutations, when he eagerly asked, "how fares your countryman, the great Washington?" "He was very well," replied the youths, brightening at the thought, that they were the countrymen of Washington; "he was very well, general, when we left America."—"Ah, gentlemen!" rejoined he, "Washington can never be otherwise than well.— The measure of his fame is full.—Posterity will talk of him with reverence as the founder of a great empire, when my name shall be lost in the vortex of Revolutions!"

Who, then, that has a spark of virtuous curiosity, but must wish to know the history of him whose name could thus awaken the sigh even of Bonaparte? But is not his history already known? Have not a thousand orators spread his fame abroad, bright as his own Potomac, when he reflects the morning sun, and flames like a sea of liquid gold, the wonder and delight of all the neighboring shores? Yes, they have indeed spread his fame abroad. . . . his fame as Generalissimo of the armies, and first President of the councils of his nation. But this is not half his fame. . . . True, he has been seen in greatness: but it is only the greatness of public character, which is no evidence of true greatness; for a public character is often an artificial one. At the head of an army or nation, where gold and glory are at stake, and where a man feels himself the burning focus of unnumbered eyes; he must be a paltry fellow, indeed, who does not play his part pretty handsomely. . . . even the common passions of pride, avarice, or ambition, will put him up to his mettle, and call forth his best and bravest doings. But let this heat and blaze of public situation and incitement be withdrawn; let him be thrust back into the shade of private life; and you shall see how soon, like a forced plant robbed of its hot-bed, he will drop his false foliage and fruit, and stand forth confessed in native stickweed sterility and worthlessness.—There was Benedict Arnold—while strutting a brigadier general on the public state, he could play you the great man, on a handsome scale—he out-marched Hannibal, and out-fought Burgoyne—he chased the British like curlews, or cooped them up like chickens! And yet in the private walks of life, in Philadelphia, he could swindle rum from the commissary's stores, and, with the aid of loose women, retail it by the gill!!—And there was the great duke of Marlborough too—his public character, a thunderbolt in war! Britain's boast, and the terror of the French! But his private character, what? Why a swindler to whom Arnold's self could hold a candle; a perfect nondescript of baseness; a shaver of farthings from the poor sixpenny pay of his own brave soldiers!!

It is not, then, in the glare of public, but in the shade of private life, that we are to look for the man. Private life, is always real life. Behind the curtain, where the eyes of the million are not upon him, and where a man can have no motive but inclination, no incitement but honest nature, there he will always be sure to act himself: consequently, if he act greatly, he must be great indeed. Hence it has been justly said, that, "our private deeds, if noble, are noblest of our lives."

Of these private deeds of Washington very little has been said. In most of the elegant orations pronounced to his praise, you see nothing of Washington below the clouds—nothing of Washington the dutiful son—the affectionate brother—the cheerful school-boy—the diligent surveyor—the neat draftsman—the laborious farmer—the widow's husband—the orphan's father—the poor man's friend. No! this is not the Washington you see; 'tis only Washington, the hero, and the Demigod—Washington the sun-beam in council, or the storm in war.

And in all the ensigns of character amidst which he is generally drawn, you see none that represent him what he really was, "the Jupiter Conservator," the friend and benefactor of men. Where's his bright ploughshare that he loved—or his wheat-crowned fields, waving in yellow ridges before the wanton breeze—or his hills whitened over with flocks—or his clover covered pastures spread with innumerous herds—or his neat-clad servants with songs rolling the heavy harvest before them? Such were the scenes of peace, plenty, and happiness, in which Washington delighted. But his eulogists have denied him these, the only scenes which belong to man the great; and have trick'd him up in the vile drapery of man the little. See! there he stands! with the port of Mars "the destroyer," dark frowning over the fields of war—the lightning of Potter's blade is by his side—the deep-mouthed cannon is before him, disgorging its flesh-mangling balls—his war-horse pants with impatience to bear him, a speedy thunderbolt, against the pale and bleeding ranks of Britain!—These are the drawings usually given of Washington; drawings masterly no doubt, and perhaps justly descriptive of him in some scenes of his life. But scenes they were, which I am sure his soul abhorred, and in which, at any rate, you see nothing of his private virtues. These old fashioned commodities are generally thrown into the back ground of the picture; and treated, as the grandees at the London and Paris routs, treat their good old aunts and grandmothers, huddling them together into the back rooms, there to wheeze and cough by themselves, and not depress the fine laudanum-raised spirits of the young sparklers. And yet it was to those old fashioned virtues that our hero owed every thing. For they in fact were the food of the great actions of him, whom men call Washington. It was they that enabled him, first to triumph over himself; then over the British; and uniformly to set such bright examples of human perfectibility and true greatness, that, compared therewith, the history of his capturing Cornwallis and Tarleton, with their buccaneering legions, sounds almost as small as the story of General Putnam's catching his wolf and her lamb-killing whelps.

Since then it is the private virtues that lay the foundation of all human excellence—since it was these that exalted Washington to be "Columbia's first and greatest Son," be it our first care to present these, in all their lustre, before the admiring eyes of our children. To them his private character is every thing; his public, hardly any thing. For how glorious soever it may have been in Washington to have undertaken the emancipation of his country; to have stemmed the long tide of adversity; to have baffled every effort of a wealthy and warlike nation; to have obtained for his countrymen the completest victory, and for himself the most unbounded power; and then to have returned that power, accompanied with all the weight of his own great character and advice to establish a government that should immortalize the blessings of liberty—however glorious, I say, all this may have been to himself, or instructive to future generals and presidents, yet does it but little concern our children. For who among us can hope that his son shall ever be called, like Washington, to direct the storm of war, or to ravish the ears of deeply listening Senates? To be constantly placing him then, before our children, in this high character, what is it but like springing in the clouds a golden Phoenix, which no mortal calibre can ever hope to reach? Or like setting pictures of the Mammoth before the mice, whom "not all the manna of Heaven" can ever raise to equality? Oh no! give us his private virtues! In these, every youth is interested, because in these every youth may become a Washington—a Washington in piety and patriotism,—in industry and honour—and consequently a Washington, in what alone deserves the name, self esteem and universal respect.

BIRTH AND EDUCATION

"Children like tender osiers take the bow;
"And as they first are form'd, forever grow."

To this day numbers of good Christians can hardly find faith to believe that Washington was, bona fide, a Virginian! "What! a buckskin!" say they with a smile. "George Washington a buckskin! pshaw! impossible! he was certainly an European: So great a man could never have been born in America."

So great a man could never have been born in America!—why that's the very prince of reasons why he should have been born here! Nature, we know, is fond of harmonies; and paria paribus, that is, great things to great, is the rule she delights to work by. Where, for example, do we look for the whale, "the biggest born of nature?" not, I trow, in a mill-pond, but in the main ocean. "There go the great ships:" and there are the sproutings of whales amidst their boiling foam.

By the same rule, where shall we look for Washington, the greatest among men, but in America—that greatest Continent, which, rising from beneath the frozen pole, stretches far and wide to the south, running almost "the whole length of this vast terrene," and sustaining on her ample sides the roaring shock of half the watery globe? And equal to its size is the furniture of this vast continent, where the Almighty has reared his cloud-capt mountains, and spread his sea-like lakes, and poured his mighty rivers, and hurled down his thundering cataracts in a style of the sublime, so far superior to any thing of the kind in the other continents, that we may fairly conclude that great men and great deeds are designed for America.

This seems to be the verdict of honest analogy; and accordingly we find America the honoured cradle of Washington, who was born on Pope's creek, in Westmoreland county, Virginia, the 22nd of February, 1732. His father, whose name was Augustin Washington, was also a Virginian: but his grandfather (John) was an Englishman, who came over and settled in Virginia in 1657.

His father, fully persuaded that a marriage of virtuous love comes nearest to angelic life, early stepped up to the altar with glowing cheeks and joy sparkling eyes, while by his side with soft warm hand, sweetly trembling in his, stood the angel-form of the lovely Miss Dandridge.

After several years of great domestic happiness, Mr. Washington was separated by death from this excellent woman, who left him and two children to lament her early fate.

Fully persuaded still, that "it is not good for man to be alone," he renewed, for the second time, the chaste delights of matrimonial love. His consort was Miss Mary Ball, a young lady of fortune, and descended from one of the best families in Virginia.

From his intermarriage with this charming girl, it would appear that our hero's father must have possessed either a very pleasing person, or highly polished manners, or perhaps both; for, from what I can learn, he was at that time at least forty years old! while she, on the other hand, was universally toasted as the belle of the Northern Neck, and in the full bloom and freshness of love-inspiring sixteen. This I have from one who tells me that he has carried down many a sett dance with her; I mean that amiable and pleasant old gentleman, John Fitzhugh, Esq. of Stafford, who was, all his life, a neighbour and intimate of the Washington family. By his first wife, Mr. Washington had two children, both sons— Lawrence and Augustin. By his second wife, he had five children, four sons and a daughter—George, Samuel, John, Charles, and Elizabeth. Those over delicate folk, who are ready to faint at thought of a second marriage, might do well to remember, that the greatest man that ever lived was the son of this second marriage.

Little George had scarcely attained his fifth year, when his father left Pope's creek, and came up to a plantation which he had in Stafford, opposite to Fredericksburg. The house in which he lived is still to be seen. It lifts its low and modest front of faded red, over the turbid waters of Rappahannock; whither, to this day, numbers of people repair, and, with emotions unutterable, looking at the weather-beaten mansion, exclaim, "Here's the house where the great Washington was born!"

But it is all a mistake; for he was born, as I said, at Pope's creek, in Westmoreland county, near the margin of his own roaring Potomac.

The first place of education to which George was ever sent, was a little "old field school," kept by one of his father's tenants, named Hobby; an honest, poor old man, who acted in the double character of sexton and schoolmaster. On his skill as a grave-digger, tradition is silent; but for a teacher of youth, his qualifications were certainly of the humbler sort; making what is generally called an A. B. C. schoolmaster. Such was the preceptor who first taught Washington the knowledge of letters! Hobby lived to see his young pupil in all his glory, and rejoiced exceedingly. In his cups—for though a sexton, he would sometimes drink, particularly on the General's birth days—he used to boast that "'twas he, who, between his knees, had laid the foundation of George Washington's greatness."

But though George was early sent to a schoolmaster, yet he was not on that account neglected by his father. Deeply sensible of the loveliness and worth of which human nature is capable, through the virtues and graces early implanted in the heart, he never for a moment, lost sight of George in those all-important respects.

To assist his son to overcome that selfish spirit, which too often leads children to fret and fight about trifles, was a notable care of Mr. Washington. For this purpose, of all the presents, such as cakes, fruit, &c. he received, he was always desired to give a liberal part to his playmates. To enable him to do this with more alacrity, his father would remind him of the love which he would thereby gain, and the frequent presents which would in return be made to him; and also would tell of that great and good God, who delights above all things to see children love one another, and will assuredly reward them for acting so amiable a part.

Some idea of Mr. Washington's plan of education in this respect, may be collected from the following anecdote, related to me twenty years ago by an aged lady, who was a distant relative, and, when a girl, spent much of her time in the family:

"On a fine morning," said she, "in the fall of 1737, Mr. Washington having little George by the hand, came to the door and asked my cousin Washington and myself to walk with him to the orchard, promising he would show us a fine sight. On arriving at the orchard, we were presented with a fine sight indeed. The whole earth, as far as we could see, was strewed with fruit: and yet the trees were bending under the weight of apples, which hung in clusters like grapes, and vainly strove to hide their blushing cheeks behind the green leaves. Now, George, said his father, look here, my son! Don't you remember when this good cousin of yours brought you that fine large apple last spring, how hardly I could prevail on you to divide with your brothers and sisters; though I promised you that if you would but do it, God Almighty would give you plenty of apples this fall. Poor George could not say a word; but hanging down his head, looked quite confused, while with his little naked toes he scratched in the soft ground. Now look up, my son, continued his father, look up, George! and see how richly the blessed God has made good my promise to you. Wherever you turn your eyes, you see the trees loaded with fine fruit; many of them indeed breaking down; while the ground is covered with mellow apples, more than you could eat, my son, in all your life time."

George looked in silence on the wide wilderness of fruit. He marked the busy humming bees, and heard the gay notes of birds; then lifting his eyes, filled with shining moisture, to his father, he softly said, "Well, Pa, only forgive me this time; and see if I ever be so stingy any more."

Some, when they look up to the oak, whose giant arms throw a darkening shade over distant acres, or whose single trunk lays the keel of a man of war, cannot bear to hear of the time when this mighty plant was but an acorn, which a pig could have demolished. But others, who know their value, like to learn the soil and situation which best produces such noble trees. Thus, parents that are wise, will listen, welled pleased, while I relate how moved the steps of the youthful Washington, whose single worth far outweighs all the oaks of Bashan and the red spicy cedars of Lebanon. Yes, they will listen delighted while I tell of their Washington in the days of his youth, when his little feet were swift towards the nests of birds; or when, wearied in the chase of the butterfly, he laid him down on his grassy couch and slept, while ministering spirits, with their roseate wings, fanned his glowing cheeks, and kissed his lips of innocence with that fervent love which makes the Heaven!

Never did the wise Ulysses take more pains with his beloved Telemachus, than did Mr. Washington with George, to inspire him with an early love of truth. "Truth, George," said he, "is the loveliest quality of youth. I would ride fifty miles, my son, to see the little boy whose heart is so honest, and his lips so pure, that we may depend on every word he says. O how lovely does such a child appear in the eyes of every body! his parents doat on him. His relations glory in him. They are constantly praising him to their children, whom they beg to imitate him. They are often sending for him to visit them; and receive him, when he comes, with as much joy as if he were a little angel, come to set pretty examples to their children.

"But, Oh! How different, George, is the case with the boy who is so given to lying, that nobody can believe a word he says! He is looked at with aversion wherever he goes, and parents dread to see him come among their children. Oh, George! my son! rather than see you come to this pass, dear as you are to my heart, gladly would I assist to nail you up in your little coffin, and follow you to your grave. Hard, indeed, would it be to me to give up my son, whose little feet are always so ready to run about with me, and whose fondly looking eyes, and sweet prattle make so large a part of my happiness. But still I would give him up, rather than see him a common liar."

"Pa," said George very seriously, "do I ever tell lies?"

"No, George, I thank God you do not, my son; and I rejoice in the hope you never will. At least, you shall never, from me, have cause to be guilty of so shameful a thing. Many parents, indeed, even compel their children to this vile practice, by barbarously beating them for every little fault: hence, on the next offence, the little terrified creature slips out a lie! just to escape the rod. But as to yourself George, you know I have always told you, and now tell you again, that, whenever by accident, you do any thing wrong, which must often be the case, as you are but a poor little boy yet, without experience or knowledge, you must never tell a falsehood to conceal it; but come bravely up, my son, like a little man, and tell me of it: and, instead of beating you, George, I will but the more honour and love you for it, my dear."

This, you'll say, was sowing good seed!—Yes, it was: and the crop, thank God, was, as I believe it ever will be, where a man acts the true parent, that is, the Guardian Angel, by his child.

The following anecdote is a case in point. It is too valuable to be lost, and too true to be doubted; for it was communicated to me by the same excellent lady to whom I am indebted for the last.

"When George," said she, "was about six years old, he was made the wealthy master of a hatchet! of which, like most little boys, he was immoderately fond, and was constantly going about chopping every thing that came in his way. One day, in the garden, where he often amused himself hacking his mother's pea-sticks, he unluckily tried the edge of his hatchet on the body of a beautiful young English cherry-tree, which he barked so terribly, that I don't believe the tree ever got the better of it. The next morning the old gentleman, finding out what had befallen his tree, which, by the by, was a great favourite, came into the house; and with much warmth asked for the mischievous author, declaring at the same time, that he would not have taken five guineas for his tree. Nobody could tell him any thing about it. Presently George and his hatchet made their appearance. "George," said his father, "do you know who killed that beautiful little cherry tree yonder in the garden?" This was a tough question; and George staggered under it for a moment; but quickly recovered himself: and looking at his father, with the sweet face of youth brightened with the inexpressible charm of all-conquering truth, he bravely cried out, "I can't tell a lie, Pa; you know I can't tell a lie. I did cut it with my hatchet."—Run to my arms, you dearest boy, cried his father in transports, run to my arms; glad am I, George, that you killed my tree;

for you have paid me for it a thousand fold. Such an act of heroism in my son is more worth than a thousand trees, though blossomed with silver, and their fruits of purest gold."

It was in this way by interesting at once both his heart and head, that Mr. Washington conducted George with great ease and pleasure along the happy paths of virtue. But well knowing that his beloved charge, soon to be a man, would be left exposed to numberless temptations, both from himself and from others, his heart throbbed with the tenderest anxiety to make him acquainted with that great being, whom to know and love, is to possess the surest defence against vice, and the best of all motives to virtue and happiness. To startle George into a lively sense of his Maker, he fell upon the following very curious, but impressive expedient:

One day he went into the garden, and prepared a little bed of finely pulverized earth, on which he wrote George's name at full, in large letters—then strewing in plenty of cabbage seed, he covered them up, and smoothed all over nicely with the roller.—This bed he purposely prepared close along side of a gooseberry walk, which happening at this time to be well hung with ripe fruit, he knew would be honoured with George's visits pretty regularly every day. Not many mornings had passed away before in came George, with eyes wild rolling, and his little cheeks, ready to burst with great news.

"O Pa! come here! come here!"

"What's the matter, my son? what's the matter?"

"O come here, I tell you, Pa: come here! and I'll show you such a sight as you never saw in all your life time."

The old gentleman suspecting what George would be at, gave him his hand, which he seized with great eagerness, and tugging him along through the garden, led him point blank to the bed whereon was inscribed, in large letters, and in all the freshness of newly sprung plants, the full name of George Washington.

"There Pa?" said George, quite in an ecstasy of astonishment, "did you ever see such a sight in all your life time?"

"Why it seems like a curious affair, sure enough, George!"

"But, Pa, who did make it there? who did make it there?"

"It grew there by chance, I suppose, my son."

"By chance, Pa! O no! no! it never did grow there by chance, Pa. Indeed that it never did!"

"High! why not, my son?"

"Why, Pa, did you ever see any body's name in a plant bed before?"

"Well, but George, such a thing might happen, though you never saw it before."

"Yes, Pa; but I did never see the little plants grow up so as to make one single letter of my name before. Now, how could they grow up so as to make all the letters of my name! and then standing one after another, to spell my name so exactly!—and all so neat and even too, at top and bottom!! O Pa, you must not say chance did all this. Indeed somebody did it; and I dare say now, Pa, you did it just to scare me, because I am your little boy."

His father smiled; and said, "Well George, you have guessed right. I indeed did it; but not to scare you, my son; but to learn you a great thing which I wish you to understand. I want, my son, to introduce you to your true Father."

"High, Pa, an't you my true father, that has loved me, and been so good to me always?"

"Yes George, I am your father, as the world calls it: and I love you very dearly too. But yet with all my love for you, George, I am but a poor good-for-nothing sort of a father in comparison of one you have."

"Aye! I know, well enough whom you mean, Pa. You mean God Almighty; don't you?"

"Yes, my son, I mean him indeed. He is your true Father, George."

"But, Pa, where is God Almighty! I did never see him yet."

"True my son; but though you never saw him, yet he is always with you. You did not see me when ten days ago I made this little plant bed, where you see your name in such beautiful green letters: but though you did not see me here, yet you know I was here!"

"Yes, Pa, that I do. I know you was here."

"Well then, and as my son could not believe that chance had made and put together so exactly the letters of his name, (though only sixteen) then how can he believe, that chance could have made and put together all those millions of things that are now so exactly fitted to his good! That my son may look at every thing around him, see! what fine eyes he has got! and a little pug nose to smell the sweet flowers! and pretty ears to hear sweet sounds! and a lovely mouth for his bread and butter! and O, the little ivory teeth to cut it for him! and the dear little tongue to prattle with his father! and precious little hands and fingers to hold his play-things!

and beautiful little feet for him to run about upon! and when my little rogue of a son is tired with running about, then the still night comes for him to lie down: and his mother sings, and the little crickets chirp him to sleep! and as soon as he has slept enough, and jumps up fresh and strong as a little buck, there the sweet golden light is ready for him! When he looks down into the water, there he sees the beautiful silver fishes for him! and up in the tree there are the apples, and peaches, and thousands of sweet fruits for him! and all, all around him, wherever my dear boy looks, he sees every thing just to his wants and wishes;—the bubbling springs with cool sweet water for him to drink! and the wood to make him sparkling fires when he is cold! and beautiful horses for him to ride! and strong oxen to work for him! and the good cow to give him milk! and bees to make sweet honey for his sweeter mouth! and the little lambs, with snowy wool, for beautiful clothes for him! Now, these and all the ten thousand thousand other good things more than my son can ever think of, and all so exactly fitted to his use and delight—Now how could chance ever have done all this for my little son? Oh George!—

He would have gone on: but George, who had hung upon his father's words with looks and eyes of all-devouring attention, here broke out—

"Oh, Pa, that's enough! that's enough! It can't be chance, indeed—it can't be chance, that made and gave me all these things."

"What was it then, do you think, my son?"

"Indeed, Pa, I don't know unless it was God Almighty!"

"Yes, George, he it was, my son, and nobody else."

"Well, but Pa, (continued George) does God Almighty give me every thing? Don't you give me some things, Pa?"

"I give you something indeed! Oh how can I give you any thing, George! I who have nothing on earth that I can call my own, no, not even the breath I draw!"

"High, Pa! isn't that great big house your house, and this garden, and the horses yonder, and oxen, and sheep, and trees, and every thing, isn't all yours, Pa?"

"Oh no! my son! no! why you make me shrink into nothing, George, when you talk of all these belonging to me, who can't even make a grain of sand! Oh, how could I, my son, have given life to those great oxen and horses, when I can't give life even to a fly?—no! for if the poorest fly were killed, it is not your father, George, nor all the men in the world, that could ever make him alive again!"

At this, George fell into a profound silence, while his pensive looks showed that his youthful soul was labouring with some idea never felt before. Perhaps it was at that moment, that the good Spirit of God ingrafted on his heart that germ of piety, which filled his after life with so many of the precious fruits of morality.

Paul Revere

[WALTER A. DYER]

Paul Revere was keenly alive to the importance of the trust thus placed in him, and he watched the course of events like a cat. No slightest detail escaped him. It was not wholly easy to get news in and out of Boston promptly, but Revere managed it. Newton had all the members of the watch under surveillance, but Peter Brackett was still a free lance, so far as the organization was concerned. And if anybody could slip through the lines, the wily Peter could. Arrangements were made whereby he could leave town quietly on foot and then ride to Concord, and the result was that Paul Revere received daily bulletins from the seat of the Provincial Government.

On Saturday, April 15th, the Congress adjourned, to reconvene in one month, but Hancock and Adams, made fully aware of their peril by messages delivered by Peter, did not return to Boston. Instead they went to Lexington and accepted the hospitality of Hancock's cousin and her husband, the Rev. Jonas Clark. Hither, in a panic after another raid on Hancock's house, came Madam Lydia

Hancock, the aunt who acted as hostess in his establishment, and with her came her young and pretty friend, Dorothy Quincy, a relative of Mr. Clark's. In spite of her panic, Madam Hancock had a method in this, for she was a shrewd and confirmed old matchmaker, and she had long ago selected Dorothy to be Hancock's bride. He had remained a bachelor altogether too long, according to her way of thinking, and Mr. Clark's quiet house seemed to her an ideal place for courting. That her plot was successful is evidenced by the fact that Hancock and Dorothy were married the following August. Meanwhile, however, the Clark house proved to be anything but the quiet rendezvous that Madam Hancock had pictured it.

In Boston Revere felt now somewhat less alarmed for Hancock and Adams, since Peter reported them prepared to leave on short notice, but he felt a growing concern for the supplies that the Committee of Safety had been collecting at Concord. They seemed dangerously near to Boston. Gage had learned through his secret informant that these stores were of considerable importance, and Revere knew that Gage knew. Any move in that direction must be thwarted or the Committee of Safety might lose what it had taken them months to collect. Revere ordered the Committee of Six and the Watch of Thirty to redouble their vigilance. They must not let the smallest trifle escape them.

The legends that attribute the leaking out of Gage's plans to the fact that his wife was an American woman of Whig sympathies have been the cause of considerable debate, but they are not needed to explain the situation. Indiscreet soldiers talked too much, and wherever there were ears, those ears were used to serve Paul Revere.

Indeed, it was very evident that some sort of expedition was being planned. The small boats of the transport fleet had been drawn up and repaired. That looked like some sort of expedition by water. On the other hand, there were military preparations reported that suggested a march by land. In any case Revere felt certain that Concord would be the objective and he laid his plans accordingly.

On Saturday evening, April 15th, Revere's patrols brought him reports that something was in the wind. Details began to reach him, and at midnight he went to Warren.

"Something is up," said he. "All the grenadiers and light infantry have been taken off sentry duty and are held in barracks. All the small boats of the transports have been launched and are lying hidden under the sterns of the men-o'-war. What do you make of it?"

"An expedition, undoubtedly," said Warren. "Perhaps they mean to cross to Charlestown in force. At any rate, you had better prepare for that contingency. They may be after Hancock and Adams at Lexington or the stores at Concord—perhaps both. There must be no sleep for us this night."

There was no sleep for Paul Revere. Indeed, the Sons of Liberty were so active about the town that Gage must have decided to postpone action until his plans were more fully matured. At all events, morning found the soldiers still in their barracks.

Warren, however, was not to be lulled into a false sense of security. He knew that Peter Brackett had warned the patriots at Lexington and Concord, but he could not feel quite content until he knew that Paul Revere himself had been to see them. Accordingly, on Sunday morning, April

16th, he summoned Revere and requested him to take the dangerous ride himself to Lexington and Concord in order to see to it that the facts were fully set before Hancock and Adams and the Committee of Safety.

This proved to be one of the most important if one of the least spectacular of all Paul Revere's rides. He managed to slip quietly out of town by way of the Neck and found the horse that was held for Peter's use. Then, jogging slowly along the back roads, attracting as little attention as possible, and making sure that Newton's men were thrown off the scent, he made his way to Lexington.

Revere did not mince matters, and Hancock, now thoroughly aroused to the seriousness of the situation, began to take immediate action. He sent out a call to the members of the Provincial Congress to meet in Watertown on April 22nd instead of May 15th. Then he sent Revere on to Concord with messages for the Committee of Safety and Supplies which was still in session there.

As a result of this timely warning, the stores were removed to places of greater security. On the following day, the 17th, they were quietly disposed of. Two four-pounders were hidden in Concord in charge of the artillery company there. Four six-pounders were sent to Groton under Colonel Prescott. Two seven-inch mortars were taken to Acton. The ammunition in the hands of Colonel Barrett, and also the intrenching implements, medical supplies, etc., were distributed in like manner among the towns of Worcester, Lancaster, Groton, Mendor, Leicester, and Sudbury. Revere, with a less anxious heart, rode home by way of Charlestown.

It proved easier to get into Boston than to get out again. On Tuesday soldiers were guarding every exit and the challenges of the sentries were more peremptory. The ferries ceased running. The *Somerset* moved from the bay into the Charles River and her guns covered the ferry ways. At 9 o'clock in the evening orders were issued forbidding all exit from the town; Boston was closed up tight.

But if the soldiers were watchful, so were the Sons of Liberty, especially the vigilant Thirty. During the evening reports reached Revere that the troops were being mustered. The movement appeared to be not toward the Neck, but toward the bottom of the Common.

At 10 o'clock Warren sent for him in great haste.

"What have you learned?" asked Warren.

"Enough to convince me," replied Revere, "that the troops will move to-night and that they will go by water rather than by land. They are not moving toward the Neck."

"I agree with you," said Warren. "Gage's promised expedition is on foot. I am told that 1,500 men have been mobilized. Hancock and Adams must be warned at once and persuaded to leave Lexington for a place of greater safety. The remaining stores are also in danger. We must guard against every chance of failure. To that end I have already dispatched William Dawes, who said that he was confident of being able to slip through the lines and across the Neck. But we must not depend on one man. You we have learned to trust. Do you cross the river and proceed through Charlestown, Revere."

"I will undertake to win through," said Revere. "But to make assurance doubly sure, I have already arranged a signal to acquaint our friends in Charlestown with what is going forward. They will take the message in case I am intercepted."

"Good," said Warren.

No further time was wasted in words. Revere started at once.

His first move was to find Peter Brackett.

"Peter," said he, "there are important tasks ahead of us all this night. I ride secretly to Lexington. Captain Pulling will also have a difficult duty to perform and he will remain here in Boston, in great danger. If he is discovered and caught, you know that Newton will see to it that short work is made of him. Newton hates Pulling almost as well as he hates me. You have two sharp eyes, Peter. Let one of them watch Newton's men, whom you know well. Keep the other on Captain Pulling and see that he is warned if danger threatens."

Peter nodded and slipped silently away.

Revere found Pulling at his home in Salem Street and quietly entered the house by a back door.

"The hour has struck," said Pulling.

"It has, John," said Revere. "And I have a hazardous task for you. If I can get cross the river, I ride express to Lexington to warn Hancock and Adams. God grant that I may be in time."

"But the river is guarded," said Pulling.

"True," replied Revere. "I may fail at the outset. But I have taken steps to get a message through in case I fail. On my return from Lexington yesterday I passed through Charlestown. There I put the case before our friend Colonel Conant. He will have a horseman ready and as soon as he sees our signals he will know what the message will be. Then he will wait a reasonable time, and if I do not appear, he will dispatch his messenger. I must hurry. With you I leave the responsibility of the signals. I depend upon your resourcefulness."

"What were the signals agreed upon?" asked Pulling.

"Lanterns in the belfry of the North Church," replied Revere. "Conant will see them. I promised to show two lanterns if the troops should embark in the boats; one if they start off by land. They are moving now, and it looks as though they would proceed by water. Make sure, John, and then show the signals."

The two friends gripped hands and Revere departed as quietly as he had come.

John Pulling lost no time. He was a vestryman in the Old North Church and he knew where to get the keys. He started at once for the home of Robert Newman, the sexton, who lived in the same street.

Reaching the house he took the precaution of peering in at the window. In the living room sat the sexton with four soldiers who were quartered on him. Pulling was perplexed. As he stood there cogitating, he heard a slight noise by his side which startled him, and then a cautious whisper.

"It's Peter Brackett. Mr. Revere told me to help you. Do you want to speak to Mr. Newman?"

"Very much I do," whispered Pulling.

"Leave that to me," said Peter.

"Be careful," said Pulling.

"I will," said Peter.

He hurried up the steps and banged at the knocker. Newman opened the door. Behind him loomed the figure of one of the soldiers.

"I am sorry to trouble you, Mr. Newman," said Peter, "but Mistress Hunter is much disturbed because no arrangements have been made for her son's funeral."

"Mistress Hunter?" echoed Newman, to whom the name meant nothing.

"If you will step out here just a minute, Mr. Newman, perhaps she can explain to you. She is much perturbed."

The weary soldier grunted and stepped back into the room while the puzzled sexton followed Peter into the shadow of a big maple.

"That was just a trick," whispered Peter in hurried explanation. "It's Captain Pulling that wants to speak with you."

Robert Newman, though not an active Son of Liberty, was known to Pulling as a faithful friend of the cause. At any rate, he had no choice but to trust him. In as few words as possible he acquainted him with the situation. Newman hesitated for a moment, and then answered, "All right; I'll chance it."

"Have you lanterns at the church?" asked Pulling.

"I have one," said the sexton. "I will fetch another and the keys."

He reentered his house, grumbling audibly, and closed the door behind him. In a short time he emerged through a kitchen window with an unlighted lantern in his hand and rejoined Pulling. Together the two made their way by a roundabout route to the church, while Peter vanished in the shadows.

The sound of marching feet was heard, and as they neared the water front they observed torches.

"The soldiers are taking to the boats," remarked Pulling. "It is by water, then, and two lanterns will be the signal."

They entered the empty church, but Pulling advised against lighting the lanterns until the last moment.

"Can you do it, Newman?" he asked. "You alone know those belfry stairs in the dark."

The sexton held back at first, but was at last persuaded.

"Light both lanterns and place them where they can be seen from the Charlestown shore," directed Pulling. "I'll remain here to keep watch."

Christ Church, or Old North, had been erected in 1723, and its graceful spire had long been a landmark for home-coming mariners. Never, however, had eyes sought it more eagerly than on that night, when Conant and his friends waited on the other side of the river for the promised signals. Slowly and somewhat fearfully the sexton mounted the creaking old stairs, while Pulling waited anxiously below.

At last Newman gained the belfry, and the watchful Conant saw first one point of light and then another.

"They come by water," said he. "It is well. Whatever may happen to Paul Revere, the warning will be sent before a British foot is set on Charlestown or Cambridge soil."

The sexton presently rejoined Pulling and they locked the door of the church behind them. Pulling slipped off toward the water front to observe the embarkation of the troops and to make sure that the lanterns were properly set, while Newman hurried home and reëntered his kitchen window.

Every available man that James Newton could command was on duty that night to guard against any leaking out of Gage's plan. And Newton had given special orders to watch Revere and Pulling, hoping that this time he might be able to catch them red-handed. Sharp eyes, therefore, spied those lanterns as soon as they flashed forth. Newton's men rushed to the church, but the door was already locked. Suspicion at once turned toward the sexton, who kept the keys.

Newton's men hurried to Newman's house, which was near by, and aroused the soldiers there. Their story was quickly told. The house was searched, and Robert Newman was found in bed. At first he appeared to have awakened from a sound sleep, and was extraordinarily stupid. The soldiers placed him under arrest and an officer, summoned to the house, began to question him.

No evidence against himself could be wormed out of the man, and at last he was released. But the officer was clever and persistent, and the sexton began to weaken under the rapid cross questioning. Finally they forced him to state that he had lent his keys to John Pulling.

That was enough for Newton's men. Here was the longed-for chance to win the reward their chief had offered. Out of the house they hurried with the soldiers, leaving the remorseful sexton to pray for the safety of his accomplice.

But there was one who had left ahead of the soldiers. Peter Brackett had been listening to the inquisition from the limb of a tree that reached close to Newman's window. As soon as he heard Pulling's name mentioned he dropped to the ground and was off like a deer.

By a happy chance he came upon Pulling who was just returning home from the water front.

"They are after you," panted Peter. "There's not a moment to be lost. No, you must not go home. I'll explain to your family. You must hide at once. Newton has sworn to have his revenge on you and he will show no mercy. You must not be taken. The old tobacco shed by the Mill Pond. Hide there and I will come to you before morning with something to eat. Meanwhile I'll try to throw them off the track."

John Pulling hated to flee, but there was no alternative. He hid himself securely and the soldiers and Newton's men never found him. The next day, with Peter Brackett's help, he disguised himself as a laborer and escaped to Nantasket with his family in a small boat, leaving all his worldly goods behind him.

To return to Paul Revere. Longfellow has made famous the ride he took that night in a poem that is spirited and unforgettable if not entirely accurate. Neither the episode of the lanterns nor the details of the ride are quite correct in that version, though it has served a noble end. Some years later Paul Revere wrote out two versions of his own which the historian may more safely follow.

Leaving his friend Pulling, assured that the signals would be shown, he hastened home for his boots and surtout and kissed his wife a hurried good-by. Then, avoiding the marching columns of red-coats, he hastened to the water front. To get across the Charles River was no easy task. All egress had been stopped at 9 o'clock. The ferry boats had been tied up and the guns of the *Somerset* covered the river.

But Revere was prepared for that. He had kept in constant readiness for such emergency a small boat, hidden beneath a cob-wharf on the Mill Pond side, in the custody of two loyal Sons of Liberty, John Richardson and Joshua Bentley, both of whom afterward fought gallantly in the Revolution. They lived near at hand

and Revere quickly found them. They brought out the boat and prepared to put off, when Revere halted them.

"The oars must be muffled," said he. "They will hear us else on the *Somerset*."

"A plague on it!" exclaimed Bentley. "We have no cloth."

"That is easily remedied, I think," said Richardson, and hurried to a house close by.

Under a window the young man gave a low whistle. The sash was stealthily raised and a hurried colloquy followed in guarded whispers. Revere heard a low feminine laugh and something white fluttered down to the ground. In triumph Richardson bore it back to the boat. It was a woman's skirt, suspiciously warm.

The thole pins were carefully wrapped in the cloth and the boat pushed out upon the water. Richardson and Bentley took the oars and Revere sat in the stern. With the utmost caution the men guided the precious craft across the river, under the very guns of the frowning man-of-war. An unwary splash or a cough would have betrayed them. It was a tense moment for Paul Revere as they crossed the *Somerset's* bows and made for the Charlestown shore. The rising moon broke through the low clouds as the men bent to their oars for the final pull. They were just in time.

They landed near the old battery in Charlestown, and there found Colonel Conant, Richard Devens, a member of the Committee of Safety, and two or three others.

"Well met, Revere," cried Conant. "We saw your signals and have a post rider all ready to start for Lexington. Shall we send him?"

"No," said Revere, "though I do thank you. I have got thus far; I will press on. The soldiers are already embarking; there is no time to lose. Can you get me a good horse?"

"At once," said Conant, and dispatched a man.

"Be cautious, Revere," warned Devens. "There are scouts upon the road. I myself came from Lexington to-day, and just after sunset I met with nine or ten British officers, armed and well mounted, going toward Concord."

"I'll be on my guard," said Revere.

The man appeared with a horse, saddled and bridled.

"It is Deacon Larkin's horse, and a good one," said the man. "I promised that no harm should befall it."

Revere laughed. "It were easy to promise," said he.

With all that had taken place, only an hour had elapsed since Revere had called on Dr. Warren. It was now about 11 o'clock, a full moon had risen, and the night was, as Revere puts it, "very pleasant." Pleased with the success of his crossing and enjoying the prospect of further adventure, he set off, riding cautiously at first.

He passed Charlestown Neck and took the open road. He had ridden a little way in the moonlight when his sharp eyes detected two horsemen waiting in the shade of a tree. The road was narrow here, and Revere saw that he would have to pass close to them. As he approached he discerned holsters and cockades; they were British officers.

He was about to make a dash for it when one of them rode directly toward him and the other took his place in the road ahead.

★   ★   ★

Revere suppressed the temptation to risk an encounter. Turning his horse short about, he made off at full speed as though to return to Charlestown. One of the officers was close at his heels, the other farther behind.

Selecting a dark spot in the road, he turned at right angles, struck off 'cross country, and made for the Medford Road. It was not easy going, for the spring mud had not dried up, but Revere knew the lay of the land like a book. His pursuer, less familiar with it, presently came to grief in a clay bank. Revere flung him back a taunting laugh. The other followed for a quarter of a mile and then gave it up.

Reaching the road, Revere let out his horse and proceeded at a rapid pace along the Mystic River to Medford. There he awoke the Captain of the minute-men.

"The British are on the way to Lexington and Concord," he cried. "They must be delayed as much as possible."

Then he dashed across the bridge and on toward Menotomy, now Arlington. Behind him the ringing church bells told him that the minute-men were gathering.

"They will fight!" he cried exultantly, urging his horse to greater speed. "The farmers will fight!"

The spirit of the situation was getting into his blood, and as he rode he shouted aloud to every farmhouse, "To arms, patriots! The red-coats are coming!"

> *"A hurry of hoofs in a village street,*
> *A shape in the moonlight, a bulk in the dark,*
> *And beneath, from the pebbles, in passing, a spark*
> *Struck out by the steed flying fearless and fleet:*
> *That was all! And yet, through the gloom and the light,*
> *The fate of a nation was riding that night."*

Back in Boston the soldiers were rapidly embarking. Warren knew that this was to be Gage's supreme effort. There was no sleep for him that night. The lives of Adams and Hancock were in dire peril; the fate of a nation hung in the balance. Would Revere be in time?

In Lexington the militia, warned by Revere the previous Sunday, were ready for whatever might happen. British officers had been seen on the road and the Clark house, with its precious occupants, was guarded by eight men under Sergeant William Monroe.

Meanwhile Deacon Larkin's horse was eating up the miles and Paul Revere was everywhere spreading the alarm. Farmers and townsmen tumbled out of bed and sought their weapons.

> *"So through the night rode Paul Revere!*
> *And so through the night went his cry of alarm*
> *To every Middlesex village and farm,—*
> *A cry of defiance and not of fear,*
> *A voice in the darkness, a knock at the door,*
> *And a word that shall echo forevermore!*
> *For, borne on the night-wind of the Past*
> *Through all our history to the last,*
> *In the hour of darkness and peril and need*
> *The people will waken and listen to hear*
> *The hurrying hoof-beats of that steed,*
> *And the midnight message of Paul Revere."*

On the stroke of twelve Revere came galloping up to Mr. Clark's door.

"Halt!" challenged Monroe. "Who goes there?"

"A friend," answered Revere, "and in a precious hurry."

"Hush!" cautioned Monroe. "Don't make so much noise. Everybody's asleep inside."

"Noise?" cried Revere. "There'll be noise soon enough. Why, man, the regulars are coming!"

The clattering hoofs and Revere's shouts had awakened Hancock, and he thrust his head out of an open window.

"Come on in, Revere," he called. "We're not afraid of you."

Revere dismounted and went inside. Mr. Clark brought candles and they were soon joined by Adams and Hancock.

"What's up, Revere?" asked Adams sleepily.

"No false alarm this time, Mr. Adams," replied Revere. "There are some 1,500 red-coats on the way from Boston. They will be here by daybreak."

"Are you sure?" demanded Adams, his face betraying his consternation.

"I saw them embarking myself," said Revere. "Dr. Warren sent me post haste to warn you, and I have alarmed everybody on the way. Hasn't William Dawes told you?"

"No," said Hancock, "no one has told us."

"That is strange," said Revere. "Dr. Warren sent Dawes first and he did not have to get across the water. He must have been intercepted. At all events, there is no time to waste. Dr. Warren said to urge you to leave on the instant. The British mean to make a thorough job of it this time. You should leave at once, Dr. Warren says, and not stop until you are safe in New York or Philadelphia."

"But," demurred Hancock, "we cannot leave the Provincial Congress in the lurch. I have called them to meet on the 22nd."

"They would be left more in the lurch if you were to be captured, Mr. Hancock. I tell you the whole British army is after you. Gage has vowed that you shall not escape."

John Hancock, for all his elegance, did not lack heroic qualities in an emergency. Though aroused to a sense of his personal peril, his first thought was for his followers and for the remaining stores. He sent word at once to Buckman's Tavern, the militia headquarters. Soon a bell raised its clamor, and militia and citizens gathered to the number of about 150.

While Hancock and Adams were taking counsel together, William Dawes arrived on a spent horse, after a difficult journey. He did not wait to tell his story but sought at once a fresh mount and proposed that he and Revere should carry the news on to Concord where there were still some valuable stores to be secreted.

After a bare half hour's rest they set off again along the Concord road. They had not proceeded far when they heard hoof-beats on the road behind them.

"There is but one of them," said Revere. "We need not fear."

Presently they were overtaken by a horseman who was evidently not a British officer.

"Good evening to you, gentlemen," said he. "It is good to have company on the road in these times."

"It is indeed," replied Revere, "so be it the company be friendly."

"I will be bold," laughed the stranger. "If you be friends of King George, we may as well part company."

"Not so," said Dawes. "We be friends of freedom, and we ride, Revere and I, to tell the militia at Concord that the British are coming."

"Then that rumor is true?" said the stranger. "And you are Paul Revere? Well met, Revere. My name is Prescott, Dr. Prescott of Concord."

"Well met, indeed," said Revere, "for I know your name as that of a loyal Son of Liberty. But have you no errand this time of night?"

"No errand but to get home," said Prescott. "I fear I lingered overlong with a certain lady in Lexington."

"So that's the quarter in which the wind sets," laughed Revere. "Well, you had best put from your mind thoughts of courting now. We must keep a sharp lookout, for scouts have been seen on the road by both Dawes and myself, and by Richard Devens earlier in the day. We may be stopped if we don't look out."

"We'd better spread the alarm as we go, in any case," said Dawes.

"I know every farmer between here and Concord. I'll attend to that," said Prescott.

So they began spreading the alarm as they rode. While Prescott and Dawes were engaged in trying to get the facts into the head of a sleepy farmer, Revere went on ahead. He had gone about 200 yards when he became aware of two horsemen in the road ahead of him. He turned and shouted back to Dawes and Prescott:

"Look out! Scouts ahead!"

The two horsemen bore down upon him at that and two more suddenly appeared from the shadow of a tree in the pasture close by. Revere was immediately surrounded and one of the horsemen clapped a pistol to his breast.

"Move an inch farther and you're a dead man," cried the officer.

Revere was unable to give a second warning and Dawes and Prescott came riding up to be stopped in like manner. Then all three were forced through a barway into the pasture.

Each one of the three fully intended to make a dash for liberty, and as soon as they reached the shadow of the tree Revere gave a yell and struck spurs to his horse. A hand clutched Dawes's bridle and held him, but Revere and Prescott started off full tilt.

Prescott was the lucky one. He turned his horse sharply to the right, jumped the stone wall, gained the road, and escaped to carry the alarm to Concord. Revere, who knew nothing of the jumping abilities of Deacon Larkin's horse, turned to the left and made for the wood at the foot of the pasture. He might have shaken his pursuers there, but as luck would have it six more horsemen emerged from the wood and blocked his way. Again a pistol was presented to Revere's breast and he was ordered to dismount. There was nothing for it but to comply. Then the leader of the six, who appeared to be a gentlemanly fellow, came forward.

"What is your name?" he demanded.

"Revere."

"Paul Revere?" asked the officer, not without a sort of respect in his tone.

"Yes."

"You ride express from Boston?"

"Yes."

The others crowded about and seemed desirous of abusing Revere, but the leader restrained them.

"He's the man we want," they said.

"He will serve us better alive than dead," said the officer.

"Gentlemen," said Revere, "I know what you are after, but you have missed your aim. You are after bigger game than me but you will not find it. I left Boston after your troops had landed at Lechmere Point and if I were not certain that the people to the distance of fifty miles into the country had been notified of your movements, I would have risked one shot before you should have taken me. We shall have 500 men here forthwith."

"But we have 1,500 coming," indiscreetly answered the officer.

"I know that well enough," said Revere, "but they will not be enough and they will not come soon enough. The whole countryside is aroused, I tell you. It is you who are in danger, not I."

Now the other four came on the scene, with the captured Dawes. One of them was Major Mitchell of the Fifth Regiment. He pointed his pistol at Revere and frowned menacingly.

"Tell me the truth or I will blow your brains out," said he.

He asked several questions and got much the same answers that Revere had given before. The soldiers were evidently disturbed by his replies and his fearless bearing. Then they took away his pistols and ordered him to remount. An officer grasped his bridle. Four other prisoners were now brought from the woods and all returned to the road. It was a Sergeant who guided Revere's horse, and he held his pistol in readiness.

"Remember," said he, "I will shoot if you attempt to escape or if any attempt at rescue appears."

On the road the soldiers arranged themselves in a circle with their prisoners in the center. Revere was too well guarded by the Sergeant to attempt escape, but the soldiers had become alarmed, some of them relaxed their vigilance, and suddenly William Dawes tore his bridle from the hand of his captor and made a dash for it.

Three of the horsemen started pell mell on his heels. He kept well ahead at first, but his horse was not a fast one, and they began to gain on him. As he approached a darkened farmhouse he raised his voice in an exultant shout.

"Hello, boys," he yelled, "I've got three of 'em!"

The ruse succeeded, the soldiers turned and fled without more ado, and Dawes escaped.

The others pressed on toward Lexington. Suddenly the report of a musket was heard.

"What was that?" cried Major Mitchell.

"An alarm gun," replied Revere quite truthfully. "The countryside is gathering. You will soon find yourselves in hot water."

"We can't be bothered with these fellows," said the Major. He caused all the prisoners to dismount except Revere, removed their saddles and bridles, turned the horses loose, and sent the men about their business. Then they rode cautiously on again.

More guns were heard. The Major ordered a halt and commanded the Sergeant to take Revere's horse, his own being fagged. The saddle and bridle were cut from the Sergeant's mount and he was turned loose. Revere was compelled to proceed on foot.

As they approached Lexington they could see the minute-men gathering. The soldiers began to look to their arms and their horses, and in the midst of the confusion Revere slipped quietly away. What eventually happened to Deacon Larkin's beloved horse, history, unfortunately, does not tell.

Meanwhile the British troops—though not the full 1,500 of them—had indeed crossed the Charles River and had landed about midnight near Phipps's Farm, Lechmere Point, Cambridge. They heard the church bells and saw the minute-men gathering as they started on the road toward Lexington. Lieutenant-Colonel Smith, who was in command of the force, alarmed at these evidences of preparedness against them, ordered a rapid march, sent back to Boston for reinforcements, and bade Major Pitcairn of the Marines, with one company, to push on ahead with all speed.

Revere, finding himself free at last, though without a horse, and knowing the roads to be filled with peril for the fugitives, hurried across the burying-ground to the Clark house. Much to his dismay he found Hancock and Adams still there. Hancock, indeed, had announced his firm intention of remaining to fight.

Revere, who understood the danger better than they, was beside himself with anxiety. He did not mince matters. Forgetting for a moment their relative positions he all but ordered them out of the house.

"The time has come to strike a blow for Liberty," said Hancock. "Shall it be said that John Hancock fled in that hour of need?"

But Adams had the wiser head of the two.

"Revere is right," said he. "This is not our business, this fighting. Remember, Hancock, we belong to the Cabinet."

Very tactfully he argued with the headstrong leader and at last, about daybreak, persuaded him to go. Hancock's secretary, Lowell, had been making the arrangements, and said that they should go at once to Woburn, and on from there the next night.

At last, when it seemed as though the British must be nearly upon them, Adams and Hancock started. Lowell and Revere accompanied them for about two miles to guard against an encounter with the scouts, and Revere at least was prepared to fight to death for them if need arose. But they were not molested, and finally Revere and Lowell, assured of their safety, turned back.

Hancock and Adams proceeded to the home of the Rev. Samuel Sewell in Woburn where they were carefully protected against capture. Dorothy Quincy and Mrs. Hancock joined them later and they were escorted by easy stages out of the dangerous country. Hancock and Dorothy were married in Fairfield, Conn., on August 28th, and thence they went on to New York and Philadelphia.

As Revere and Lowell turned back toward Lexington, the latter bethought him of a trunk filled with valuable papers belonging to Hancock.

"Those must certainly be rescued," said Lowell, "or I shall sweat for it. They must be sent on to Philadelphia."

"Where are they?" asked Revere.

"In the tavern," said Lowell.

"Well, then let us get them," said Revere. "That is certainly no safe place for them."

As they hurried on they met a man on horseback.

"What news?" cried Revere.

"The troops are less than two miles away," shouted the man as he dashed past on his errand.

Lowell's face turned a sickly hue, but Revere urged him to hurry on.

"Thank God, Hancock and Adams are safe," said he. "They started none too soon."

Revere stopped for a moment at the Clark house to give the ladies tidings of Hancock and then hastened with Lowell to the tavern. From a chamber window they could see the troops approaching up the road in the distance.

"We have no time to get this away now," said Revere, as they bore the trunk down stairs. "We must hide it in Mr. Clark's garret. It will look like any other trunk up there, if a search should be made. Judging by what is acting here they may have small chance to search for anything but the way back to Boston."

As he spoke they were passing through a body of fifty or sixty militia standing with weapons ready. Lowell, taking the small trunk in his arms, started on a run for the Clark house. Revere tarried.

He beheld about 800 British soldiers, with a mounted officer at their head, appear around both sides of the meeting-house. Facing them, across the green, was the handful of minute-men.

As Revere started on toward the Clark house he heard a pistol shot, followed by two musket shots. Then he turned just in time to see the troops fire a volley.

Nathan Hale

[JAMES PARTON]

eneral Washington wanted a man. It was in September, 1776, at the City of New York, a few days after the battle of Long Island. The swift and deep East River flowed between the two hostile armies, and General Washington had as yet no system established for getting information of the enemy's movements and intentions. He never needed such information so much as at that crisis.

What would General Howe do next? If he crossed at Hell Gate, the American army, too small in numbers, and defeated the week before, might be caught on Manhattan Island as in a trap, and the issue of the contest might be made to depend upon a single battle; for in such circumstances defeat would involve the capture of the whole army. And yet General Washington was compelled to confess:

"We cannot learn, nor have we been able to procure the least information of late."

Therefore he wanted a man. He wanted an intelligent man, cool-headed, skillful, brave, to cross the East River to Long Island, enter the enemy's camp, and get information as to his strength and intentions. He went to Colonel Knowlton, commanding a remarkably efficient regiment from Connecticut, and requested him to ascertain if this man, so sorely needed, could be found in his command. Colonel Knowlton called his officers together, stated the wishes of General Washington, and, without urging the enterprise upon any individual, left the matter to their reflections.

Captain Nathan Hale, a brilliant youth of twenty-one, recently graduated from Yale College, was one of those who reflected upon the subject. He soon reached a conclusion. He was of the very flower of the young men of New England, and one of the best of the younger soldiers of the patriot army. He had been educated for the ministry, and his motive in adopting for a time the profession of arms was purely patriotic. This we know from the familiar records of his life at the time when the call to arms was first heard.

In addition to his other gifts and graces, he was handsome, vigorous, and athletic, all in an extraordinary degree. If he had lived in our day he might have pulled the stroke-oar at New London, or pitched for the college nine.

The officers were conversing in a group. No one had as yet spoken the decisive word. Colonel Knowlton appealed to a French sergeant, an old soldier of former wars, and asked him to volunteer.

"No, no," said he. "I am ready to fight the British at any place and time, but I do not feel willing to go among them to be hung up like a dog."

Captain Hale joined the group of officers. He said to Colonel Knowlton:

"I will undertake it."

Some of his best friends remonstrated. One of them, afterwards the famous general William Hull, then a captain in Washington's army, has recorded Hale's reply to his own attempt to dissuade him.

"I think," said Hale, "I owe to my country the accomplishment of an object so important. I am fully sensible of the consequences of discovery and capture in such a situation. But for a year I have been attached to the army, and have not rendered any material service, while receiving a compensation for which I make no return. I wish to be useful, and every kind of service necessary for the public good becomes honorable by being necessary."

He spoke, as General Hull remembered, with earnestness and decision, as one who had considered the matter well, and had made up his mind.

Having received his instructions, he traveled fifty miles along the Sound as far as Norwalk in Connecticut. One who saw him there made a very wise remark upon him, to the effect that he was "too good-looking" to go as a spy. He could not deceive. "Some scrubby fellow ought to have gone." At Norwalk he assumed the disguise of a Dutch schoolmaster, putting on a suit of plain brown clothes, and a round, broad-brimmed hat. He had no difficulty in crossing the Sound, since he bore an order from General Washington which placed at his disposal all the vessels belonging to Congress. For several days everything appears to have gone well with him, and there is reason to believe that he passed through the entire British army without detection or even exciting suspicion.

Finding the British had crossed to New York, he followed them. He made his way back to Long Island, and nearly reached the point opposite Norwalk where he had originally landed. Rendered perhaps too bold by success, he went into a well-known and popular tavern, entered into conversation with the guests, and made himself very agreeable. The tradition is that he made himself too agreeable. A man present suspecting or knowing that he was not the character he had assumed, quietly left the room, communicated his suspicions to the captain of a British ship anchored near, who dispatched a boat's crew to capture and bring on board the agreeable stranger. His true character was immediately revealed. Drawings of some of the British works, with notes in Latin, were found hidden in the soles of his shoes. Nor did he attempt to deceive his captors, and the English captain, lamenting, as he said, that "so fine a fellow had fallen into his power," sent him to New York in one of his boats, and with him the fatal proofs that he was a spy.

September twenty-first was the day on which he reached New York—the day of the great fire which laid one-third of the little city in ashes. From the time of his departure from General Washington's camp to that of his return to New York was about fourteen days. He was taken to General Howe's headquarters at the Beekman mansion, on the East River, near the corner of the present Fifty-first Street and First Avenue. It is a strange coincidence that this house to which he was brought to be tried as a spy was the very one from which Major Andre departed when he went to West Point. Tradition says that Captain Hale was examined in a greenhouse which then stood in the garden of the Beekman mansion.

Short was his trial, for he avowed at once his true character. The British general signed an order to his provost-marshal directing him to receive into his custody the prisoner convicted as a spy, and to see him hanged by the neck "to-morrow morning at daybreak."

Terrible things are reported of the manner in which this noble prisoner, this admirable gentleman and hero, was treated by his jailer and executioner. There are savages in every large army, and it is possible that this provost-marshal was one of them. It is said that he refused him writing-materials, and afterwards, when Captain Hale had been furnished them by others, destroyed before his face his last letters to his mother and to the young lady to whom he was engaged to be married. As those letters were never received this statement may be true. The other alleged horrors of the execution it is safe to disregard, because we know that it was conducted in the usual form and in the presence of many spectators and a considerable body of troops. One fact shines out from the distracting confusion of that morning, which will be cherished to the latest posterity as a precious ingot of the moral treasure of the American people. When asked if he had anything to say, Captain Hale replied:

"I only regret that I have but one life to lose for my country."

The scene of his execution was probably an old graveyard in Chambers Street, which was then called Barrack Street. General Howe formally notified General Washington of his execution. In recent years, through the industry of investigators, the pathos and sublimity of these events have been in part revealed.

In 1887 a bronze statue of the young hero was unveiled in the State House at Hartford. Mr. Charles Dudley Warner delivered a beautiful address suitable to the occasion, and Governor Lounsberry worthily accepted the statue on behalf of the State. It is greatly to be regretted that our knowledge of this noble martyr is so slight; but we know enough to be sure that he merits the veneration of his countrymen.

David Crockett

[JOHN S. C. ABBOTT]

Crockett was very fond of hunting-adventures, and told stories of these enterprises in a racy way, peculiarly characteristic of the man. The following narrative from his own lips, the reader will certainly peruse with much interest.

"I was sitting by a good fire in my little cabin, on a cool November evening, roasting potatoes I believe, and playing with my children, when some one halloed at the fence. I went out, and there were three strangers, who said they come to take an elk-hunt. I was glad to see 'em, invited 'em in, and after supper we cleaned our guns. I took down old Betsey, rubbed her up, greased her, and laid her away to rest. She is a mighty rough old piece, but I love her, for she and I have seen hard times. She mighty seldom tells me a lie. If I hold her right, she always sends the ball where I tell her. After we were all fixed, I told 'em hunting-stories till bedtime.

"Next morning was clear and cold, and by times I sounded my horn, and my dogs came howling 'bout me, ready for a chase. Old Rattler was a little lame—a bear bit him in the shoulder; but Soundwell, Tiger, and the rest of 'em were all mighty anxious. We got a bite, and saddled our horses. I went by to git a neighbor to drive for us, and off we started for the *Harricane*. My dogs looked mighty wolfish; they kept jumping on one another and growling. I knew they were run mad for a fight, for they hadn't had one for two or three days. We were in fine spirits, and going 'long through very open woods, when one of the strangers said, 'I would give my horse now to see a bear.'

"Said I, 'Well, give me your horse,' and I pointed to an old bear, about three or four hundred yards ahead of us, feeding on acorns.

"I had been looking at him some time, but he was so far off; I wasn't certain what it was. However, I hardly spoke before we all strained off, and the woods fairly echoed as we harked the dogs on. The old bear didn't want to run, and he never broke till we got most upon him; but then he buckled for it, I tell you. When they overhauled him he just rared up on his hind legs, and he boxed the dogs 'bout at a mighty rate. He hugged old Tiger and another, till he dropped 'em nearly lifeless; but the others worried him, and after a while they all come to, and they give him trouble. They are mighty apt, I tell you, to give a bear trouble before they leave him.

"'Twas a mighty pretty fight—'twould have done any one's soul good to see it, just to see how they all rolled about. It was as much as I could do to keep the strangers from shooting him; but I wouldn't let 'em, for fear they would kill some of my dogs. After we got tired seeing 'em fight, I went in among 'em, and the first time they got him down I socked my knife in the old bear. We then hung him up, and went on to take our elk-hunt. You never seed fellows so delighted as them strangers was. Blow me, if they didn't cut more capers, jumping about, than the old bear. 'Twas a mighty pretty fight, but I believe I seed more fun looking at them than at the bear.

"By the time we got to the *Harricane,* we were all rested, and ripe for a drive. My dogs were in a better humor, for the fight had just taken off the wiry edge. So I placed the strangers at the stands through which I thought the elk would pass, sent the driver way up ahead, and I went down below.

"Everything was quiet, and I leaned old Betsey 'gin a tree, and laid down. I s'pose I had been lying there nearly an hour, when I heard old Tiger open. He opened once or twice, and old Rattler gave a long howl; the balance joined in, and I knew the elk were up. I jumped up and seized my rifle. I could hear nothing but one continued roar of all my dogs, coming right towards me. Though I was an old hunter, the music made my hair stand on end. Soon after they first started, I heard one gun go off, and my dogs stopped, but not long, for they took a little tack towards where I had placed the strangers. One of them fired, and they dashed back, and circled round way to my left. I run down 'bout a quarter of a mile, and I heard my dogs make a bend like they were coming to me. While I was listening, I heard the bushes breaking still lower down, and started to run there.

"As I was going 'long, I seed two elks burst out of the *Harricane* 'bout one hundred and thirty or forty yards below me. There was an old buck and a doe. I stopped, waited till they got into a clear place, and as the old fellow made a leap, I raised old Bet, pulled trigger, and she spoke out. The smoke blinded me so, that I couldn't see what I did; but as it cleared away, I caught a glimpse of only one of them going through the bushes; so I thought I had the other. I went up, and there lay the old buck kicking. I cut his throat, and by that time, Tiger and two of my dogs came up. I thought it singular that all my dogs wasn't there, and I began to think they had killed another. After the dogs had bit him, and found out he was dead, old Tiger began to growl, and curled himself up between his legs. Everything had to stand off then, for he wouldn't let the devil himself touch him.

"I started off to look for the strangers. My two dogs followed me. After gitting away a piece, I looked back, and once in a while I could see old Tiger git up and shake the elk, to see if he was really dead, and then curl up between his legs agin. I found the strangers round a doe elk the driver had killed; and one of 'em said he was sure he had killed one lower down. I asked him if he had horns. He said he didn't see any. I put the dogs on where he said he had shot, and they didn't go fur before they came to a halt. I went up, and there lay a fine buck elk; and though his horns were four or five feet long, the fellow who shot him was so scared that he never saw them. We had three elk, and a bear; and we managed to git it home, then butchered our game, talked over our hunt, and had a glorious frolic."

Crockett served in the Legislature for two years, during which time nothing occurred of special interest. These were the years of 1823 and 1824. Colonel Alexander was then the representative, in the National Legislature, of the district in which Crockett lived. He had offended his constituents by voting for the Tariff. It was proposed to run Crockett for Congress in opposition to him. Crockett says:

"I told the people that I could not stand that. It was a step above my knowledge; and I know'd nothing about Congress matters."

They persisted; but he lost the election; for cotton was very high, and Alexander urged that it was in consequence of the Tariff. Two years passed away, which Crockett spent in the wildest adventures of hunting. He was a true man of the woods with no ambition for any better home than the log cabin he occupied. There was no excitement so dear to him as the pursuit and capture of a grizzly bear. There is nothing on record, in the way of hunting, which surpasses the exploits of this renowned bear-hunter. But there is a certain degree of sameness in these narratives of skill and endurance which would weary the reader.

In the fall of 1825, Crockett built two large flat-boats, to load with staves for the making of casks, which he intended to take down the river to market. He employed a number of hands in building the boat and splitting out the staves, and engaged himself in these labors "till the bears got fat." He then plunged into the woods, and in two weeks killed fifteen. The whole winter was spent in hunting with his son and his dogs. His workmen continued busy getting the staves, and when the rivers rose with the spring floods, he had thirty thousand ready for the market.

With this load he embarked for New Orleans. His boats without difficulty floated down the Obion into the majestic Mississippi. It was the first time he had seen the rush of these mighty waters. There was before him a boat voyage of nearly fifteen hundred miles, through regions to him entirely unknown. In his own account of this adventure he writes:

"When I got into the Mississippi I found all my hands were bad scared. In fact, I believe I was scared a little the worst of any; for I had never been down the river, and I soon discovered that my pilot was as ignorant of the business as myself. I hadn't gone far before I determined to lash the two boats together. We did so; but it made them so heavy and obstinate that it was next akin to impossible to do any thing at all with them, or to guide them right in the river.

"That evening we fell in company with some Ohio boats, and about night we tried to land, but we could not. The Ohio men hollered to us to go on and run all night. We took their advice, though we had a good deal rather not. But we couldn't do any other way. In a short distance we got into what is called the Devil's Elbow. And if any place in the wide creation has its own proper name I thought it was this. Here we had about the hardest work that I was ever engaged in in my life, to keep out of danger. And even then we were in it all the while. We twice attempted to land at Wood Yards, which we could see, but couldn't reach.

"The people would run out with lights, and try to instruct us how to get to shore; but all in vain. Our boats were so heavy that we could not take them much any way except the way they wanted to go, and just the way the current would carry them. At last we quit trying to land, and concluded just to go ahead as well as we could, for we found we couldn't do any better.

"Some time in the night I was down in the cabin of one of the boats, sitting by the fire, thinking on what a hobble we had got into; and how much better bear-hunting was on hard land, than floating along on the water, when a fellow had to go ahead whether he was exactly willing or not. The hatch-way of the cabin came slap down, right through the top of the boat; and it was the only way out, except a small hole in the side which we had used for putting our arms through to dip up water before we lashed the boats together.

"We were now floating sideways, and the boat I was in was the hindmost as we went. All at once I heard the hands begin to run over the top of the boat in great confusion, and pull with all their might. And the first thing I know'd after this we went broadside full tilt against the head of an island, where a large raft of drift timber had lodged. The nature of such a place would be, as everybody knows, to suck the boats down and turn them right under this raft; and the uppermost boat would, of course, be suck'd down and go under first. As soon as we struck, I bulged for my hatchway, as the boat was turning under sure enough. But when I got to it, the water was pouring through in a current as large as the hole would let it, and as strong as the weight of the river would force it. I found I couldn't get out here, for the boat was now turned down in such a way that it was steeper than a house-top. I now thought of the hole in the side, and made my way in a hurry for that.

"With difficulty I got to it, and when I got there, I found it was too small for me to get out by my own power, and I began to think that I was in a worse box than ever. But I put my arms through, and hollered as loud as I could roar, as the boat I was in hadn't yet quite filled with water up to my head; and the hands who were next to the raft, seeing my arms out, and hearing me holler, seized them, and began to pull. I told them I was sinking, and to pull my arms off, or force me through, for now I know'd well enough it was neck or nothing, come out or sink.

"By a violent effort they jerked me through; but I was in a pretty pickle when I got through. I had been sitting without any clothing over my shirt; this was torn off, and I was literally skinn'd like a rabbit. I was, however, well pleased to get out in any way, even without shirt or hide; as before I could straighten myself on the boat next to the raft, the one they pull'd me out of went entirely under, and I have never seen it any more to this day. We all escaped on to the raft, where we were compelled to sit all night, about a mile from land on either side. Four of my company were bareheaded, and three barefooted; and of that number I was one. I reckon I looked like a pretty cracklin ever to get to Congress!

"We had now lost all our loading, and every particle of our clothing, except what little we had on; but over all this, while I was sitting there, in the night, floating about on the drift, I felt happier and better off than I ever had in my life before, for I had just made such a marvellous escape, that I had forgot almost everything else in that; and so I felt prime.

"In the morning about sunrise, we saw a boat coming down, and we hailed her. They sent a large skiff, and took us all on board, and carried us down as far as Memphis. Here I met with a friend, that I never can forget as long as I am able to go ahead at anything; it was a Major

Winchester, a merchant of that place; he let us all have hats, and shoes, and some little money to go upon, and so we all parted.

"A young man and myself concluded to go on down to Natchez, to see if we could hear anything of our boats; for we supposed they would float out from the raft, and keep on down the river. We got on a boat at Memphis, that was going down, and so cut out. Our largest boat, we were informed, had been seen about fifty miles below where we stove, and an attempt had been made to land her, but without success, as she was as hard-headed as ever.

"This was the last of my boats, and of my boating; for it went so badly with me along at the first, that I had not much mind to try it any more. I now returned home again, and, as the next August was the Congressional election, I began to turn my attention a little to that matter, as it was beginning to be talked of a good deal among the people."

Cotton was down very low. Crockett could now say to the people: "You see the effects of the Tariff." There were two rival candidates for the office, Colonel Alexander and General Arnold. Money was needed to carry the election, and Crockett had no money. He resolved, however, to try his chances. A friend loaned him a little money to start with; which sum Crockett, of course, expended in whiskey, as the most potent influence, then and there, to secure an election.

"So I was able," writes Crockett, "to buy a little of the 'creature,' to put my friends in a good humor, as well as the other gentlemen, for they all treat in that country; not to get elected, of course, for that would be against the law, but just to make themselves and their friends feel their keeping a little."

The contest was, as usual, made up of drinking, feasting, and speeches. Colonel Alexander was an intelligent and worthy man, who had been public surveyor. General Arnold was a lawyer of very respectable attainments. Neither of these men considered Crockett a candidate in the slightest degree to be feared. They only feared each other, and tried to circumvent each other.

On one occasion there was a large gathering, where all three of the candidates were present, and each one was expected to make a speech. It came Crockett's lot to speak first. He knew nothing of Congressional affairs, and had sense enough to be aware that it was not best for him to attempt to speak upon subjects of which he was entirely ignorant. He made one of his funny speeches, very short and entirely non-committal. Colonel Alexander followed, endeavoring to grapple with the great questions of tariffs, finance, and internal improvements, which were then agitating the nation.

General Arnold then, in his turn, took the stump, opposing the measures which Colonel Alexander had left. He seemed entirely to ignore the fact that Crockett was a candidate. Not the slightest allusion was made to him in his speech. The nervous temperament predominated in the man, and he was easily annoyed. While speaking, a large flock of guinea-hens came along, whose peculiar and noisy cry all will remember who have ever heard it. Arnold was greatly disturbed, and at last requested some one to drive the fowls away. As soon as he had finished his speech, Crockett again mounted the stump, and ostensibly addressing Arnold, but really addressing the crowd, said, in a loud voice, but very jocosely:

"Well, General, you are the first man I ever saw that understood the language of fowls. You had not the politeness even to allude to me in your speech. But when my little friends the guinea-hens came up, and began to holler 'Crockett, Crockett, Crockett,' you were ungenerous enough to drive them all away."

This raised such a universal laugh that even Crockett's opponents feared that he was getting the best of them in winning the favor of the people. When the day of election came, the popular bear-hunter beat both of his competitors by twenty-seven hundred and forty-seven votes. Thus David Crockett, unable to read and barely able to sign his name, became a member of Congress, to assist in framing laws for the grandest republic earth has ever known. He represented a constituency of about one hundred thousand souls.

An intelligent gentleman, travelling in West Tennessee, finding himself within eight miles of Colonel Crockett's cabin, decided to call upon the man whose name had now become quite renowned. This was just after Crockett's election to Congress, but before he had set out for Washington. There was no road leading to the lonely hut. He followed a rough and obstructed path or trail, which was indicated only by blazed trees, and which bore no marks of being often travelled.

At length he came to a small opening in the forest, very rude and uninviting in its appearance. It embraced eight or ten acres. One of the humblest and least tasteful of log huts stood in the centre. It was truly a cabin, a mere shelter from the weather. There was no yard;

there were no fences. Not the slightest effort had been made toward ornamentation. It would be difficult to imagine a more lonely and cheerless abode.

Two men were seated on stools at the door, both in their shirt-sleeves, engaged in cleaning their rifles. As the stranger rode up, one of the men rose and came forward to meet him. He was dressed in very plain homespun attire, with a black fur cap upon his head. He was a finely proportioned man, about six feet high, apparently forty-five years of age, and of very frank, pleasing, open countenance. He held his rifle in his hand, and from his right shoulder hung a bag made of raccoon skin, to which there was a sheath attached containing a large butcher-knife.

"This is Colonel Crockett's residence, I presume," said the stranger.

"Yes," was the reply, with a smile as of welcome.

"Have I the pleasure of seeing that gentleman before me?" the stranger added.

"If it be a pleasure," was the courtly reply, "you have, sir."

"Well, Colonel," responded the stranger, "I have ridden much out of my way to spend a day or two with you, and take a hunt."

"Get down, sir," said the Colonel, cordially. "I am delighted to see you. I like to see strangers. And the only care I have is that I cannot accommodate them as well as I could wish. I have no corn, but my little boy will take your horse over to my son-in-law's. He is a good fellow, and will take care of him."

Leading the stranger into his cabin, Crockett very courteously introduced him to his brother, his wife, and his daughters. He then added:

"You see we are mighty rough here. I am afraid you will think it hard times. But we have to do the best we can. I started mighty poor, and have been rooting 'long ever since. But I hate apologies. What I live upon always, I think a friend can for a day or two. I have but little, but that little is as free as the water that runs. So make yourself at home."

Mrs. Crockett was an intelligent and capable woman for one in her station in life. The cabin was clean and orderly, and presented a general aspect of comfort. Many trophies of the chase were in the house, and spread around the yard. Several dogs, looking like war-worn veterans, were sunning themselves in various parts of the premises.

All the family were neatly dressed in homemade garments. Mrs. Crockett was a grave, dignified woman, very courteous to her guests. The daughters were remarkably pretty, but very diffident. Though entirely uneducated, they could converse very easily, seeming to inherit their father's fluency of utterance. They were active and efficient in aiding their mother in her household work. Colonel Crockett, with much apparent pleasure, conducted his guest over the small patch of ground he had grubbed and was cultivating. He exhibited his growing peas and pumpkins, and his little field of corn, with as much apparent pleasure as an Illinois farmer would now point out his hundreds of acres of waving grain. The hunter seemed surprisingly well informed. As we have mentioned, nature had endowed him with unusual strength of mind, and with a memory which was almost miraculous. He never forgot anything he had heard. His electioneering tours had been to him very valuable schools of education. Carefully he listened to all the speeches and the conversation of the intelligent men he met with.

John Quincy Adams was then in the Presidential chair. It was the year 1827. Nearly all Crockett's constituents were strong Jackson-men. Crockett, who afterward opposed Jackson, subsequently said, speaking of his views at that time:

"I can say on my conscience, that I was, without disguise, the friend and supporter of General Jackson upon his principles, as he had laid them down, and as I understood them, before his election as President."

Alluding to Crockett's political views at that time, his guest writes, "I held in high estimation the present Administration of our country. To this he was opposed. His views, however, delighted me. And were they more generally adopted we should be none the loser. He was opposed to the Administration, and yet conceded that many of its acts were wise and efficient, and would have received his cordial support. He admired Mr. Clay, but had objections to him. He was opposed to the Tariff, yet, I think, a supporter of the United States Bank. He seemed to have the most horrible objection to binding himself to any man or set of men. He said, 'I would as lieve be an old coon-dog as obliged to do what any man or set of men would tell me to do. I will support the present Administration as far as I would any other; that is, as far as I believe its views to be right. I will pledge myself to support no Administration. I had rather be politically damned than hypocritically immortalized.'"

In the winter of 1827, Crockett emerged from his cabin in the wilderness for a seat in Congress. He was so poor that he had not money enough to pay his expenses to Washington. His election had cost him one hundred and fifty dollars, which a friend had loaned him. The same friend advanced one hundred dollars more to help him on his journey.

"When I left home," he says, "I was happy, devilish, and full of fun. I bade adieu to my friends, dogs, and rifle, and took the stage, where I met with much variety of character, and amused myself when my humor prompted. Being fresh from the backwoods, my stories amused my companions, and I passed my time pleasantly.

"When I arrived at Raleigh the weather was cold and rainy, and we were all dull and tired. Upon going into the tavern, where I was an entire stranger, the room was crowded, and the crowd did not give way that I might come to the fire. I was rooting my way to the fire, not in a good humor, when some fellow staggered up towards me, and cried out, 'Hurrah for Adams.'

"Said I, 'Stranger, you had better hurrah for hell, and praise your own country.'

"'And who are you?' said he. I replied:

"'I am that same David Crockett, fresh from the backwoods, half horse, half alligator, a little touched with the snapping-turtle. I can wade the Mississippi, leap the Ohio, ride upon a streak of lightning, and slip without a scratch down a honey-locust. I can whip my weight in wildcats, and, if any gentleman pleases, for a ten-dollar bill he can throw in a panther. I can hug a bear too close for comfort, and eat any man opposed to General Jackson.'"

All eyes were immediately turned toward this strange man, for all had heard of him. A place was promptly made for him at the fire. He was afterward asked if this wondrous outburst of slang was entirely unpremeditated. He said that it was; that it had all popped into his head at once; and that he should never have thought of it again, had not the story gone the round of the newspapers.

"I came on to Washington," he says, "and drawed two hundred and fifty dollars, and purchased with it a check on the bank in Nashville, and enclosed it to my friend. And I may say, in truth, I sent this money with a mighty good will, for I reckon nobody in this world loves a friend better than me, or remembers a kindness longer."

Soon after his arrival at Washington he was invited to dine with President Adams, a man of the highest culture, whose manners had been formed in the courts of Europe. Crockett, totally unacquainted with the usages of society, did not know what the note of invitation meant, and inquired of a friend, the Hon. Mr. Verplanck. He says:

"I was wild from the backwoods, and didn't know nothing about eating dinner with the big folks of our country. And how should I, having been a hunter all my life? I had eat most of my dinners on a log in the woods, and sometimes no dinner at all. I knew, whether I ate dinner with the President or not was a matter of no importance, for my constituents were not to be benefited by it. I did not go to court the President, for I was opposed to him in principle, and had no favors to ask at his hands. I was afraid, however, I should be awkward, as I was so entirely a stranger to fashion; and in going along, I resolved to observe the conduct of my friend Mr. Verplanck, and to do as he did. And I know that I did behave myself right well."

Some cruel wag wrote the following ludicrous account of this dinner-party, which went the round of all the papers as veritable history. The writer pretended to quote Crockett's own account of the dinner.

"The first thing I did," said Davy, "after I got to Washington, was to go to the President's. I stepped into the President's house. Thinks I, who's afeard. If I didn't, I wish I may be shot. Says I, 'Mr. Adams, I am Mr. Crockett, from Tennessee.' So, says he, 'How d'ye do, Mr. Crockett?' And he shook me by the hand, although he know'd I went the whole hog for Jackson. If he didn't, I wish I may be shot.

"Not only that, but he sent me a printed ticket to dine with him. I've got it in my pocket yet. I went to dinner, and I walked all around the long table, looking for something that I liked. At last I took my seat beside a fat goose, and I helped myself to as much of it as I wanted. But I hadn't took three bites, when I looked away up the table at a man they called *Tash* (attaché). He was talking French to a woman on t'other side of the table. He dodged his head and she dodged hers, and then they got to drinking wine across the table.

"But when I looked back again my plate was gone, goose and all. So I jist cast my eyes down to t'other end of the table, and sure enough I seed a white man walking off with my plate. I says, 'Hello, mister, bring back my plate.' He fetched it back in a hurry, as you may think. And when he set it down before me, how do you think it was? Licked as clean as my hand. If it wasn't, I wish I may be shot!

"Says he, 'What will you have, sir?' And says I, 'You may well say that, after stealing my goose.' And he began to laugh. Then says I, 'Mister, laugh if you please; but I don't half-like sich tricks upon travellers.' I then filled my plate with bacon and greens. And whenever I looked up or down the table, I held on to my plate with my left hand.

"When we were all done eating, they cleared everything off the table, and took away the table-cloth. And what do you think? There was another cloth under it. If there wasn't, I wish I may be shot! Then I saw a man coming along carrying a great glass thing, with a glass handle below, something like a candlestick. It was stuck full of little glass cups, with something in them that looked good to eat. Says I, 'Mister, bring that thing here.' Thinks I, let's taste them first. They were mighty sweet and good, so I took six of them. If I didn't, I wish I may be shot!"

This humorous fabrication was copied into almost every paper in the Union. The more respectable portion of Crockett's constituents were so annoyed that their representative should be thus held up to the contempt of the nation, that Crockett felt constrained to present a reliable refutation of the story. He therefore obtained and published certificates from three gentlemen, testifying to his good behavior at the table. Hon. Mr. Verplanck, of New York, testified as follows:

"I dined at the President's, at the time alluded to, in company with you, and I had, I recollect, a good deal of conversation with you. Your behavior there was, I thought, perfectly becoming and proper. And I do not recollect, or believe, that you said or did anything resembling the newspaper account."

Two other members of Congress were equally explicit in their testimony.

During Crockett's first two sessions in Congress he got along very smoothly, cooperating generally with what was called the Jackson party. In 1829 he was again reelected by an overwhelming majority. On the 4th of March of this year, Andrew Jackson was inaugurated President of the United States. It may be doubted whether there ever was a more honest, conscientious man in Congress than David Crockett. His celebrated motto, "Be sure that you are right, and then go ahead," seemed ever to animate him. He could neither be menaced or bribed to support any measure which he thought to be wrong. Ere long he found it necessary to oppose some of Jackson's measures. We will let him tell the story in his own truthful words:

"Soon after the commencement of this second term, I saw, or thought I did, that it was expected of me that I would bow to the name of Andrew Jackson, and follow him in all his motions, and windings, and turnings, even at the expense of my conscience and judgment. Such a thing was new to me, and a total stranger to my principles. I know'd well enough, though, that if I didn't 'hurrah' for his name, the hue and cry was to be raised against me, and I was to be sacrificed, if possible. His famous, or rather I should say his *infamous* Indian bill was brought forward, and I opposed it from the purest motives in the world. Several of my colleagues got around me, and told me how well they loved me, and that I was ruining myself. They said this was a favorite measure of the President, and I ought to go for it. I told them I believed it was a wicked, unjust measure, and that I should go against it, let the cost to myself be what it might; that I was willing to go with General Jackson in everything that I believed was honest and right; but, further than this, I wouldn't go for him or any other man in the whole creation.

"I had been elected by a majority of three thousand five hundred and eighty-five votes, and I believed they were honest men, and wouldn't want me to vote for any unjust notion, to please Jackson or any one else; at any rate, I was of age, and determined to trust them. I voted against this Indian bill, and my conscience yet tells me that I gave a good, honest vote, and one that I believe will not make me ashamed in the day of judgment. I served out my term, and though many amusing things happened, I am not disposed to swell my narrative by inserting them.

"When it closed, and I returned home, I found the storm had raised against me sure enough; and it was echoed from side to side, and from end to end of my district, that I had turned against Jackson. This was considered the unpardonable sin. I was hunted down like a wild varment, and in this hunt every little newspaper in the district, and every little pinhook lawyer was engaged. Indeed, they were ready to print anything and everything that the ingenuity of man could invent against me."

In consequence of this opposition, Crockett lost his next election, and yet by a majority of but seventy votes. For two years he remained at home hunting bears. But having once tasted the pleasures of political life, and the excitements of Washington, his silent rambles in the woods had lost much of their ancient charms. He was again a candidate at the ensuing election, and, after a very warm contest gained the day by a majority of two hundred and two votes.

★   ★   ★

COLONEL CROCKETT, having been reelected again repaired to Washington. During the session, to complete his education, and the better to prepare himself as a legislator for the whole nation, he decided to take a short trip to the North and the East. His health had also begun to fail, and his physicians advised him to go. He was thoroughly acquainted with the Great West. With his rifle upon his shoulder, in the Creek War, he had made wide explorations through the South. But the North and the East were regions as yet unknown to him.

On the 25th of April, 1834, he left Washington for this Northern tour. He reached Baltimore that evening, where he was invited to a supper by some of the leading gentlemen. He writes:

"Early next morning, I started for Philadelphia, a place where I had never been. I sort of felt lonesome as I went down to the steamboat. The idea of going among a new people, where there are tens of thousands who would pass me by without knowing or caring who I was, who are all taken up with their own pleasures or their own business, made me feel small; and, indeed, if any one who reads this book has a grand idea of his own importance, let him go to a big city, and he will find that he is not higher valued than a coonskin.

"The steamboat was the Carroll of Carrollton, a fine craft, with the rum old Commodore Chaytor for head man. A good fellow he is—all sorts of a man—bowing and scraping to the ladies, nodding to the gentlemen, cursing the crew, and his right eye broad-cast upon the 'opposition line,' all at the same time. 'Let go!' said the old one, and off we walked in prime style.

"Our passage down Chesapeake Bay was very pleasant. In a very short run we came to a place where we were to get on board the rail-cars. This was a clean new sight to me. About a dozen big stages hung on to one machine. After a good deal of fuss we all got seated and moved slowly off; the engine wheezing as though she had the tizzic. By-and-by, she began to take short breaths, and away we went, with a blue streak after us. The whole distance is seventeen miles. It was run in fifty-five minutes.

"At Delaware City, I again embarked on board of a splendid steamboat. When dinner was ready, I set down with the rest of the passengers. Among them was Rev. O. B. Brown, of the Post-Office Department, who sat near me. During dinner he ordered a bottle of wine, and called upon me for a toast. Not knowing whether he intended to compliment me, or abash me among so many strangers, or have some fun at my expense, I concluded to go ahead, and give him and his like a blizzard. So our glasses being filled, the word went round, 'A toast from Colonel Crockett.' I give it as follows: 'Here's wishing the bones of tyrant kings may answer in hell, in place of gridirons, to roast the souls of Tories on.' At this the parson appeared as if he was stumpt. I said, 'Never heed; it was meant for where it belonged.' He did not repeat his invitation, and I eat my dinner quietly.

"After dinner I went up on the deck, and saw the captain hoisting three flags. Says I, 'What does that mean?' He replied, that he was under promise to the citizens of Philadelphia, if I was on board, to hoist his flags, as a friend of mine had said he expected I would be along soon.

"We went on till we came in sight of the city and as we advanced towards the wharf, I saw the whole face of the earth covered with people, all anxiously looking on towards the boat. The captain and myself were standing on the bow-deck; he pointed his finger at me, and people slung their hats, and huzzaed for Colonel Crockett. It struck me with astonishment to hear a strange people huzzaing for me, and made me feel sort of queer. It took me so uncommon unexpected, as I had no idea of attracting attention. But I had to meet it, and so I stepped on to the wharf, where the folks came crowding around me, saying, 'Give me the hand of an honest man.' I did not know what all this meant: but some gentleman took hold of me, and pressing through the crowd, put me into an elegant barouche, drawn by four fine horses; they then told me to bow to the people: I did so, and with much difficulty we moved off. The streets were crowded to a great distance, and the windows full of people, looking out, I suppose, to see the wild man. I thought I had rather be in the wilderness with my gun and dogs, than to be attracting all that fuss. I had never seen the like before, and did not know exactly what to say or do. After some time we reached the United States Hotel, in Chesnut Street.

"The crowd had followed me filling up the street, and pressing into the house to shake hands. I was conducted up stairs, and walked out on a platform, drew off my hat, and bowed round to the people. They cried out from all quarters, 'A speech, a speech, Colonel Crockett.'

"After the noise had quit, so I could be heard, I said to them the following words:

"'Gentlemen of Philadelphia:

"'My visit to your city is rather accidental. I had no expectation of attracting any uncommon attention. I am travelling for my health, without the least wish of exciting the people in such times of high political feeling. I do not wish to encourage it. I am unable at this time to find language suitable to return my gratitude to the citizens of Philadelphia. However, I am almost induced to believe it flattery—perhaps a burlesque. This is new to me, yet I see nothing but friendship in your faces; and if your curiosity is to hear the backwoodsman, I will assure you I am illy prepared to address this most enlightened people. However, gentlemen, if this is a curiosity to you, if you will meet me to-morrow, at one o'clock, I will endeavor to address you, in my plain manner.'

"So I made my obeisance to them, and retired into the house."

It is true that there was much of mere curiosity in the desire to see Colonel Crockett. He was a strange and an incomprehensible man. His manly, honest course in Congress had secured much respect. But such developments of character as were shown in his rude and vulgar toast, before a party of gentlemen and ladies, excited astonishment. His notoriety preceded him, wherever he went; and all were alike curious to see so strange a specimen of a man.

The next morning, several gentlemen called upon him, and took him in a carriage to see the various objects of interest in the city. The gentlemen made him a present of a rich seal, representing two horses at full speed, with the words, "Go Ahead." The young men also made him a present of a truly magnificent rifle. From Philadelphia he went to New York. The shipping astonished him. "They beat me all hollow," he says, "and looked for all the world like a big clearing in the West, with the dead trees all standing."

There was a great crowd upon the wharf to greet him. And when the captain of the boat led him conspicuously forward, and pointed him out to the multitude, the cheering was tremendous. A committee conducted him to the American Hotel, and treated him with the greatest distinction. Again he was fêted, and loaded with the greatest attentions. He was invited to a very splendid supper, got up in his honor, at which there were a hundred guests. The Hon. Judge Clayton, of Georgia, was present, and make a speech which, as Crockett says, fairly made the tumblers hop.

Crockett was then called up, as the "undeviating supporter of the Constitution and the laws." In response to this toast, he says,

"I made a short speech, and concluded with the story of the red cow, which was, that as long as General Jackson went straight, I followed him; but when he began to go this way, and that way, and every way, I wouldn't go after him; like the boy whose master ordered him to plough across the field to the red cow. Well, he began to plough, and she began to walk; and he ploughed all forenoon after her. So when the master came, he swore at him for going so crooked. 'Why, sir,' said the boy, 'you told me to plough to the red cow, and I kept after her, but she always kept moving.'"

His trip to New York was concluded by his visiting Jersey City to witness a shooting-match with rifles. He was invited to try his hand. Standing, at the distance of one hundred and twenty feet, he fired twice, striking very near the centre of the mark. Some one then put up a quarter of a dollar in the midst of a black spot, and requested him to shoot at it. The bullet struck the coin, and as Crockett says "made slight-of-hand work with it."

From New York he went to Boston. There, as the opponent of some of President Jackson's measures which were most offensive to the New England people, he was fêted with extraordinary enthusiasm. He dined and supped, made speeches, which generally consisted of but one short anecdote, and visited nearly all the public institutions.

Just before this, Andrew Jackson had received from Harvard University the honorary title of LL.D. Jackson was no longer a favorite of Crockett. The new distinguished guest, the renowned bear-hunter, was in his turn invited to visit Harvard. He writes:

"There were some gentlemen that invited me to go to Cambridge, where the big college or university is, where they keep ready-made titles or nick-names to give people. I would not go, for I did not know but they might stick an LL.D. on me before they let me go; and I had no idea of changing 'Member of the House of Representatives of the United States,' for what stands for 'lazy, lounging dunce,' which I am sure my constituents would have translated my new title to be. Knowing that I had never taken any degree, and did not own to any—except a small degree of good sense not to pass for what I was not—I would not go it. There had been one doctor made from Tennessee already, and I had no wish to put on the cap and bells.

"I told them that I did not go to this branding school; I did not want to be tarred with the same stick; one dignitary was enough from Tennessee; that as far as my learning went, I would stand over it, and spell a strive or two with any of them, from *a-b-ab* to *crucifix,* which was where I left off at school."

A gentleman, at a dinner-party, very earnestly invited Crockett to visit him. He returned the compliment by saying:

"If you ever come to my part of the country, I hope you will call and see me."

"And how shall I find where you live?" the gentleman inquired.

"Why, sir," Crockett answered, "run down the Mississippi till you come to the Obion River. Run a small streak up that; jump ashore anywhere, and inquire for me."

From Boston, he went to Lowell. The hospitality he had enjoyed in Boston won his warmest commendation. At Lowell, he was quite charmed by the aspect of wealth, industry, and comfort which met his eye. Upon his return to Boston, he spent the evening, with several gentlemen and ladies at the pleasant residence of Lieutenant-Governor Armstrong. In reference to this visit, he writes:

"This was my last night in Boston, and I am sure, if I never see the place again, I never can forget the kind and friendly manner in which I was treated by them. It appeared to me that everybody was anxious to serve me, and make my time agreeable. And as a proof that comes home—when I called for my bill next morning, I was told there was no charge to be paid by me, and that he was very much delighted that I had made his house my home. I forgot to mention that they treated me so in Lowell—but it is true. This was, to me, at all events, proof enough of Yankee liberality; and more than they generally get credit for. In fact, from the time I entered New England, I was treated with the greatest friendship; and, I hope, never shall forget it; and I wish all who read this book, and who never were there, would take a trip among them. If they don't learn how to make money, they will know how to use it; and if they don't learn industry, they will see how comfortable everybody can be that turns his hands to some employment."

Crockett was not a mere joker. He was an honest man, and an earnest man; and under the tuition of Congress had formed some very decided political principles, which he vigorously enforced with his rude eloquence.

When he first went to Congress he was merely a big boy, of very strong mind, but totally uninformed, and uncultivated. He very rapidly improved under the tuition of Congress; and in some degree awoke to the consciousness of his great intellectual imperfections. Still he was never diffident. He closed one of his off-hand after-dinner speeches in Boston, by saying:

"Gentlemen of Boston, I come here as a private citizen, to see you, and not to show myself. I had no idea of attracting attention. But I feel it my duty to thank you, with my gratitude to you, and with a gratitude to all who have given a plain man, like me, so kind a reception. I come from a great way off. But I shall never repent of having been persuaded to come here, and get a knowledge of your ways, which I can carry home with me. We only want to do away prejudice and give the people information.

"I hope, gentlemen, you will excuse my plain, unvarnished ways, which may seem strange to you here. I never had but six months' schooling in all my life. And I confess, I consider myself a poor tyke to be here addressing the most intelligent people in the world. But I think it the duty of every representative of the people, when he is called upon, to give his opinions. And I have tried to give you a little touch of mine."

Crockett returned to Washington just in time to be present at the closing scenes, and then set out for home. So much had been said of him in the public journals, of his speeches and his peculiarities, that his renown now filled the land.

★   ★   ★

Crockett's return to his home was a signal triumph all the way. At Baltimore, Philadelphia, Pittsburgh, Cincinnati, Louisville, crowds gathered to greet him. He was feasted, received presents, was complimented, and was incessantly called upon for a speech. He was an earnest student as he journeyed along. A new world of wonders were opening before him. Thoughts which he never before had dreamed of were rushing into his mind. His eyes were ever watchful to see all that was worthy of note. His ear was ever listening for every new idea. He scarcely ever looked at the printed page, but perused with the utmost diligence the book of nature. His comments upon what he saw indicate much sagacity.

At Cincinnatti and Louisville, immense crowds assembled to hear him. In both places he spoke quite at length. And all who heard him were surprised at the power he displayed. Though his speech was rude and unpolished, the clearness of his views, and the intelligence he manifested, caused the journals generally to speak of him in quite a different strain from that which they had been accustomed to use. Probably never did a man make so much intellectual progress, in the course of a few months, as David Crockett had made in that time. His wonderful memory of names, dates, facts, all the intricacies of statistics, was such, that almost any statesman might be instructed by his addresses, and not many men could safely encounter him in argument. The views he presented upon the subject of the Constitution, finance, internal improvements, etc., were very surprising, when one considers the limited education he had enjoyed. At the close of these agitating scenes he touchingly writes:

"In a short time I set out for my own home; yes, my own home, my own soil, my humble dwelling, my own family, my own hearts, my ocean of love and affection, which neither circumstances nor time can dry up. Here, like the wearied bird, let me settle down for a while, and shut out the world."

But hunting bears had lost its charms for Crockett. He had been so flattered that it is probable that he fully expected to be chosen President of the United States. There were two great parties then dividing the country, the Democrats and the Whigs. The great object of each was to find an *available* candidate, no matter how unfit for the office. The leaders wished to elect a President who would be, like the Queen of England, merely the ornamental figure-head of the ship of state, while their energies should propel and guide the majestic fabric. For a time some few thought it possible that in the popularity of the great bear-hunter such a candidate might be found.

Crockett, upon his return home, resumed his deer-skin leggins, his fringed hunting-shirt, his fox-skin cap, and shouldering his rifle, plunged, as he thought, with his original zest, into the cheerless, tangled, marshy forest which surrounded him. But the excitements of Washington, the splendid entertainments of Philadelphia, New York, and Boston, the flattery, the speech-making, which to him, with his marvellous memory and his wonderful fluency of speech, was as easy as breathing, the applause showered upon him, and the gorgeous vision of the Presidency looming up before him, engrossed his mind. He sauntered listlessly through the forest, his bear-hunting energies all paralyzed. He soon grew very weary of home and of all its employments, and was eager to return to the infinitely higher excitements of political life.

General Jackson was then almost idolized by his party. All through the South and West his name was a tower of strength. Crockett had originally been elected as a Jackson-man. He had abandoned the Administration, and was now one of the most inveterate opponents of Jackson. The majority in Crockett's district were in favor of Jackson. The time came for a new election of a representative. Crockett made every effort, in his old style, to secure the vote. He appeared at the gatherings in his garb as a bear-hunter, with his rifle on his shoulder. He brought 'coonskins to buy whiskey to treat his friends. A 'coonskin in the currency of that country was considered the equivalent for twenty-five cents. He made funny speeches. But it was all in vain.

Greatly to his surprise, and still more to his chagrin, he lost his election. He was beaten by two hundred and thirty votes. The whole powerful influence of the Government was exerted against Crockett and in favor of his competitor. It is said that large bribes were paid for votes. Crockett wrote, in a strain which reveals the bitterness of his disappointment:

"I am gratified that I have spoken the truth to the people of my district, regardless of the consequences. I would not be compelled to bow down to the idol for a seat in Congress during life. I have never known what it was to sacrifice my own judgment to gratify any party; and I have no doubt of the time being close at hand when I shall be rewarded for letting my tongue speak what my heart thinks. I have suffered myself to be politically sacrificed to save my country from ruin and disgrace; and if I am never again elected, I will have the gratification to know that I have done my duty. I may add, in the words of the man in the play, 'Crockett's occupation's gone.'"

Two weeks after this he writes, "I confess the thorn still rankles, not so much on my own account as the nation's. As my country no longer requires my services, I have made up my mind to go to Texas. My life has been one of danger, toil, and privation. But these difficulties I had to encounter at a time when I considered it nothing more than right good sport to surmount them. But now I start upon my own hook, and God only grant that it may be strong enough to support the weight that may be hung upon it. I have a new row to hoe, a long and rough one; but come what will, I will go ahead."

Just before leaving for Texas, he attended a political meeting of his constituents. The following extract from his autobiography will give the reader a very vivid idea of his feelings at the time, and of the very peculiar character which circumstances had developed in him:

"A few days ago I went to a meeting of my constituents. My appetite for politics was at one time just about as sharp set as a saw-mill, but late events have given me something of a surfeit, more than I could well digest; still, habit, they say, is second natur, and so I went, and gave them a piece of my mind touching 'the Government' and the succession, by way of a codicil to what I have often said before.

"I told them, moreover, of my services, pretty straight up and down, for a man may be allowed to speak on such subjects when others are about to forget them; and I also told them of the manner in which I had been knocked down and dragged out, and that I did not consider it a fair fight anyhow they could fix it. I put the ingredients in the cup pretty strong I tell you, and I concluded my speech by telling them that I was done with politics for the present, and that they might all go to hell, and I would go to Texas."

A party of American adventurers, then called filibusters, had gone into Texas, in the endeavor to wrest that immense and beautiful territory, larger than the whole Empire of France, from feeble, distracted, miserable Mexico, to which it belonged. These filibusters were generally the most worthless and desperate vagabonds to be found in all the Southern States. Many Southern gentlemen of wealth and ability, but strong advocates of slavery, were in cordial sympathy with this movement, and aided it with their purses, and in many other ways. It was thought that if Texas could be wrested from Mexico and annexed to the United States, it might be divided into several slaveholding States, and thus check the rapidly increasing preponderance of the free States of the North.

To join in this enterprise, Crockett now left his home, his wife, his children. There could be no doubt of the eventual success of the undertaking. And in that success Crockett saw visions of political glory opening before him. I determined, he said, "to quit the States until such time as honest and independent men should again work their way to the head of the heap. And as I should probably have some idle time on hand before that state of affairs would be brought about, I promised to give the Texans a helping hand on the high road to freedom."

He dressed himself in a new deerskin hunting-shirt, put on a foxskin cap with the tail hanging behind, shouldered his famous rifle, and cruelly leaving in the dreary cabin his wife and children whom he cherished with an "ocean of love and affection," set out on foot upon his perilous adventure. A day's journey through the forest brought him to the Mississippi River. Here he took a steamer down that majestic stream to the mouth of the Arkansas River, which rolls its vast flood from regions then quite unexplored in the far West. The stream was navigable fourteen hundred miles from its mouth.

Arkansas was then but a Territory, two hundred and forty miles long and two hundred and twenty-eight broad. The sparsely scattered population of the Territory amounted to but about thirty thousand. Following up the windings of the river three hundred miles, one came to a cluster of a few straggling huts, called Little Rock, which constitutes now the capital of the State.

Crockett ascended the river in the steamer, and, unencumbered with baggage, save his rifle, hastened to a tavern which he saw at a little distance from the shore, around which there was assembled quite a crowd of men. He had been so accustomed to public triumphs that he supposed that they had assembled in honor of his arrival. "Strange as it may seem," he says, "they took no more notice of me than if I had been Dick Johnson, the wool-grower. This took me somewhat aback;" and he inquired what was the meaning of the gathering.

He found that the people had been called together to witness the feats of a celebrated juggler and gambler. The name of Colonel Crockett had gone through the nation; and gradually it became noised abroad that Colonel Crockett was in the crowd. "I wish I may be shot," Crockett says, "if I wasn't looked upon as almost as great a sight as Punch and Judy."

He was invited to a public dinner that very day. As it took some time to cook the dinner, the whole company went to a little distance to shoot at a mark. All had heard of Crockett's skill. After several of the best sharp-shooters had fired, with remarkable accuracy, it came to Crockett's turn. Assuming an air of great carelessness, he raised his beautiful rifle, which he called Betsey, to his shoulder, fired, and it so happened that the bullet struck exactly in the centre of the bull's-eye. All were astonished, and so was Crockett himself. But with an air of much indifference he turned upon his heel, saying, "There's no mistake in Betsey."

One of the best marksmen in those parts, chagrined at being so beaten, said, "Colonel, that must have been a chance shot."

"I can do it," Crockett replied, "five times out of six, any day in the week."

"I knew," he adds, in his autobiography, "it was not altogether as correct as it might be; but when a man sets about going the big figure, halfway measures won't answer no how."

It was now proposed that there should be a second trial. Crockett was very reluctant to consent to this, for he had nothing to gain, and everything to lose. But they insisted so vehemently that he had to yield. As what ensued does not redound much to his credit, we will let him tell the story in his own language.

"So to it again we went. They were now put upon their mettle, and they fired much better than the first time; and it was what might be called pretty sharp shooting. When it came to my turn, I squared myself, and turning to the prime shot, I gave him a knowing nod, by way of showing my confidence; and says I, 'Look out for the bull's-eye, stranger.' I blazed away, and I wish I may be shot if I didn't miss the target. They examined it all over, and could find neither hair nor hide of my bullet, and pronounced it a dead miss; when says I, 'Stand aside and let me look, and I warrant you I get on the right trail of the critter,' They stood aside, and I examined the bull's-eye pretty particular, and at length cried out, 'Here it is; there is no snakes if it ha'n't followed the very track of the other.' They said it was utterly impossible, but I insisted on their searching the hole, and I agreed to be stuck up as a mark myself, if they did not find two bullets there. They searched for my satisfaction, and sure enough it all come out just as I had told them; for I had picked up a bullet that had been fired, and stuck it deep into the hole, without any one perceiving it. They were all perfectly satisfied that fame had not made too great a flourish of trumpets when speaking of me as a marksman: and they all said they had enough of shooting for that day, and they moved that we adjourn to the tavern and liquor."

The dinner consisted of bear's meat, venison, and wild turkey. They had an "uproarious" time over their whiskey. Crockett made a coarse and vulgar speech, which was neither creditable to his head nor his heart. But it was received with great applause.

The next morning Crockett decided to set out to cross the country in a southwest direction, to Fulton, on the upper waters of the Red River. The gentlemen furnished Crockett with a fine horse, and five of them decided to accompany him, as a mark of respect, to the River Washita, fifty miles from Little Rock. Crockett endeavored to raise some recruits for Texas, but was unsuccessful. When they reached the Washita, they found a clergyman, one of those bold, hardy pioneers of the wilderness, who through the wildest adventures were distributing tracts and preaching the gospel in the remotest hamlets.

He was in a condition of great peril. He had attempted to ford the river in the wrong place, and had reached a spot where he could not advance any farther, and yet could not turn his horse round. With much difficulty they succeeded in extricating him, and in bringing him safe to the shore. Having bid adieu to his kind friends, who had escorted him thus far, Crockett crossed the river, and in company with the clergyman continued his journey, about twenty miles farther west toward a little settlement called Greenville. He found his new friend to be a very charming companion. In describing the ride, Crockett writes:

"We talked about politics, religion, and nature, farming, and bear-hunting, and the many blessings that an all-bountiful Providence has bestowed upon our happy country. He continued to talk upon this subject, travelling over the whole ground as it were, until his imagination glowed, and his soul became full to overflowing; and he checked his horse, and I stopped mine also, and a stream of eloquence burst forth from his aged lips, such as I have seldom listened to: it came from the overflowing fountain of a pure and grateful heart. We were alone in the wilderness, but as he proceeded, it seemed to me as if the tall trees bent their tops to listen; that the mountain stream laughed out joyfully as it bounded on like some living thing that the fading flowers of autumn smiled, and sent forth fresher fragrance, as if conscious that they would revive in spring; and even the sterile rocks seemed to be endued with some mysterious influence. We were alone in the wilderness, but all things told me that God was there. The thought renewed my strength and courage. I had left my country, felt somewhat like an outcast, believed that I had been neglected and lost sight of. But I was now conscious that there was still one watchful Eye over me; no matter whether I dwelt in the populous cities, or threaded the pathless forest alone; no matter whether I stood in the high places among men, or made my solitary lair in the untrodden wild, that Eye was still upon me. My very soul leaped joyfully at the thought. I never felt so grateful in all my life. I never loved my God so sincerely in all my life. I felt that I still had a friend.

"When the old man finished, I found that my eyes were wet with tears. I approached and pressed his hand, and thanked him, and says I, 'Now let us take a drink.' I set him the example, and he followed it, and in a style too that satisfied me, that if he had ever belonged to the temperance society, he had either renounced membership, or obtained a dispensation. Having liquored, we proceeded on our journey, keeping a sharp lookout for mill-seats and plantations as we rode along.

"I left the worthy old man at Greenville, and sorry enough I was to part with him, for he talked a great deal, and he seemed to know a little about everything. He knew all about the history of the country; was well acquainted with all the leading men; knew where all the good lands lay in most of Western States.

"He was very cheerful and happy, though to all appearances very poor. I thought that he would make a first-rate agent for taking up lands, and mentioned it to him. He smiled, and pointing above, said, 'My wealth lies not in this world.'"

From Greenville, Crockett pressed on about fifty or sixty miles through a country interspersed withe forests and treeless prairies, until he reached Fulton. He had a letter of introduction to one of the prominent gentlemen here, and was received with marked distinction. After a short visit he disposed of his horse; he took a steamer to descend the river several hundred miles to Natchitoches, pronounced Nakitosh, a small straggling village of eight hundred inhabitants, on the right bank of the Red River, about two hundred miles from its entrance into the Mississippi.

In descending the river there was a juggler on board, who performed many skilful juggling tricks. and by various feats of gambling won much money from his dupes. Crockett was opposed to gambling in all its forms. Becoming acquainted with the juggler and, finding him at heart a well-meaning, good-natured fellow, he endeavored to remonstrate with him upon his evil practices.

"I told him," says Crockett, "that it was a burlesque on human nature, that an able-bodied man, possessed of his full share of good sense, should voluntarily debase himself, and be indebted for subsistence to such a pitiful artifice.

"'But what's to be done, Colonel?' says he. 'I'm in the slough of despond, up to the very chin. A miry and slippery path to travel.'

"'Then hold your head up,' says I, 'before the slough reaches your lips.'

"'But what's the use?' says he: 'it's utterly impossible for me to wade through; and even if I could, I should be in such a dirty plight, that it would defy all the waters in the Mississippi to wash me clean again. No,' he added in a desponding tone, 'I should be like a live eel in a frying-pan, Colonel, sort of out of my element, if I attempted to live like an honest man at this time o' day.'

"'That I deny. It is never too late to become honest,' said I. 'But even admit what you say to be true—that you cannot live like an honest man—you have at least the next best thing in your power, and no one can say nay to it.'

"'And what is that?'

"'Die like a brave one. And I know not whether, in the eyes of the world, a brilliant death is not preferred to an obscure life of rectitude. Most men are remembered as they died, and not as they lived. We gaze with admiration upon the glories of the setting sun, yet scarcely bestow a passing glance upon its noonday splendor.'

"'You are right; but how is this to be done?'

"'Accompany me to Texas. Cut aloof from your degrading habits and associates here, and, in fighting for the freedom of the Texans, regain your own.'

"The man seemed much moved. He caught up his gambling instruments, thrust them into his pocket, with hasty strides traversed the floor two or three times, and then exclaimed:

"'By heaven, I will try to be a man again. I will live honestly, or die bravely. I will go with you to Texas.'"

To confirm him in his good resolution, Crockett "asked him to liquor." At Natchitoches, Crockett encountered another very singular character. He was a remarkably handsome young man, of poetic imagination, a sweet singer, and with innumerable scraps of poetry and of song ever at his tongue's end. Honey-trees, as they were called, were very abundant in Texas. The prairies were almost boundless parterres of the richest flowers, from which the bees made large quantities of the most delicious honey. This they deposited in the hollows of trees. Not only was the honey valuable, but the wax constituted a very important article of commerce in Mexico, and brought a high price, being used for the immense candles which they burned in their churches. The bee-hunter, by practice, acquired much skill in coursing the bees to their hives.

This man decided to join Crockett and the juggler in their journey over the vast prairies of Texas. Small, but very strong and tough Mexican ponies, called mustangs, were very cheap. They were found wild, in droves of thousands, grazing on the prairies. The three adventurers mounted their ponies, and set out on their journey due west, a distance of one hundred and twenty miles, to Nacogdoches. Their route was along a mere trail, which was called the old Spanish road. It led over vast prairies, where there was no path, and where the bee-hunter was their guide, and through forests where their course was marked only by blazed trees.[1]

The next morning they crossed the river and pushed on for the fortress of Alamo. When within about twenty miles of San Antonio, they beheld about fifteen mounted men, well armed, approaching them at full speed. Crockett's party numbered five. They immediately dismounted, made a rampart of their horses, and with the muzzles of their rifles pointed toward the approaching foe, were prepared for battle.

It was a party of Mexicans. When within a few hundred yards they reined in their horses, and the leader, advancing a little, called out to them in Spanish to surrender.

"We must have a brush with those blackguards," said the pirate. "Let each one single out his man for the first fire. They are greater fools than I take them for if they give us a chance for a second shot. Colonel, just settle the business with that talking fellow with the red feather. He's worth any three of the party."

"Surrender, or we fire!" shouted the fellow with the red feather. The pirate replied, with a piratic oath, "Fire away."

---

[1]Crockett and his party are soon joined by a disreputably looking old man they nickname "Pirate." For the next while, they undergo various trials and adventures, eventually fetching up in San Antonio.

"And sure enough," writes Crockett, "they took his advice, for the next minute we were saluted with a discharge of musketry, the report of which was so loud that we were convinced they all had fired. Before the smoke had cleared away we had each selected our man, fired, and I never did see such a scattering among their ranks as followed. We beheld several mustangs running wild without their riders over the prairie, and the balance of the company were already retreating at a more rapid gait than they approached. We hastily mounted and commenced pursuit, which we kept up until we beheld the independent flag flying from the battlements of the fortress of Alamo, our place of destination. The fugitives succeeded in evading our pursuit, and we rode up to the gates of the fortress, announced to the sentinel who we were, and the gates were thrown open; and we entered amid shouts of welcome bestowed upon us by the patriots."

★   ★   ★

The fortress of Alamo is just outside of the town of Bexar, on the San Antonio River. The town is about one hundred and forty miles from the coast, and contained, at that time, about twelve hundred inhabitants. Nearly all were Mexicans, though there were a few American families. In the year 1718, the Spanish Government had established a military outpost here; and in the year 1721, a few emigrants from Spain commenced a flourishing settlement at this spot. Its site is beautiful, the air salubrious, the soil highly fertile, and the water of crystal purity.

The town of Bexar subsequently received the name of San Antonio. On the tenth of December, 1835, the Texans captured the town and citadel from the Mexicans.

These Texan Rangers were rude men, who had but little regard for the refinements or humanities of civilization. When Crockett with his companions arrived, Colonel Bowie, of Louisiana, one of the most desperate of Western adventurers, was in the fortress. The celebrated bowie-knife was named after this man. There was but a feeble garrison, and it was threatened with an attack by an overwhelming force of Mexicans under Santa Anna. Colonel Travis was in command. He was very glad to receive even so small a reinforcement. The fame of Colonel Crockett, as one of the bravest of men, had already reached his ears.

"While we were conversing," writes Crockett, "Colonel Bowie had occasion to draw his famous knife, and I wish I may be shot if the bare sight of it wasn't enough to give a man of a squeamish stomach the colic. He saw I was admiring it, and said he, 'Colonel, you might tickle a fellow's ribs a long time with this little instrument before you'd make make him laugh.'"

According to Crockett's account, many shameful orgies took place in the little garrison. They were evidently in considerable trepidation, for a large force was gathering against them, and they could not look for any considerable reinforcements from any quarter. Rumors were continually reaching them of the formidable preparations Santa Anna was making to attack the place. Scouts ere long brought in the tidings that Santa Anna, President of the Mexican Republic, at the head of sixteen hundred soldiers, and accompanied by several of his ablest generals, was within six miles of Bexar. It was said that he was doing everything in his power to enlist the warlike Comanches in his favor, but that they remained faithful in their friendship to the United States.

Early in the month of February, 1836, the army of Santa Anna appeared before the town, with infantry, artillery, and cavalry. With military precision they approached, their banners waving, and their bugle-notes bearing defiance to the feeble little garrison. The Texan invaders, seeing that they would soon be surrounded, abandoned the town to the enemy, and fled to the protection of the citadel. They were but one hundred and fifty in number. Almost without exception they were hardy adventurers, and the most fearless and desperate of men. They had previously stored away in the fortress all the provisions, arms, and ammunition, of which they could avail themselves. Over the battlements they unfurled an immense flag of thirteen stripes, and with a large white star of five points, surrounded by the letters "Texas." As they raised their flag, they gave three cheers, while with drums and trumpets they hurled back their challenge to the foe.

The Mexicans raised over the town a blood-red banner. It was their significant intimation to the garrison that no quarter was to be expected. Santa Anna, having advantageously posted his troops, in the afternoon sent a summons to Colonel Travis, demanding an unconditional surrender, threatening, in case of refusal, to put every man to the sword. The only reply Colonel Travis made was to throw a cannon-shot into the town. The Mexicans then opened fire from their batteries, but without doing much harm.

In the night, Colonel Travis sent the old pirate on an express to Colonel Fanning, who, with a small military force, was at Goliad, to entreat him to come to his aid. Goliad was about four days' march from Bexar. The next morning the Mexicans renewed their fire from a battery about three hundred and fifty yards from the fort. A three-ounce ball struck the juggler on the breast, inflicting a painful but not a dangerous wound.

Day after day this storm of war continued. The walls of the citadel were strong, and the bombardment inflicted but little injury. The sharpshooters within the fortress struck down many of the assailants at great distances.

"The bee-hunter," writes Crockett, "is about the quickest on the trigger, and the best rifle-shot we have in the fort. I have already seen him bring down eleven of the enemy, and at such a distance that we all thought that it would be a waste of ammunition to attempt it." Provisions were beginning to become scarce, and the citadel was so surrounded that it was impossible for the garrison to cut its way through the lines and escape.

Under date of February 28th, Crockett writes in his Journal:

"Last night our hunters brought in some corn, and had a brush with a scout from the enemy beyond gunshot of the fort. They put the scout to flight, and got in without injury. They bring accounts that the settlers are flying in all quarters, in dismay, leaving their possessions to the mercy of the ruthless invader, who is literally engaged in a war of extermination more brutal than the untutored savage of the desert could be guilty of. Slaughter is indiscriminate, sparing neither sex, age, nor condition. Buildings have been burnt down, farms laid waste, and Santa Anna appears determined to verify his threat, and convert the blooming paradise into a howling wilderness. For just one fair crack at that rascal, even at a hundred yards' distance, I would bargain to break my Betsey, and never pull trigger again. My name's not Crockett if I wouldn't get glory enough to appease my stomach for the remainder of my life.

"The scouts report that a settler by the name of Johnson, flying with his wife and three little children, when they reached the Colorado, left his family on the shore, and waded into the river to see whether it would be safe to ford with his wagon. When about the middle of the river he was seized by an alligator, and after a struggle was dragged under the water, and perished. The helpless woman and her babes were discovered, gazing in agony on the spot, by other fugitives, who happily passed that way, and relieved them. Those who fight the battles experience but a small part of the privation, suffering, and anguish that follow in the train of ruthless war. The cannonading continued at intervals throughout the day, and all hands were kept up to their work."

The next day he writes: "I had a little sport this morning before breakfast. The enemy had planted a piece of ordnance within gunshot of the fort during the night, and the first thing in the morning they commenced a brisk cannonade, point blank against the spot where I was snoring. I turned out pretty smart and mounted the rampart. The gun was charged again; a fellow stepped forth to touch her off, but before he could apply the match, I let him have it, and he keeled over. A second stepped up, snatched the match from the hand of the dying man, but the juggler, who had followed me, handed me his rifle, and the next instant the Mexican was stretched on the earth beside the first. A third came up to the cannon. My companion handed me another gun, and I fixed him off in like manner. A fourth, then a fifth seized the match, who both met with the same fate. Then the whole party gave it up as a bad job, and hurried off to the camp, leaving the cannon ready charged where they had planted it. I came down, took my bitters, and went to breakfast."

In the course of a week the Mexicans lost three hundred men. But still reinforcements were continually arriving, so that their numbers were on the rapid increase. The garrison no longer cherished any hope of receiving aid from abroad.

Under date of March 4th and 5th, 1836, we have the last lines which Crockett ever penned.

"March 4th. Shells have been falling into the fort like hail during the day, but without effect. About dusk, in the evening, we observed a man running toward the fort, pursued by about half a dozen of the Mexican cavalry. The bee-hunter immediately knew him to be the old pirate, who had gone to Goliad, and, calling to the two hunters, he sallied out of the fort to the relief of the old man, who was hard pressed. I followed close after. Before we reached the spot the Mexicans were close on the heels of the old man, who stopped suddenly, turned short upon his pursuers, discharged his rifle, and one of the enemy fell from his horse. The chase was renewed, but finding that he would be overtaken and cut to pieces, he now turned again, and, to the amazement of the enemy, became the assailant in his turn. He clubbed his gun, and dashed among them like a wounded tiger, and they fled like sparrows. By this time we reached the spot, and, in the ardor of the moment, followed some

distance before we saw that our retreat to the fort was cut off by another detachment of cavalry. Nothing was to be done but fight our way through. We were all of the same mind. 'Go ahead!' cried I; and they shouted, 'Go ahead, Colonel!' We dashed among them, and a bloody conflict ensued. They were about twenty in number, and they stood their ground. After the fight had continued about five minutes, a detachment was seen issuing from the fort to our relief, and the Mexicans scampered off, leaving eight of their comrades dead upon the field. But we did not escape unscathed, for both the pirate and the bee-hunter were mortally wounded, and I received a sabre-cut across the forehead. The old man died without speaking, as soon as we entered the fort. We bore my young friend to his bed, dressed his wounds, and I watched beside him. He lay, without complaint or manifesting pain, until about midnight, when he spoke, and I asked him if he wanted anything. 'Nothing,' he replied, but drew a sigh that seemed to rend his heart, as he added, 'Poor Kate of Nacogdoches.' His eyes were filled with tears, as he continued, 'Her words were prophetic, Colonel,' and then he sang in a low voice, that resembled the sweet notes of his own devoted Kate:

> 'But toom cam' the saddle, all bluidy to see,
> And hame came the steed, but hame never came he.'

He spoke no more, and a few minutes after died. Poor Kate, who will tell this to thee?"

The romantic bee-hunter had a sweetheart by the name of Kate in Nacogdoches. She seems to have been a very affectionate and religious girl. In parting, she had presented her lover with a Bible, and in anguish of spirit had expressed her fears that he would never return from his perilous enterprise.

The next day, Crockett simply writes, "*March 5th.* Pop, pop, pop! Bom, bom, bom! throughout the day. No time for memorandums now. Go ahead! Liberty and Independence forever."

Before daybreak on the 6th of March, the citadel of the Alamo was assaulted by the whole Mexican army, then numbering about three thousand men. Santa Anna in person commanded. The assailants swarmed over the works and into the fortress. The battle was fought with the utmost desperation until daylight. Six only of the Garrison then remained alive. They were surrounded, and they surrendered. Colonel Crockett was one. He at the time stood alone in an angle of the fort, like a lion at bay. His eyes flashed fire, his shattered rifle in his right hand, and in his left a gleaming bowie-knife streaming with blood. His face was covered with blood flowing from a deep gash across his forehead. About twenty Mexicans, dead and dying, were lying at his feet. The juggler was also there dead. With one hand he was clenching the hair of a dead Mexican, while with the other he had driven his knife to the haft in the bosom of his foe.

The Mexican General Castrillon, to whom the prisoners had surrendered, wished to spare their lives. He led them to that part of the fort where Santa Anna stood surrounded by his staff. As Castrillon marched his prisoners into the presence of the President, he said:

"Sir, here are six prisoners I have taken alive. How shall I dispose of them?"

Santa Anna seemed much annoyed, and said, "Have I not told you before how to dispose of them? Why do you bring them to me?"

Immediately several Mexicans commenced plunging their swords into the bosoms of the captives. Crockett, entirely unarmed, sprang, like a tiger, at the throat of Santa Anna. But before he could reach him, a dozen swords were sheathed in his heart, and he fell without a word or a groan. But there still remained upon his brow the frown of indignation, and his lip was curled with a smile of defiance and scorn.

And thus was terminated the earthly life of this extraordinary man. In this narrative it has been the object of the writer faithfully to record the influences under which Colonel Crockett was reared, and the incidents of his wild and wondrous life, leaving it with the reader to form his own estimate of the character which these exploits indicate. David Crockett has gone to the tribunal of his God, there to be judged for all the deeds done in the body. Beautifully and consolingly the Psalmist has written:

"Like as a father pitieth his children, so the Lord pitieth them that fear him. For he knoweth our frame; he remembereth that we are dust."

John Brown

[WALTER HAWKINS]

T he birth of John Brown is recorded in the following laconic style by his father in a little
autobiography he wrote for his children in the
closing days of his life. 'In 1800, May 8, John was born
one hundred years after his great-grandfather; nothing
else very uncommon.' In the year mentioned the family were living at Torrington, Connecticut, whence they
shortly removed to Ohio, then the haunt of the Red
Indian. They were of the pioneer farming class, which
has supplied so many of the shapers of American history. The one great honour in their pedigree was that
they descended from a man of the *Mayflower*—Peter
Brown, a working carpenter who belonged to that
famous ship's company. We might say, indeed, that the
story of John Brown flows from the events of 1620, the
year of the *Mayflower*. Two landings on the American
coast that year were destined to be memorable. In
August a Dutch vessel disembarked the first cargo of
imported slaves—twenty of them; and that day slavery

struck deep root in the new land. And in November of that same year the *Mayflower,* with her very different cargo of brave freemen, dropped anchor in Cape Cod Bay. The stream of ill results from that first landing and the stream of Puritan blood, generous in its passion for liberty, that flowed unimpoverished from Peter Brown through generations of sturdy ancestors—these are the streams destined to meet turbulently and to supply us with our story. Owen Brown, the father of John, thus testifies to his own fidelity to the tradition of liberty. 'I am an Abolitionist. I know we are not loved by many. I wish to tell how I became one. Our neighbour lent my mother a slave for a few days. I used to go out into the field with him, and he used to carry me on his back, and I fell in love with him.' There we have the clue to the history of the household of the Browns for the next two generations. They fell in love with the despised negro, and this glorious trait passed like an heritage from generation to generation.

There is a letter extant which supplies us with the best information on John Brown's own boyhood. It was written for a lad in a wealthy home where he stayed in later days, who had asked him many questions about his experiences in early life. He humorously calls it a 'short story of a certain boy of my acquaintance I will call John.' A few extracts will reveal his character in the forming. Here, for instance, you may trace the conscientiousness (often morbid) which was so marked a feature in his later days. 'I cannot tell you of anything in the first four years of John's life worth mentioning save that at that early age he was tempted by three large brass pins belonging to a girl who lived in the family, and stole them. In this he was detected by his mother; and after having a full day to think of the wrong, received from her a thorough whipping.' He adds, 'I must not neglect to tell you of a very foolish and bad habit to which John was somewhat addicted. I mean, telling lies, generally to screen himself from blame or from punishment. He could not well endure to be reproached, and now I think had he been oftener encouraged to be entirely frank, by making frankness a kind of atonement for some of his faults, he would not have had to struggle so long with this mean habit.'

A story is told of John's schooldays which is an amusing and quite characteristic instance of his ethical eccentricities. For a short time he and his younger brother Salmon were at a school together, and Salmon was guilty of some offence which was condoned by the master. John had serious concern for the effect this might have upon his brother's morals, and he sought the lenient teacher and informed him that the fault was much deprecated by their father at home, and he was sure castigation there would have been inevitable. He therefore desired it should be duly inflicted, as otherwise he should feel compelled to act as his father's proxy. Finding discipline was still lax, he proceeded with paternal solemnity to administer it himself. His brother acknowledged that this was done with reluctant fidelity! Truly the moral instincts of the family were worthy of their Puritan ancestry.

Although naturally self-conscious and shy, his precociousness in boyhood, bringing him into association, as it did, with much older folk, bred a somewhat arrogant manner. The rule he exercised over younger members of the family also made him somewhat domineering, a fault which he diligently sought to correct in later life. At fifteen he had become a miniature man of business and was driving cattle on long journeys with all the confidence of mid-age. The letter from which we have already quoted has one or two more passages which may enlighten us as to his rearing. Still writing in the third person, he says, 'John had been taught from earliest childhood to fear God and keep His commandments, and though quite sceptical he had always by turns felt much doubt as to his future well being. He became to some extent a convert to Christianity, and ever after a firm believer in the divine authenticity of the Bible. With this book he became very familiar, and possessed a most unusual memory of its entire contents.' Here are hints as to his early pursuits: 'After getting to Ohio in 1805, he was for some time rather afraid of the Indians and their rifles, but this soon wore off, and he used to hang about them quite as much as was consistent with good manners and learned a trifle of their talk. His father learned to dress deer-skins, and at six years old John was installed a young buck-skin. He was, perhaps, rather observing, as he ever after remembered the entire process of deer-skin dressing, so that he could at any time dress his own leather, such as squirrel, racoon, cat, wolf, and dog skins, and also learned to make whiplashes, which brought him some change at times, and was of considerable service in many ways. He did not become much of a scholar. He would always choose to stay at home and work hard rather than be sent to school, and during the warm season might generally be seen barefooted and bareheaded, with buck-skin breeches suspended often with one leather strap over his shoulder, but sometimes with two. To be sent off through the wilderness alone to very considerable distances was particularly his delight; in this he was often indulged, so that by the time he was twelve years old he was sent off more than a hundred miles with companies of cattle. He followed up with tenacity whatever he set about so long as it answered his general purpose, and thence he rarely failed in some good degree to effect the things he undertook.'

'From fifteen years and upward he felt a good deal of anxiety to learn, but could only read and study a little, both for want of time and on account of inflammation of the eyes. He managed by the help of books, however, to make himself tolerably well acquainted with common arithmetic and surveying, which he practised more or less after he was twenty years old.'

'John began early in life to discover a great liking to fine cattle, horses, sheep, and swine; and as soon as circumstances would enable him, he began to be a practical shepherd—it being a calling for which, in early life, he had a kind of enthusiastic longing, together with the idea that as a business it bade fair to afford him the means of carrying out his greatest principal object.'

Here we touch the keynote of this life of manifold outward occupations, but of one consuming desire. That principal object filled his horizon even in childhood. He loved to tell how, like his father before him, he fell captive to the slave's dumb plea and pledged his whole strength to the chivalrous task of breaking his fetters. It happened on this wise. In those long journeys he was allowed to take, he was the 'business guest'

of a slaveowner, who was pleased with his resourcefulness at such an age. He was the object of curious attention, and was treated as 'company' at table. On the
estate was a young negro just his own age, and as intelligent as he. Young John struck up an acquaintance
with him, and could not fail to contrast the fashion in
which he himself was pampered with the way the
young darkie was coarsely treated with scant fare and
ill-housing. His frequent thrashings seemed to bruise
young John's spirit as much as they did his flesh. They
were not always administered with the orthodox whip,
but with a shovel or anything else that came first to
hand. Young John pondered long upon this contrast,
and tells us how the iniquity of slavery was borne in
upon his young heart, and he was drawn to this little
coloured playmate, who had neither father nor mother
known to him. The Bible was the final court of appeal
in the Brown family, and the verdict of that court was
that they two—the slave and the guest—were brothers,
so henceforth the instinct of fraternal loyalty drew
young John to 'swear eternal war with slavery.' That
vow, never recanted or forgotten, became the text of
his life. It interprets all his vagaries and reconciles what
else were hopeless inconsistencies. It was a devout
obsession which made him a wanderer all his days, and
in the end carried him to prison and to death. To a
child a great call had come, and a child's voice had
replied, 'Speak, Lord, Thy servant heareth.' And ears
and heart tingled at messages that seemed to come
from the Unseen.

THE LONG WAITING-TIME

For over thirty years did this man both 'hope and quietly wait for the salvation of the Lord' to come for the slaves of his land. The interval is full of interest for those who care to watch the development of a life-purpose. Only for three or four years was he destined to figure in the eyes of the world. Those years, as we shall hereafter see, were crowded with events; but for a generation he felt an abiding conviction of impending destiny.

There is something fateful about the constant indications of this spirit of readiness. His commercial pursuits were multifarious, but none of them was greatly successful. At Hudson, Ohio, till 1825, and afterwards at Richmond, Pennsylvania, he was tanner, land-surveyor, and part of the time postmaster. He became skilful at his father's business of tanning, but is a typical Yankee in the facility with which he turns his hand to anything.

From 1835 to 1839 he was at Franklin, Ohio, where we find him adding to his former occupations the breeding of horses, and also dabbling in land speculation, with the result that he became bankrupt. But when he failed in business he set to work to pay his debts in full. His death found him still striving to achieve that end. He was regarded as whimsical and stubborn, yet through years of struggle, endeavour, and even failure he was known as trusty and honourable.

From 1841 to 1846 he lived at Richfield, Ohio, where he took to shepherding and wool-dealing, which he continued in 1849 at Springfield, Massachusetts. He seems to have developed much capacity for wool-testing. When he came to England with a cargo of wool, some English dealers sought to practise a fraudulent joke upon his quick fingers. They stripped a poodle of the best of his fleece and handed it to the oracular Yankee with the inquiry, 'What would you do with that wool?' But there was wisdom in him down to the finger-ends, for he rolled it there, and in a moment handed it back with the confounding retort, 'Gentlemen, if you have any machinery in England for working up dog's hair I would advise you to put this into it.'

Had he known how to sell wool as well as he knew how to test it; had he known how to sell his sheep as well as he knew hundreds of sheep faces apart, and like a diviner could interpret their inarticulate language; had he been as apt upon the market as he was upon the farm, he might have made money. As it was, there was never more than enough for the wants of a severely plain household life.

But this business record was (and herefrom its frequent misfortune may have largely proceeded) in no wise the history of John Brown. We must catch, if we can, indications of the unfolding of his soul, and of the inward preparation for what he felt was his divine destiny; and these may best be gathered as we watch the simple home life of the family. At an early age, while residing at Hudson, Ohio, he married his first wife, Dianthe Lusk; and though he was but twenty years of age, his was no rash choice. A description by one who had been brought up with her may be fitly quoted: 'Plain but attractive, because of a quiet amiable disposition, sang beautifully, almost always sacred music; she had a place in the wood not far from the house where she used to go alone to pray.' John Brown, servant as he already accounted himself of the

Invisible Powers, is drawn to one who thus communes with the Unseen. She will have sympathy with his moral aims and a source of strength when he may be absent from her in pursuit of them. The sketch proceeds, 'She was pleasant but not funny; she never said what she did not mean.' Here, truly, was the wife for a man in dead earnest and who could keep a boyish oath even unto death. For twelve years she proved a good comrade, and of the seven children of this marriage five survived, from whom testimonies concerning the domestic life are forthcoming.

The wife who succeeded her (Mary Ann Day) seems to have been no less a help-meet in his enterprises. Thirteen children, many of whom died young, were the offspring of this second marriage, so that in a hereditary sense the soul of John Brown may be said to have marched on.

He infected all his children with his passionate love of liberty. Many are his cares for their spiritual welfare. Some of them sorely tried his patience by their aloofness from the Christian conventions that were dear to him; he yearns over their souls as he fears their experience of the inner working of grace is not as his own, but they swerved not in their allegiance to the cause of the slave. Let us avail ourselves of some of their memories of their remarkable father. How early the house became a city of refuge for the runaway negro we learn from the eldest son, who tells us he can just recollect a timid knock at the door of the log cabin where they lived. A fugitive slave and his wife were there, for they had heard that there were a couple residing in the house who loved the negro and would lend him a rescuing hand. They were speedily made to know they were welcome, and the negress, relieved of her last fear, takes young John in a motherly fashion upon her knee and kisses him. He almost instinctively scampers off to rub the black from his face. Returning, he watches his mother giving them supper. Presently Father's extraordinarily quick ear detects the sound of horsehoofs half a mile away; weapons are thrust into the hands of the terrified pair, and they are taken out to the woody swamps behind the house to lie in hiding. Father then returns, only to discover that it is a false alarm, whereupon he sallies forth to bring them into shelter and warmth once more, and tells the assembled family on their arrival how he had difficulty in the dark in recognizing the hiding-place and really discovered them at length by hearing the beating of their frightened hearts. No wonder. Quick as any faculty he had was that of hearing a slave's heart beat. Had it not been for that keen instinct there would have been no tale to tell of John Brown.

The daughter says her earliest memory is of her father's great arms about her as he sang to her his favourite hymn:

> *Blow ye the trumpet, blow*
> *The gladly solemn sound:*
> *Let all the nations know*
> *To earth's remotest bound.*
> *The year of Jubilee is come,*
> *Return, ye ransomed sinners, home.*

Then, ceasing, he would tell her with heart brimming with tenderness of poor little black children who were slaves. What were slaves? she wanted to know. And he was ready enough to tell her of those who were riven from father and mother and sold for base coin, whom in some States it was illegal to teach their A B C, but quite lawful to flog; and then the daughter would be asked, by way of application to his moving discourse, if she would like some of them to come some time and share her home and food.

Thus continually to that rising family there was unfolded the horror of the slavery system. That horror had faded in the minds of many in the Northern States whose ancestry had held freedom dear; while in the Southern States, for the most part, the possession of your fellow creatures as if they were so much farm stock had become too familiar a feature of common life to evoke any conscientious misgiving, much less shame. The enormous additions to the cotton trade had made slave labour increasingly gainful, and the capital invested in this living property was immense. Careful rearing of slaves for the market as well as their purchase brought wealth to many, and fierce was the resentment when any one publicly criticized the institution. There was by no means an absence of humane regard for the well being of the negroes; a kind of patriarchal tenderness towards them was distinctly 'good form.' But there was the deadly fact that they were human goods and chattels, with no civil rights worth mentioning—for laws in their defence were practically worthless, seeing they could not appear as witnesses in the court. Public whipping-houses were provided for the expeditious correction of the refractory, and a mere suspicion of intent to escape was legal justification for the use of the branding-irons upon their flesh. If they did contrive to escape there were dogs bred on purpose to hunt them down. If the slave resisted his master's will he might be slain, and the law would not graze the master's head. Domestic security he had none, for wife might be wrenched from husband or child from mother according to the state of the market. And, strangest of all to our ears, the pulpits of the South extolled slavery as appointed of Heaven, and solemnly quoting the prophecy that Ham should be the servant of his brethren, the pulpiteer would ask who would dare to resist the will of God Most High? Not content to hold their views tenaciously, the slave-holders and their followers dealt out threatenings and slaughter to all who by lip or pen opposed them. The household of Brown pondered all this invasion of the great natural right of freedom, and with one accord pined for the opportunity of checking, or, it might be, ending it.

It is on record how they were taught to repeat their father's vow. It was in 1839, when they were living at Franklin, Ohio, that he called them around him, and on bended knee declared the secret mission with which, he believed, High Heaven had charged him—to labour by word or sword, by any means opportunity might offer, for the overthrow of slavery, which he believed to be the very citadel of evil in America. 'Swear, children, swear,' said he; and from that little group in the log house there went up an appeal for a blessing upon their oath—an oath which they could truly protest was likely to bring nought to them but peril, disaster, and, perchance, death, but which they were well assured must bring glory to Eternal God. And so their oath was registered in heaven.

For many years it was only in indirect ways they could promote their end. Early they gave themselves to help the tentative endeavours that were often on foot to educate those slaves who did make good their escape, and especially to train them to independent agriculture, so that evidence might be afforded that they could use their liberty to good purpose, and become useful citizens. The Browns were always active in promoting such apprenticeship to freedom.

The last stage in what we may call the long preparation of John Brown for the prominent labours of his life reveals still further how the passionate love of the cause of liberty burned as a fire in the bones of this family. They were attracted by the proposal of Gerrit Smith, to celebrate the passing of West Indian Emancipation with the offer of 100,000 acres of his wild land in the north of New York State for coloured families to settle upon. Eager for the success of the experiment, Brown and his sons were prepared to start pioneering in the new region, so as to be near at hand to encourage and assist the new settlers. Prepared to choose their location as they deemed the exigencies of the great cause demanded, they settled at North Elba in what was then a wilderness in Essex county, and commenced to live a life of sterner simplicity than before, hewing in the forests, and clearing with axe and fire the land which they then proceeded to cultivate, obtaining food and clothes as those must who have neither store nor tailor near. There, with one room beneath that served by day, and two rooms overhead that served by night, they lived, and not discontentedly, for if there was little space or grandeur within there was plenty without; and John Brown, who was no mere conqueror of Nature, but a lover of her beauty, revelled in the glories of that untamed land, with its mountains wooded to their summits, with its frowning gorges and rushing torrents and its richly scented air. Best of all there were black settlers around whom they could help and thus forward their life-work, proving that the race they vowed should be free could appreciate and justify the boon.

HOW THE CALL CAME

Thus, then, did this family live their life of preparation. But eventful days were at hand, and John Brown felt that his real life-work had yet to come. 'I have never,' he said, 'for twenty years made any business arrangement that would prevent me at any time from answering the call of the Lord. I have kept my affairs in such a condition that in two weeks I could wind them up and be ready to obey that call, permitting nothing to stand in the way of duty, neither wife, children, nor worldly goods; whenever the time should come, I was ready.' Now truly it seemed as if 'God's judgements' were to be abroad in the earth, as if He was 'travelling in the greatness of His strength, mighty to save' the oppressed; as if 'the Day of Vengeance' were in His heart, and the 'Year of His redeemed was come'; and, said John Brown's heart, 'He shall find one loyal henchman; I am ready.'

John Brown's call seemed to come after this wise. The enrollment of each New State in the Union was the occasion of fierce contention as to whether the territories should be free or whether slavery should be permitted. Each party had sought at such junctures to score an advantage, for the balance was often a very fine one between them.

The spirit of compromise had from the earliest days prevailed upon the thorny question. Washington was against slavery. Statesmen like Adams, Franklin, Madison, and Munroe had opposed it; but others had been willing to purchase the preservation of Union by concessions to the South, and toleration had been their consistent policy.

The Missouri compromise in 1820 had apparently settled the question as to the new State of Kansas, for all future States north of the latitude 36d 30m were to be free. But at the enrolment of Kansas the slave party circumvented this statute, and ensured local option for the State upon this matter. In 1854 the new State of Kansas proceeded to determine for itself once and for all by popular election the grave question whether she was to be a Slave or a Free State. But in these young States, which were being almost daily reinforced by new residents, each at once entitled to vote, the slave party saw a rare opportunity for the manufacture of faggot votes. What was to hinder the inhabitants of Missouri, the neighbouring State—who were slavery men—from going over in a body and voting! Couldn't men migrate and change their minds? Scandalous, you say. It was. But the scandal was actually perpetrated. None other than the acting Vice-President of the United States advised this course, and he found many ready to improve upon his instructions. One official stated: 'To those who have qualms of conscience as to violating laws, State or National, I say the time has come when such impositions must be disregarded, since your rights and property are at stake. And I advise you one and all to enter every election district in Kansas and vote at the point of the bowie-knife and the revolver.''

Thus, a thousand strong, with two cannon in their procession, the armed ruffians went to vote at an election out of their own State. If brave election judges protested—and some did, in spite of cocked pistols at their heads (like true lawyers ready to die for justice' sake)—and required the mob to establish their claims, they were overpowered; the ruffians seized the ballot-boxes, and in the end there were 4,908 votes cast, though there were only 1,410 genuine voters in the State. Such was the deliberate report of a committee years after. The Legislature thus elected met and were suffered to make a Statute Book for the young State. Penalties of imprisonment and death were liberally appointed for all who should dare to resist the institution of slavery.

With such legislation to shield their lawlessness, ruffians belonging to the class of 'mean whites' commenced a series of barbarous outrages in the interests of the slave-holders—a series sickening to contemplate. Two instances may be quoted which are typical:

A ruffian bets that he will scalp an Abolitionist in true Indian fashion, and rides out in search of his prey. A gentleman known to be opposed to slavery is met in a gig and shot; and, taking his scalp, the drunken fiend rides back, and producing the promised spoil, claims his due.

Another leader of the Free-State men is surrounded by these desperate ruffians, and his skull and brain are cloven with a hatchet. In fiendish glee they dance upon the almost breathless man, who vainly pleads, 'Do not abuse me, I am dying.' The only response is a shower of tobacco juice from their filthy lips into his pleading eyes. With his last breath he says, 'It is in a good cause,' and so dies—slaughtered because he dared to say others should share in his right of liberty. True, dying man, the cause is good and will triumph, though thou and many others die first!

Such scenes roused the ire of the long-suffering Free-State men of Kansas. Redress there was none, save in their own right arm, for, as Emerson says, 'A plundered man might take his case to the court and find the ring-leader who has robbed him dismounting from his own horse and unbuckling his knife to sit as judge.'

They were not without allies. There might be no government aid from Washington, but throughout the North were men who loved the cause of Abolition better than their own ease, and they came in ever-increasing numbers. Amongst them were several of Brown's upgrown sons, followed by their father, ready to settle in this new State, where they might turn the tide of public opinion in favour of Freedom.

Thus slowly the ranks of the righteous lovers of liberty were replenished, and they began to form into bands for mutual protection, farming and soldiering by turns as necessity dictated.

Some of John Brown's Northern friends, who knew the stuff of which he was made, and saw that if Freedom had no blow struck on her behalf she would be driven by outrage-mongers out of Kansas, equipped him with money and rifles, or, as they had come to be called, 'Beecher Bibles'—a tribute to Henry Ward Beecher's ardent championship of advanced views upon the slavery question.

On October 6, 1855, he arrived at Osawatomie, and we find him writing cheery words to his brave second wife and their family whom he had left, telling them to hope in God and comfort one another, humbly trusting they may meet again on God's earth, and if not—for his vow is 'to the death'—that they may meet in God's heaven. Of that second wife—heroine in obscurity, sharer of the oath which ever knit the household in one, mother of thirteen children—we might say much, but her spirit breathes in these words she speaks concerning her solitary days:

'That was the time in my life when all my religion, all my philosophy, and all my faith in God's goodness were put to the test. My husband was away from home, prostrated by sickness; I was helpless from illness; in one week three of my little ones died of dysentery—this but three months before the birth of another child. Three years after this sad time another little one, eighteen months old, was burned to death. Yet even in these trials God upheld me.'

Such was the wife who, while John Brown fought for liberty, grudged him not to such a cause, and patiently trained others who should bear his name worthily in days to come.

BIBLE AND SWORD

John Brown was now at his work; no longer the mere fingers, but the soul of him had found a task. He set before himself this object, to free Kansas from the slave-holders' grip.

The Free-State men had met and agreed to pay no taxes to a Legislature illegally elected. They organized a rival government, and brought themselves into violent antagonism to the Federal Authorities at Washington—

for President Pierce and his Cabinet, which included the renowned Jefferson Davis, backed the pro-slavery Legislature and its following of ruffians. The town of Lawrence, which the Free Staters held, was taken and pillaged by a wild mob under the leadership of the United States Marshal, and we find the Browns in a company marching to its relief. There was much skirmishing, during which two of Brown's sons were taken prisoners. Only the constant vigilance and undaunted courage of a few desperately bold men kept heart in the lovers of liberty. But they (often led by John Brown) escaped the government officials who sought to arrest them and sped to the help of those who were marked as the victims of the marauders. So slowly did the Federal Authorities awake to the situation that for a time there seemed little protection to be expected for persecuted lovers of liberty.

We must now form some estimate of the two sides in this irregular warfare in which John Brown all through the summer of 1856 was so prominently engaged.

On the one hand were those whom the slave-holders relied upon for the most part to do their dirty work—ruffians, many of them from the neighbouring State; men who did not work, but who lived a wild life—not cultivating a tract of land around their rude dwelling-place like honest settlers, but fishing, shooting, and thieving for a living—preferring the atmosphere of a Slave State as more favourable to their life of lawlessness and plunder, and finding inspiration in the whisky-bottle for such deeds of devilry as have been described.

Upon the other side, waging a guerilla warfare—for little else was possible against enemies who preferred sneaking outrages to pitched battles—were little companies of some score or two. Captain John Brown's company was ever to the fore. He felt that outrage had gone far enough unchecked, and that it was time honest men took the aggressive and struck terror into cowards' hearts. They were not without fierceness, but it was the fruit of honest anger. Rifles in their judgement went not ill with Bible-reading and prayer—but we have heard of such before. Armed Roundheads and Scotch Covenanters combined prayer with sword exercise. In this camp, morning and evening prayers were an institution; uncivil treatment of prisoners was a gross offence; no intoxicating liquors were permitted. One by-law runs: 'All profane, vulgar, or ungentlemanly talk shall be discountenanced.' What! do these rough men set themselves up to be gentlemen! Yes, according to Emerson's own meaning when he says of Brown's supporters:

'All gentlemen, of course, are on his side. I do not mean by "gentlemen" people of scented hair and perfumed handkerchiefs, but men of gentle blood and generosity, "fulfilled with all nobleness," who, like the Cid, give the outcast leper a share of their bed; like the dying Sidney, pass the cup of cold water to the wounded soldier who needs it more. For what is the oath of gentle blood and knighthood! What but to protect the weak and lowly against the strong oppressor! Nothing is more absurd than to complain of this sympathy, or to complain of a party of men united in opposition to slavery. As well complain of gravity or the ebb of the tide. Who makes the Abolitionist! The slaveholder. The sentiment of mercy is the natural recoil which the laws of the universe provide to protect mankind from destruction by savage passions. And our blind statesmen go up and down, with committees of vigilance and safety, hunting for the origin of this new heresy. They will need a very vigilant committee, indeed, to find its birthplace, and a very strong force to root it up. For the arch-abolitionist, older than Brown, and older than the Shenanndoah Mountains, is Love, whose other name is Justice—which was before Alfred, before Lycurgus, before Slavery, and will be after it.'

John Brown and, at one time, six of his sons were in the company. Many were rejected who offered for service, not for lack of physical stature, but moral. 'I would rather,' said John Brown, 'have the smallpox, yellow fever, and cholera all together in my camp than a man without principles. It is a mistake to think that bullies are the best fighters. Give me God-fearing men—men who respect themselves; and with a dozen of them, I will oppose a hundred of these ruffians.' These are the men, then, who were found in Kansas woods, with bare heads and unkempt locks, in red-topped boots and blue shirts, taking their hasty meals or fitful sleep, their horses tied to the tree-trunks ready for swift mounting at the first signal of danger. No sounds of revelry betray their hiding-place; the spirit of the man in their midst, with Puritan nobility in his rugged face, and a strange, awe-inspiring unworldliness in his talk, has entered into them. No novice is he in the affairs of either world— this or the Unseen. At night he will look up to the stars that glitter above the still camp and talk like a theologian, moralizing upon the fact that while God's stars are unerring in their courses God's human creatures are so erratic. But he is no mere dreamer; you may see him, when the enemy is known to be near, sleeping in his saddle, with his gun across it, that he may be no sooner awake than ready. One who knew not of this habit was once imprudent enough to touch him in his sleep, as he wanted to speak to him; he had only time to knock up the swiftly pointed barrel with his hand and John Brown's bullet grazed the intruder's shoulder.

One of the first deeds in this campaign, and the one that certainly first turned the tide and caused the pro-slavery ruffians to feel that they had need to look to their own safety, and would not be suffered with impunity to murder whom they chose and fire honest men's houses like fiends let loose, was the midnight massacre at Pottawatomie. Along a certain creek there lived five of these incendiaries and outrage-mongers who were specially notorious. A report reached Brown that they were sworn to sweep the neighbourhood clear of Abolitionists, not forgetting 'those Browns.' That they were to be kept in terror by such a gang seemed to Brown an unrighteous state of things, and he formed the desperate design of visiting them first. But he loved not slaughter for slaughter's sake. Not only could he strike upon occasion, but he could be just in his rough-and-ready fashion. He argued within himself, 'I shall be right in killing these men if I am sure they intend these murders, but I will not act upon mere report.' Disguising himself, he started with two men to carry a surveyor's chain, and one to carry a flag. No coward was this man. He would put his life in peril rather than act on mere suspicion. So he ran his lines past the houses of these five men, and they naturally came out to see what this surveying business was. Brown told them, as he looked through his instrument and waved the flagman to this side or that.

'Yours is a grand country. Are there many Abolitionists about here?' In his pocket-book he jotted down the answer 'Yes,' and, swearing great oaths, they told him that they meant to sweep the region clear of them in a week. 'Are there some called Brown?' 'Yes,' and man by man they swore the Browns should be killed by their hands. Back he went saying to himself, 'If I understand the Book these are murderers, they have committed murder in their hearts.' Ere many nights were passed eight men were requisitioned from the camp. They stole forth armed with short cutlasses, and next morning the ghastly news spread abroad that five corpses had been found by that creek. John Brown, Jr., said, 'The only statement that I ever heard my father make in regard to this was "I did not myself kill any of those men at Pottawatomie, but I am as fully responsible as if I did."' It was a terrible act; we cannot wonder that it came as a great shock to many who had the cause of liberty at heart, but when questioned about it the old man was always reticent, and would only say, 'God is my Judge.'

The result was unmistakable. From that moment John Brown's name became a terror to the evildoers of that quarter. The free settlers felt there was another fate than extermination for them, and the impotent administration at Washington first began to see that this hitherto submissive majority of free settlers must be reckoned with. A writer said years after, 'It was like a clap of thunder from a clear sky.' There are acts that can only be morally estimated by a careful consideration of the prevailing circumstances, and in this case they are such as we, well housed and protected folk, thank God, know not. Those who knew this man through and through were swift to testify, 'Whatever may be thought of John Brown's acts, John Brown himself was right.' No personal end had he to serve; his harvest was privation, suffering, death. He had no personal vengeance to wreak, and when revengeful words were spoken in his hearing he soon lifted the conversation to a sublime level.

'That,' said he, 'is not a Christian spirit. If I thought I had one bit of the spirit of revenge I would never lift my hand. I do not make war on slave-holders, but on slavery.'

Henceforth John Brown's little band was famous. A few days after the Pottawatomie tragedy we find him engaging a company under Captain Fate, who professed, with doubtful authority, to be the emissary of the Government. Hearing after prayer meeting one Sunday they are in the neighbourhood, he is quickly in pursuit as soon as night has set in, and in the morning with a handful of men he is exchanging brisk fire with the enemy. Presently Fred Brown, a wild-looking man of the woods, who has been left in charge of the horses, comes riding upon a pony none too large for its ungainly burden. He waves his long arms, shouting, 'Come on, boys, we've got 'em surrounded and cut off their communications.' The enemy are scared at the apparition, and their captain, thinking there is no fathoming the plots of these Browns, sends a lieutenant forward with a flag of truce. John Brown asks, 'Are you captain!' 'No.' 'I will talk with him, not with you.' Captain Fate advances with much parley. 'Any proposition to make?' impatiently asks John Brown. 'No.' Then he (John Brown) has one—unconditional surrender; and with eight men he has soon secured twenty prisoners. So all through that summer Brown was wellnigh ubiquitous in harassing the enemy, and their dispatches betray their terror of him by ludicrous exaggerations of his achievements. But it is certain he lived as nearly up to his terrible reputation as he could. At Franklin, at Washington Creek, and at Osawatomie we find him in evidence. Here are extracts from his letters in reference to the attack made by the pro-slavery men at the last-mentioned place. 'On the morning of August 30 an attack was made by the ruffians on Osawatomie, numbering some 400, by whose scouts our dear Frederick was shot dead.' (This was his son, and it was by a Methodist preacher's rifle he was killed. Such was the support which the pulpit sometimes gave in those turbulent days to the slavery cause.) 'At this time I was about three miles off, where I had some fourteen or fifteen men over-night that had just enlisted under me. These I collected with some twelve or fifteen more, and in about three-quarters of an hour I attacked them from a wood with thick undergrowth.

'With this force we threw them into confusion for about fifteen or twenty minutes, during which time we killed or wounded from seventy to eighty of the enemy—as they say—and then we escaped as we could with one killed, two or three wounded, and as many more missing. Jason (another son) fought bravely by my side. I was struck by a partly spent shot which bruised me some, but did not injure me seriously. "Hitherto the Lord has helped me, notwithstanding my afflictions."'

Later there was a futile attack upon Lawrence by 2,700 of the Border ruffians, and while the governor claimed afterwards the credit for the failure of the attack, it is certain that his dilatory intervention had less to do with the result than the prompt action of a couple of hundred defenders of the place who made a dash outwards towards the advancing rabble. Mounted on a grocer's box in the main street, John Brown thus addressed them before action: 'If they come up and attack don't yell, but remain still. Wait till they get within twenty-five yards of you: get a good object: be sure you see the hind sight of your gun—then fire. A great deal of powder and lead is wasted on aiming too high. You had better aim at their legs than at their heads. In either case, be sure of the hind sights of your guns. It is from the neglect of this that I myself have so many times escaped; for if all the bullets that have ever been aimed at me had hit, I should have been as full of holes as a riddle.'

All these skirmishes from a military point of view were trivial, but from a political standpoint they were crucial. They saved Kansas, and made free election at length possible. Brown and his men were 'incarnate earnestness,' says one writer, and it was that fervent devotion which made all that followed possible. It became impossible for a government to wink at arson and murder. 'Take more care to end life well than to live long,' the old man used to say, and he exemplified his doctrine.

His reckless bravery was proverbial. After one of their successful skirmishes a wounded Missourian wished greatly to see the redoubtable John Brown before he died. The captain went to the wagon where he lay and said, 'Here I am; take a good look at me; we wish you all no harm. Stay at home, leave us alone, and we shall be friends. I wish you well.' The dying man looked at him from head to foot, and, reaching out his hand, said, 'I don't see as you are so bad. You don't look or talk like it.

I thank you.' Clasping his hand, the old captain said, 'God bless you,' and his tears were the Amen. Thus tender was he ever with his prisoners, despite his fierceness.

At length the United States Government saw the free settlers were in no abject mood, and stepped in to their relief. John Brown saw the dawn of better days, and then travelled away northward, worn and sick, with a fugitive slave as a kind of trophy hidden in his wagon. Before long he found security and peace for a while at North Elba, New York, at the house of Gerrit Smith.

THE UNDERGROUND RAILWAY

We now find John Brown busy for a while in the Northern States addressing Abolitionist meetings, collecting funds for the cause, and co-operating with the Anti-slavery Committees, of which there were several thousands. In many homes where the friends of freedom lived he was a welcome guest, not least welcomed by the children, who always seemed to refresh his weary heart. 'Out of the mouths of children,' as the psalmist says (according to one version), 'God gives strength to true men.' You might often have seen him holding up a little two-year-old child, saying, 'When John Brown is hanged as a traitor she can say she used to stand on John Brown's hand.' He was no false prophet!

Now also he was able to revisit, after two years' absence, the old homestead where his wife and children were awaiting him, down to the little one whom he had left an infant in the cradle. 'Come,' says the strange father to the little prattler, 'I have sung it to all of them; I must sing it to you.'

Blow ye the trumpet, blow
The gladly solemn sound:
Let all the nations know
To earth's remotest bound.
The year of Jubilee is come,
Return, ye ransomed sinners, home.

In strains to which a soul on fire gave enchantment and a tunefulness of their own he sang that song of Moses and the Lamb, telling of the Jewish charter of Liberty to which Christ in His turn gave larger meaning; and the little eyes in the room beheld a transfigured face which they remembered when he had ceased blowing the trumpet of Jubilee, and when they sang the same hymn as they laid him beneath the sod outside that cabin door.

But not long could he stay at home. The year of Jubilee for all these bondmen was his one thought, and he found friends who regarded him as a tried man and were prepared to trust him implicitly. Such men as Beecher and Theodore Parker gave him help spiritual; men like the wealthy Stearns gave him help financial to the extent of many thousand dollars, and were content to know that John Brown, however he spent it (and concerning his plans he was always reticent), would have but one object—liberty to the captive.

One way in which it was spent was in the working of what was then known as the underground railway. The opportunist statesman—Henry Clay—had led many Northern voters to tolerate the passing of the Fugitive Slave Law, under which the Federal Government facilitated the enforced return of fugitive slaves found in free states to the plantations of the South. And the Abolitionists in the North, as a set-off against this detested legislation, gave themselves with much zest to aid the runaway slave. If a slave could escape to the swamps or the forest and elude the bloodhounds on his track, he knew that at certain points he would find those who were prepared to house him, and, passing him on secretly from station to station, ensure his arrival at a terminus where he would be safe for life. That was Canada, the country where the Union Jack waves—the flag of 'Britons' who 'never shall be slaves' and are prepared to grant to all the priceless boon they claim themselves. This escape was called 'shaking the paw of the lion.' May that British lion never be transformed into a sleek tiger; may his paw ever be outreached to a runaway slave, and his roar be a terror to all who would market in human flesh and blood!

This chain of well-known houses and locations was called the underground railway; and, spite of penalties of imprisonment oft inflicted, it never lacked porters or guards; and if the trains did not always run to time it was because they were very cautious against accident. Some 30,000 passengers were probably conveyed on this line. You will not be surprised to find John Brown an active 'guard,' and under the name of 'Shubel Morgan' or 'Hawkins' he did good service there. See him making his way with twelve fugitive slaves from Missouri, through Kansas, Nebraska, Iowa, Illinois, and Michigan to Canada. It is the dead of winter, and the rough wagons travel heavily and slowly along the drifted roads. There is a price on his head in these Southern States— 3,250 dollars offered conjointly by the Governor of Missouri and President Pierce—and the stations are sometimes thirty miles apart. They come to a creek, and there is the State Marshal awaiting them with eighty armed men—for he thought he had better have a good force, as he heard it was John Brown he might encounter. John puts his host of twenty-three men all told into battle array in front of the wagons, and gives the laconic order, 'Now go straight at 'em, boys, they are sure to run.' Into the water his men charge—but the baptism of water is all they are fated to pass through; there is no baptism of fire to follow, for, scared at the impulsive charge, and filled with vague terror at that irrepressible John Brown, the Marshal springs upon his horse and skedaddles. His men scramble to their horses. Some cannot untie them from the shrubs quickly enough; several animals carry two men, and, to complete the ludicrousness of the scene, one man, fearing he might be too late, grips fast the tail of the steed to which the proper rider has just set spurs, and, vainly trying to spring on behind, is seen with his feet off the ground, being whirled through the air. A few prisoners are speedily added to Brown's little company, who, thinking it is perhaps prudent to keep men off horseback who were so prone to flight, orders them to walk.

But he has ideas of courtesy, has this rough old warrior, and says he means them no unkindness and will walk with them. Such a favourable opportunity must in no wise be missed, so the old soldier-prophet gives them his mind upon the wickedness of slave-holding and the meanness of slave-hunting, which discourse, let us hope, is not wholly unfruitful. When he has held them for one night he thinks they have been brought far enough from their haunts to prevent further mischief, and sets them free. That one night spent with him they are not likely to forget. He would not so much as allow them the privilege of swearing. 'No taking of God's name in vain gentlemen; if there is a God you will gain nothing, and if there is none you are fools indeed.' Such is the old man's plain argument.

One of them, a harum-scarum young physician, is taken specially under charge by John Brown. Before retiring Brown desires him to pray. 'I can't pray,' he says, with an oath. 'What, did your mother never teach you?' asks Brown. 'Oh yes,' he replies; 'but that was a long time ago.' 'Well, you still remember the prayer she taught you?' continued Brown. 'Yes,' is the answer. 'Say that for want of a better,' is the order. Then, to the amusement of all, the poor doctor repeats the rhyme:

> *And now I lay me down to sleep,*
> *I pray the Lord my soul to keep.*

Said the young doctor after he was released, 'John Brown knows more about religion than any man I ever met. He never used harsh language; we were treated like gentlemen; we shared food with them. Only it went against the grain to be guarded by niggers.'

Thus the journey proceeds. As they get farther north there is more bark than bite about the opposition they encounter. In the street at one town where they are sheltered, Brown strolls alone and finds a champion of slavery haranguing the crowd and denouncing Brown as a reckless, bloody outlaw, a coward who skulked and would never fight in the open. Warming to a climax the orator proclaims, 'If I could get a sight of him I would shoot him on the spot; I would never give him a chance to steal any more slaves.' 'My friend,' says a plain-looking countryman—no other than John Brown himself—on the outskirts of the throng, 'you talk very brave; and as you will never have a better opportunity to shoot old Brown than right here and now, you can have a chance.' But his powder was damped—or his courage!

Now the journey is over. The twelve fugitives have become thirteen, for a little infant has been born on the march, never to know, thank God, the horrors the mother has left behind. The child is named after his deliverer 'John Brown,' who conducts them safely across the ferry and places them under the shelter of the Union Jack on the Canadian shore. Then the old man reverently pronounces his 'Nunc dimittis,' 'Lord, now lettest thou Thy servant depart in peace, for mine eyes have seen Thy salvation.' 'I could not brook the thought that any ill should befall them, least of all that they should be taken back to slavery. The arm of Jehovah has protected us.' Before many months those rescued ones were weeping at the news that John Brown was condemned to die, and were saying 'Would that we could die instead.'

HARPER'S FERRY

John Brown now prepared for his final effort, for the enterprise he had espoused and the sacrifice he had sworn to make for it were to be completed by his death. 'There is no way of deliverance but by blood,' had become his settled conviction upon this slavery question. And truly it seemed so. The Slave States were waxing fiercer in their unholy enterprise. The reopening of the market for freshly imported slaves from Africa was openly advocated—indeed, prices were offered for the best specimens, as if it were a mere cattle trade. 'For sale, 400 negroes just landed,' was placarded in Southern streets; and to complete the grim situation a prize was proposed for the best sermon in defence of the slave trade. Surely the Lord gave not 'the word,' but 'great was the company of the preachers' who were prepared to publish it.

John Brown felt that the fullness of time was come for a desperate stroke. Desperate indeed it was. From a military point of view it was madness. He resolved to hire a farm in Maryland, near to the great armoury at Harper's Ferry in the Slave State of Virginia, and there diligently and silently to store arms. Then with a small company he would seize Harper's Ferry. Having possessed himself of its stores, he would retreat to the mountains, where he hoped there would be considerable rallying to his standard. Holding his own amid mountain fastnesses of which he had acquired an intimate knowledge, he thought he might at last become strong enough to make terms with the Government.

We next find him passing as Isaac Smith, a Maryland farmer—known to his neighbours as a demure, somewhat eccentric, son of the soil. Three of his sons, true to the vow, were with him. Little thought the farmers around that hard by that farmhouse a few thousand weapons were stored and that a little band of mysterious strangers was gathering there, but so it was. To the last there was much opposition to Brown's impulsive scheme. Once, indeed, he resigned leadership, but the little group passed a horrible five minutes of bereavement and then re-elected him with many promises of support. Sublime old madman!—if mad indeed he was! Had he not made them all feel like himself, 'that they have but one life and once to die; and if they lose their lives perchance it will do more for the cause than their lives would be worth in any other way?'

Ah! the old man's soul had entered into them—it kept them 'marching on.' In the dark, wet night of October 16, 1859, they mustered quietly. The captain addressed them, and he was no reckless destroyer of human life who thus spake:

'Gentlemen, let me press this one thing on your minds. You all know how dear life is to you, and how dear your lives are to your friends; and in remembering that, consider that the lives of others are as dear. Do not therefore take the life of any one if you can possibly avoid it, but if it is necessary to take life in order to save your own, then make sure work of it.'

Two of them were deputed to hasten, when the town was in their hands, to Colonel Washington's house, four miles distant—to seize him, free his slaves, and take the relic of the house, the famed sword of his illustrious ancestor George Washington, that with this in hand John Brown might head the campaign. That feat they actually performed, and for one brief day their leader bore that sword.

Silently marched that little band of about a score under shelter of the darkness. They had their plans complete, even a Constitution ready framed, should they be successful. The telegraph wires were cut. They contrived to terrify all on guard without firing a shot, and as the sun rose, Harper's Ferry, arsenal, armoury, and rifle works, and many prisoners were in the hands of John Brown. The day wore on, but the expected reinforcements came not; the spreading news, however, brought hostile troops around the captured place, and they hourly increased. Brown took not his one chance of escape to the mountains—why, it is difficult to say. In prison afterwards he said his weakness in yielding to the entreaties of his prisoners ruined him. 'It was the first time I ever lost command of myself, and now I am punished for it,' he added. At another time when questioned he gave fatalistic answers, and said it was 'ordained so ages before the world was made.' By afternoon he was on the defensive within the armoury, and a fierce fight ensued. Even then his simple notions of justice were uppermost, and to the last as his men fired from the portholes he would be heard saying of some one passing in the street, 'That man is unarmed don't shoot.' Two of his sons— Watson and Oliver Brown— were pierced with bullets. As he straightened out the limbs of the second, he said, 'This is the third son I have lost in the cause.' Always the cause! The night fell and the fight was in abeyance, but in the morning he was summoned to surrender, and refused, saying he would die there. At length the engine-house, their last resort, held stubbornly, was captured, and Brown fell, wounded by the sword of a young lieutenant who had marked him for his stroke. One of his prisoners who was by says truly of his last fight, 'Almost any other man who saw his sons fall would have exacted life for life, but he spared all of us who were in his power.' Of the force of twenty-two men, ten were killed, seven captured and hanged, and five escaped. On the other side six were killed and eight wounded.

He was now a captive, suffered to recover from his wounds that he might die a felon's death. Many were those who, from various motives, came to see the wounded prisoner, and from many interviews reported at the time we may take a few extracts:

Q. Can you tell us who furnished money for your expedition? A. I furnished most of it myself. I cannot implicate others. It is by my own folly I have been taken. I could have saved myself had I not yielded to my feelings.

Q. If you would tell us who sent you, who provided means, it would be valuable information. A. I will answer freely and faithfully about what concerned myself, anything I can with honour, but not about others. It was my own prompting and that of my Maker or the devil—whichever you please to ascribe it to—I acknowledge no master in human form.

Q. Why came you here? A. To liberate the slaves— the cry of the oppressed is my only reason. I respect the rights of the poorest coloured folk as much as those of the most wealthy and powerful.

Q. How do you justify your acts? A. I think, my friend, you are guilty of a great wrong against God and humanity—I say it without wishing to be offensive and it would be perfectly right for any one to free those you wickedly hold in bondage. I am not here to gratify revenge, but because I pity those who have none to help them.

Q. Do you consider this a religious movement? A. The greatest service man can render to God.

Q. Do you consider yourself an instrument in the hands of Providence? A. I do.

Q. Brown, suppose you had every nigger in the United States, what would you do with them? A. Set them free.

Said Governor Wise of Virginia, 'Mr. Brown, the silver of your hair is reddened by the blood of crime, and you should eschew these hard words and think of eternity. You are committing felony by these sentiments.' Brown replied, 'Governor, I have by all appearances not more than fifteen or twenty years the start of you in the journey to eternity, and whether my time has to be long or short I am equally prepared to go. There is an eternity behind and an eternity before, and this speck in the centre, however long, is but comparatively a minute. The difference between your tenure and mine is trifling, and you have all of you a heavy responsibility and it behoves you to prepare more than it does me.'

The Governor's public testimony was: 'They are mistaken who took Brown to be a madman. He is a bundle of the best nerves I ever saw. He is a man of clear head, of courage, fortitude, and simple ingenuousness. He is cool, collected, and indomitable; and it is but just to him to say that he was humane to his prisoners, and he inspired me with great trust in his integrity as a man of truth. He is a fanatic, vain and garrulous, but firm, truthful, and intelligent. He professes to be a Christian in communion with the Congregational Church of the North, and openly preaches his purpose of universal emancipation, and the negroes themselves were to be the agents, by means of arms, led on by white commanders. Colonel Washington says that he was the coolest and firmest man he ever saw in defying danger and death. With one son dead by his side, and another shot through, he felt the pulse of his dying son with one hand, held his rifle with the other, and commanded his men with the utmost composure, encouraging them to be firm, and to sell their lives as dearly as they could.'

The trial for treason and murder took place in the Virginian Court on October 27-31, ere he had recovered. He pleaded for delay till his health allowed him to give more attention to his defence, but the request was refused. So, weak and wounded, he had to lie upon his pallet with a blanket thrown over him. His words were few, and to the same effect as those we have quoted. There was only one verdict possible in that court—guilty—and he was sentenced to be hanged. Technically there was no other course possible. The calm verdict of the *Cambridge Modern History* upon the raid is correct: 'It was the mad folly of an almost crazed fanatic . . . the stain still upon him of the bloodiest of the lawless work done in the name of Freedom; a terrible outlaw because an outlaw for conscience' sake; intense to the point of ungovernable passion—heeding nothing but his own will and sense of right; a revolutionist upon principle; a lawless incendiary, and yet seeking nothing for himself.'

But while we feel the veracity of these words there comes to our mind one of Charles Kingsley's impulsive sayings: 'Get hold of one truth, let it blaze in your sky like a Greenland sun, never setting day or night. See it in everything, and everything in it. The world will call you a bigot and fanatic, and then fifty years after will wonder how it was the bigot and fanatic managed to do so much more than all the sensible men round about him.'

John Brown vindicated that opinion.

Harriet Tubman

[SARAH H. BRADFORD]

The title I have given my black heroine, The Moses of Her People, may seem a little ambitious, considering that this Moses was a woman, and that she succeeded in piloting only three or four hundred slaves from the land of bondage to the land of freedom.

But I only give her here the name by which she was familiarly known, both at the North and the South, during the years of terror of the Fugitive Slave Law, and during our last Civil War, in both of which she took so prominent a part.

And though the results of her unexampled heroism were not to free a whole nation of bond-men and bond-women, yet this object was as much the desire of her heart, as it was of that of the great leader of Israel. Her cry to the slave-holders, was ever like his to Pharaoh, "Let my people go!" and not even he imperiled life and limb more willingly, than did our courageous and self-sacrificing friend.

Her name deserves to be handed down to posterity, side by side with the names of Jeanne D'Arc, Grace Darling, and Florence Nightingale, for not one of these women, noble and brave as they were, has shown more courage, and power of endurance, in facing danger and death to relieve human suffering, than this poor black woman.

After her almost superhuman efforts in making her own escape from slavery, and then returning to the South nineteen times, and bringing away with her over three hundred fugitives, she was sent by Governor Andrew of Massachusetts to the South at the beginning of the War, to act as spy and scout for our armies, and to be employed as hospital nurse when needed.

Here for four years she labored without any remuneration, and during the time she was acting as nurse, never drew but twenty days' rations from our Government. She managed to support herself, as well as to take care of the suffering soldiers. Secretary Seward exerted himself in every possible way to procure her a pension from Congress, but red-tape proved too strong even for him, and her case was rejected, because it did not come under any recognized law.

★　★　★

It would be impossible here to give a detailed account of the journeys and labors of this intrepid woman for the redemption of her kindred and friends, during the years that followed. Those years were spent in work, almost by night and day, with the one object of the rescue of her people from slavery. All her wages were laid away with this sole purpose, and as soon as a sufficient amount was secured, she disappeared from her Northern home, and as suddenly and mysteriously she appeared some dark night at the door of one of the cabins on a plantation, where a trembling band of fugitives, forewarned as to time and place, were anxiously awaiting their deliverer. Then she piloted them North, traveling by night, hiding by day, scaling the mountains, fording the rivers, threading the forests, lying concealed as the pursuers passed them. She, carrying the babies, drugged with paregoric, in a basket on her arm. So she went *nineteen* times, and so she brought away over three hundred pieces of living and breathing "property," with God given souls.

The way was so toilsome over the rugged mountain passes, that often the *men* who followed her would give out, and foot-sore, and bleeding, they would drop on the ground, groaning that they could not take another step. They would lie there and die, or if strength came back, they would return on their steps, and seek their old homes again. Then the revolver carried by this bold and daring pioneer, would come out, while pointing it at their heads she would say, "Dead niggers tell no tales; you go on or die!" And by this heroic treatment she compelled them to drag their weary limbs along on their northward journey.

But the pursuers were after them. A reward of $40,000 was offered by the slave-holders of the region from whence so many slaves had been spirited away, for the head of the woman who appeared so mysteriously, and enticed away their property, from under the very eyes of its owners. Our sagacious heroine has been in the car, having sent her frightened party round by some so-called "Under-ground Railway," and has heard this advertisement, which was posted over her head, read by others of the passengers. She never could read or write herself, but knowing that suspicion would be likely to fall upon any black woman traveling North, she would turn at the next station, and journey towards the South. Who would suspect a fugitive with such a price set upon her head, of rushing at railway speed into the jaws of destruction? With a daring almost heedless, she went even to the very village where she would be most likely to meet one of the masters to whom she had been hired; and having stopped at the Market and bought a pair of live fowls, she went along the street with her sun-bonnet well over her face, and with the bent and decrepit air of an aged woman. Suddenly on turning a corner, she spied her old master coming towards her. She pulled the string which tied the legs of the chickens; they began to flutter and scream, and as her master passed, she was stooping and busily engaged in attending to the fluttering fowls. And he went on his way, little thinking that he was brushing the very garments of the woman who had dared to steal herself, and others of his belongings.

At one time the pursuit was very close and vigorous. The woods were scoured in all directions, every house was visited, and every person stopped and questioned as to a band of black fugitives, known to be fleeing through that part of the country. Harriet had a large party with her then; the children were sleeping the sound sleep that opium gives; but all the others were on the alert, each one hidden behind his own tree, and silent as death. They had been long without food, and were nearly famished; and as the pursuers seemed to have passed on, Harriet decided to make the attempt to reach a certain "station of the underground railroad" well known to her; and procure food for her starving party. Under cover of the darkness, she started, leaving a cowering and trembling group in the woods, to whom a fluttering leaf, or a moving animal, were a sound of dread, bringing their hearts into their throats. How long she is away! has she been caught and carried off, and if so what is to become of them? Hark! there is a sound of singing in the distance, coming nearer and nearer.

And these are the words of the unseen singer, which I wish I could give you as I have so often heard them sung by herself:

> *Hail, oh hail, ye happy spirits,*
> *Death no more shall make you fear,*
> *Grief nor sorrow, pain nor anguish,*
> *Shall no more distress you dere.*

> *Around Him are ten thousand angels*
> *Always ready to obey command;*
> *Dey are always hovering round you,*
> *Till you reach de heavenly land.*

> *Jesus, Jesus will go wid you,*
> *He will lead you to his throne;*
> *He who died, has gone before you,*
> *Trod de wine-press all alone.*

> *He whose thunders shake creation,*
> *He who bids de planets roll;*

He who rides upon the tempest,
And whose scepter sways de whole.
Dark and thorny is de pathway,
Where de pilgrim makes his ways;
But beyond dis vale of sorrow,
Lie de fields of endless days.

The air sung to these words was so wild, so full of plaintive minor strains, and unexpected quavers, that I would defy any white person to learn it, and often as I heard it, it was to me a constant surprise. Up and down the road she passes to see if the coast is clear, and then to make them certain that it is *their* leader who is coming, she breaks out into the plaintive strains of the song, forbidden to her people at the South, but which she and her followers delight to sing together:

Oh go down, Moses,
Way down into Egypt's land,
Tell old Pharaoh,
Let my people go.

Oh Pharaoh said he would go cross,
Let my people go,
And don't get lost in de wilderness,
Let my people go.

Oh go down, Moses,
Way down into Egypt's land,
Tell old Pharaoh,
Let my people go.

You may hinder me here, but you can't up dere,
Let my people go,
He sits in de Hebben and answers prayer,
Let my people go!

Oh go down, Moses,
Way down into Egypt's land,
Tell old Pharaoh,
Let my people go.

And then she enters the recesses of the wood, carrying hope and comfort to the anxious watchers there. One by one they steal out from their hiding places, and are fed and strengthened for another night's journey.

And so by night travel, by signals, by threatenings, by encouragement, through watchings and fastings, and I may say by direct interpositions of Providence, and miraculous deliverances, she brought her people to what was then their land of Canaan; the State of New York. But alas! this State did not continue to be their refuge. For in 1850, I think, the Fugitive Slave Law was put in force, which bound the people north of Mason and Dixon's line, to return to bondage any fugitive found in their territories.

"After that," said Harriet, "I wouldn't trust Uncle Sam wid my people no longer, but I brought 'em all clar off to Canada."

On her seventh or eighth journey, she brought with her a band of fugitives, among whom was a very remarkable man, whom I knew only by the name of

"Joe." Joe was a noble specimen of a negro, enormously tall, and of splendid muscular development. He had been hired out by his master to another planter, for whom he had worked for six years, saving him all the expense of an overseer, and taking all trouble off from his hands. He was such a very valuable piece of property, and had become so absolutely necessary to the planter to whom he was hired, that he determined to buy him at any cost. His old master held him proportionately high. But by paying one thousand dollars down, and promising to pay another thousand in a certain time, the purchase was made, and this chattel passed over into the hands of a new owner.

The morning after the purchase was completed, the new master came riding down on a tall, powerful horse into the negro quarter, with a strong new rawhide in his hand, and stopping before Joe's cabin, called to him to come out. Joe was just eating his breakfast, but with ready obedience, he hastened out at the summons. Slave as he was, and accustomed to scenes of brutality, he was surprised when the order came, "Now, Joe, strip, and take a licking." Naturally enough, he demurred at first, and thought of resisting the order; but he called to mind a scene he had witnessed a few days before in the field, the particulars of which are too horrible to be given here, and he thought it the wisest course to submit; but first he tried a gentle remonstrance.

"Mas'r," said he, "habn't I always been faithful to you? Habn't I worked through sun an' rain, early in de mornin' an' late at night; habn't I saved you an oberseer by doin' his work? Hab you anything to complain agin me?"

"No, Joe, I have no complaint to make of you. You're a good nigger, an' you've always worked well. But you belong to *me* now; you're *my* nigger, and the first lesson my niggers have to learn is that I am master and they belong to me, and are never to resist anything I order them to do. So I always begin by giving them a good licking. Now strip and take it."

Joe saw that there was no help for him, and that for the time he must submit. He stripped off his clothing, and took his flogging without a word, but as he drew his shirt up over his torn and bleeding back, he said to himself: "Dis is de first an' de last." As soon as he was able he took a boat, and under cover of the night, rowed down the river, and made his way to the cabin of "Old Ben," Harriet's father, and said to him: "Nex' time *Moses* comes, let me know."

It was not long after this time, that the mysterious woman appeared—the woman on whom no one could lay his finger—and men, women, and children began to disappear from the plantations. One fine morning Joe was missing, and call as loud as he might, the master's voice had no power to bring him forth. Joe had certainly fled; and his brother William was gone, and Peter and Eliza. From other plantations other slaves were missing, and before their masters were awake to the fact, the party of fugitives, following their intrepid leader, were far on their way towards liberty.

The adventures of this escaping party would of themselves fill a volume. They hid in potato holes by day, while their pursuers passed within a few feet of them; they were passed along by friends in various disguises; they scattered and separated; some traveling by boat, some by wagons, some by cars, others on foot, to meet at some specified station of the under-ground railroad. They met at the house of Sam Green, the man who was afterwards sent to prison for ten years for having a copy of "Uncle Tom's Cabin" in his house. And so, hunted and hiding and wandering, they found themselves at last at the entrance of the long bridge which crosses the river at Wilmington, Delaware.

No time had been lost in posting up advertisements and offering rewards for the capture of these fugitives; for Joe in particular the reward offered was very high. First a thousand dollars, then fifteen hundred, and then two thousand, "an' all expenses clar an' clean for his body in Easton Jail." This high reward stimulated the efforts of the officers who were usually on the lookout for escaping fugitives, and the added rewards for others of the party, and the high price set on Harriet's head, filled the woods and highways with eager hunters after human prey. When Harriet and her companions approached the long Wilmington Bridge, a warning was given them by some secret friend, that the advertisements were up, and the bridge was guarded by police officers. Quick as lightning the plans were formed in her ready brain, and the terrified party were separated and hidden in the houses of different friends, till her arrangements for their further journey were completed.

There was at that time residing in Wilmington an old Quaker, whom I may call *my* "friend," for though I never saw his face, I have had correspondence with him in reference to Harriet and her followers. This man, whose name was Thomas Garrett, and who was well known in those days to the friends of the slave, was a man of a wonderfully large and generous heart, through whose hands during those days of distress and horror, no less than three thousand self-emancipated men, women and children passed on their way to freedom. He gave heart, hand, and means to aid these poor fugitives, and to our brave Harriet he often rendered most efficient help in her journeys back and forth.

He was the proprietor of a very large shoe establishment; and not one of these poor travelers ever left his house without a present of a new pair of shoes and other needed help. No sooner had this good man received intelligence of the condition of these poor creatures, than he devised a plan to elude the vigilance of the officers in pursuit, and bring Harriet and her party across the bridge. Two wagons filled with bricklayers were engaged, and sent over; this was a common sight there, and caused no remark. They went across the bridge singing and shouting, and it was not an unexpected thing that they should return as they went. After nightfall (and, fortunately, the night was very dark) the same wagons recrossed the bridge, but with an unlooked-for addition to their party. The fugitives were lying close together on the bottom of the wagons; the bricklayers were on the seats, still singing and shouting; and so they passed the guards, who were all unsuspicious of the nature of the load contained in the wagons, or of the amount of property thus escaping their hands.

The good man, Thomas Garrett, who was in a very feeble state of health when he last wrote me, and has now gone to his reward, supplied them with all needed comforts, and sent them on their way refreshed, and with renewed courage. And Harriet here set up her Ebenezer, saying, "Thus far hath the Lord helped me!" But many a danger, and many a fright, and many a deliverance awaited them, before they reached the city of New York. And even there they were not safe, for the Fugitive Slave Law was in operation, and their only refuge was Canada, which was now their promised land.

They finally reached New York in safety: and this goes almost without saying, for I may as well mention here that of the three hundred and more fugitives whom Harriet piloted from slavery, not one was ever recaptured, though all the cunning and skill of white men, backed by offered rewards of large sums of money, were brought into requisition for their recovery.

As they entered the anti-slavery office in New York, Mr. Oliver Johnson rose up and exclaimed, "Well, Joe, I am glad to see the man who is worth $2,000 to his master." At this Joe's heart sank. "Oh, Mas'r, how did you know me!" he panted. "Here is the advertisement in our office," said Mr. Johnson, "and the description is so close that no one could mistake it." And had he come through all these perils, had he traveled by day and night, and suffered cold and hunger, and lived in constant fear and dread, to find that far off here in New York State, he was recognized at once by the advertisement? How, then, was he ever to reach Canada?

"And how far off is Canada?" he asked. He was shown the map of New York State, and the track of the railroad, for more than three hundred miles to Niagara, where he would cross the river, and be free. But the way seemed long and full of dangers. They were surely safer on their own tired feet, where they might hide in forests and ditches, and take refuge in the friendly underground stations; but here, where this large party would be together in the cars, surely suspicion would fall upon them, and they would be seized and carried back. But Harriet encouraged him in her cheery way. He must not give up now. "De Lord had been with them in six troubles, and he would not desert them in de seventh." And there was nothing to do but to go on. As Moses spoke to the children of Israel, when compassed before and behind by dangers, so she spake to her people, that they should "go forward."

Up to this time, as they traveled they had talked and sung hymns together, like Pilgrim and his friends, and Joe's voice was the loudest and sweetest among them; but now he hanged his harp upon the willows, and could sing the Lord's songs no more.

"From dat time," in Harriet's language, "Joe was silent; he talked no more; he sang no more; he sat wid his head on his hand, an' nobody could 'rouse him, nor make him take any intrust in anything."

They passed along in safety through New York State, and at length found themselves approaching the Suspension Bridge. They could see the promised land on the other side. The uninviting plains of Canada seemed to them,

> "Sweet fields beyond the swelling flood,
> All dressed in living green;"

but they were not safe yet. Until they reached the center of the bridge, they were still in the power of their pursuers, who might at any pause enter the car, and armed with the power of the law, drag them back to slavery. The rest of the party were happy and excited; they were simple, ignorant creatures, and having implicit trust in their leader, they felt safe when with her, and no immediate danger threatened them. But Joe was of a different mould. He sat silent and sad, always thinking of the horrors that awaited him if recaptured. As it happened, all the other passengers were people who sympathized with them, understanding them to be a band of fugitives, and they listened with tears, as Harriet and all except poor Joe lifted up their voices and sang:

I'm on the way to Canada,
That cold and dreary land,
De sad effects of slavery,
I can't no longer stand;
I've served my Master all my days,
Widout a dime reward,
And now I'm forced to run away,
To flee de lash, abroad;

Farewell, ole Master, don't think hard of me,
I'm traveling on to Canada, where all de slaves are free.

De hounds are baying on my track,
Ole Master comes behind,
Resolved that he will bring me back,
Before I cross the line;
I'm now embarked for yonder shore,
Where a man's a man by law,

De iron horse will bear me o'er,
To "shake de lion's paw;"

Oh, righteous Father, wilt thou not pity me,
And help me on to Canada, where all de slaves are free.

Oh I heard Queen Victoria say,
That if we would forsake,
Our native land of slavery,
And come across de lake;
Dat she was standing on de shore,
Wid arms extended wide,
To give us all a peaceful home,
Beyond de rolling tide;

Farewell, ole Master, don't think hard of me,
I'm traveling on to Canada, where all de slaves are free.

No doubt the simple creatures with her expected to cross a wide lake instead of a rapid river, and to see Queen Victoria with her crown upon her head, waiting with arms extended wide, to fold them all in her embrace. There was now but "one wide river to cross," and the cars rolled on to the bridge. In the distance was heard the roar of the mighty cataract, and now as they neared the center of the bridge, the falls might be clearly seen. Harriet was anxious to have her companions see this wonderful sight, and succeeded in bringing all to the windows, except Joe. But Joe still sat with his head on his hands, and not even the wonders of Niagara could draw him from his melancholy musings. At length as Harriet knew by the rise of the center of the bridge, and the descent immediately after, the line of danger was passed; she sprang across to Joe's side of the car, and shook him almost out of his seat, as she shouted, "Joe! you've shook de lion's paw!" This was her phrase for having entered on the dominions of England. But Joe did not understand this figurative expression. Then she shook him again, and put it more plainly, "Joe, you're in Queen Victoria's dominions! You're a free man!"

Then Joe arose. His head went up, he raised his hands on high, and his eyes, streaming with tears, to heaven, and then he began to sing and shout:

> *"Glory to God and Jesus too,*
> *One more soul got safe;*
> *Oh, go and carry the news,*
> *One more soul got safe."*

> *"Joe, come and look at the falls!"*

> *"Glory to God and Jesus too,*
> *One more soul got safe."*

> *"Joe! it's your last chance. Come and see de falls!"*

> *"Glory to God and Jesus too,*
> *One more soul got safe."*

And this was all the answer. The train stopped on the other side; and the first feet to touch British soil, after those of the conductor, were those of poor Joe.

Loud roared the waters of Niagara, but louder still ascended the Anthem of praise from the overflowing heart of the freeman. And can we doubt that the strain was taken up by angel voices and echoed and re-echoed through the vaults of heaven:

> *Glory to God in the highest,*
> *Glory to God and Jesus too,*
> *For all these souls now safe.*

"The white ladies and gentlemen gathered round him," said Harriet, "till I couldn't see Joe for the crowd, only I heard his voice singing, 'Glory to God and Jesus too,' louder than ever." A sweet young lady reached over her fine cambric handkerchief to him, and as Joe wiped the great tears off his face, he said, "Tank de Lord! dere's only one more journey for me now, and dat's to Hebben!"

General Custer

[**FRANCES FULLER VICTOR**]

eneral Terry left Fort Abraham Lincoln on the Missouri River, May 17th 1876, with his division, consisting of the 7th Cavalry under Lieut. Col. George A. Custer, three companies of infantry, a battery of Gatling guns, and 45 enlisted scouts. His whole force, exclusive of the wagon-train drivers, numbered about 1000 men. His march was westerly, over the route taken by the Stanley expedition in 1873.

On the 11th of June, Terry reached the south bank of the Yellowstone at the mouth of Powder River, where by appointment he met steamboats, and established his supply camp. A scouting party of six companies of the 7th Cavalry under Major M. A. Reno was sent out June 10th, which ascended Powder River to its forks, crossed westerly to Tongue River and beyond, and discovered, near Rosebud River, a heavy Indian trail about ten days old leading westward toward Little Big Horn River. After following this trail a short distance Reno returned to the Yellowstone and rejoined his regiments, which then marched, accompanied by steamboats, to the mouth of Rosebud River where it encamped June 21st. Communication by steamboats and scouts had previously been opened with Col. John Gibbon, whose column was at this time encamped on the north side of the Yellowstone, near by.

Col. Gibbon of the 7th Infantry had left Fort Ellis in Montana about the middle of May, with a force consisting of six companies of his regiment, and four companies of the 2d Cavalry under Major J. S. Brisbin. He had marched eastward down the north bank of the Yellowstone to the mouth of the Rosebud, where he encamped about June 1st.

Gen. Terry now consulted with Gibbon and Custer, and decided upon a plan for attacking the Indians who were believed to be assembled in large numbers near Big Horn River. Custer with his regiment was to ascend the valley of the Rosebud, and then turn towards Little Big Horn River, keeping well to the south. Gibbon's troops were to cross the Yellowstone at the mouth of Big Horn River, and march up the Big Horn to its junction with the Little Big Horn, to co-operate with Custer. It was hoped that the Indians would thus be brought between the two forces so that their escape would be impossible.

Col. Gibbon's column was immediately put in motion for the mouth of the Big Horn. On the next day, June 22d, at noon, Custer announced himself ready to start, and drew out his regiment. It consisted of 12 companies, numbering 28 officers and 747 soldiers. There were also a strong detachment of scouts and guides, several civilians, and a supply train of 185 pack mules. Gen. Terry reviewed the column in the presence of Gibbon and Brisbon and it was pronounced in splendid condition. "The officers clustered around Terry for a final shake of the hand, the last good-bye was said, and in the best of spirits, filled with high hopes, they galloped away—many of them to their death."

Gen. Terry's orders to Custer were as follows:—

> Camp at the mouth of Rosebud River,
> June 22d, 1876.

Lieut. Col. Custer, 7th Cavalry.

Colonel: The Brigadier General Commanding directs that as soon as your regiment can be made ready for the march, you proceed up the Rosebud in pursuit of the Indians whose trail was discovered by Major Reno a few days ago. It is, of course, impossible to give any definite instructions in regard to this movement, and, were it not impossible to do so, the Department Commander places too much confidence in your zeal, energy, and ability to wish to impose upon you precise orders which might hamper your action when nearly in contact with the enemy. He will, however, indicate to you his own views of what your action should be, and he desires that you should conform to them unless you shall see sufficient reason for departing from them. He thinks that you should proceed up the Rosebud until you ascertain definitely the direction in which the trail above spoken of leads. Should it be found (as it appears to be almost certain that it will be found) to turn towards the Little Big Horn, he thinks that you should still proceed southward perhaps as far as the head waters of the Tongue, and then turn toward the Little Big Horn, feeling constantly, however, to your left, so as to preclude the possibility of the escape of the Indians to the south or south-east by passing around your left flank. The column of Col. Gibbon is now in motion for the mouth of the Big Horn. As soon as it reaches that point it will cross the Yellowstone, and move up at least as far as the forks of the Big and Little Big Horn. Of course its future movements must be controlled by circumstances as they arise; but it is hoped that the Indians, if up on the Little Big Horn, may be so nearly inclosed by the two columns that their escape will be impossible. The Department Commander desires that on your way up the Rosebud you should thoroughly examine the upper part of Tulloch's Creek, and that you should endeavor to send a scout through to Col. Gibbon's column with information of the result of your examination. The lower part of this creek will be examined by a detachment from Col. Gibbon's command. The supply steamer will be pushed up the Big Horn as far as the forks of the river are found to be navigable for that space, and the Department Commander, who will accompany the column of Col. Gibbon, desires you to report to him there not later than the expiration of the time for which your troops are rationed, unless in the meantime you receive further orders.

Respectfully, &c.,

E. W. Smith, Captain 18th Infantry,

Acting Assistant Adjutant General.

After proceeding southerly up the Rosebud for about seventy miles, Custer, at 11 P.M. on the night of the 24th, turned westerly towards Little Big Horn River. The next morning while crossing the elevated land between the two rivers, a large Indian village was discovered about fifteen miles distant, just across Little Big

Horn River. Custer with characteristic promptness decided to attack the village at once.

One company was escorting the train at the rear. The balance of the force was divided into three columns. The trail they were on led down to the stream at a point some distance south of the village. Major Reno, with three companies under Capt. T. H. French, Capt. Myles Moylan, and Lieut. Donald McIntosh, was ordered to follow the trail, cross the stream, and charge down its north bank. Capt. F. W. Benteen, with his own company and two others under Capt. T. B. Weir and Lieut. E. S. Godfrey, was sent to make a detour to the south of Reno. The other five companies of the regiment, under the immediate command of Custer, formed the right of the little army.

On reaching the river Reno crossed it as ordered, and Custer with his five companies turned northerly into a ravine running behind the bluffs on the east side of the stream.

★   ★   ★

The supply steamer Far West with Gen. Terry and Col. Gibbon on board, which steamed up the Yellowstone on the evening of June 23d, overtook Gibbon's troops near the mouth of the Big Horn early on the morning of the 24th; and by 4 o'clock P.M. of the same day, the entire command with the animals and supplies had been ferried over to the south side of the Yellowstone. An hour later the column marched out to and across Tulloch's Creek, and then encamped for the night.

At 5 o'clock on the morning of the 25th, (Sunday) the column was again in motion; and after marching 22 miles over a country so rugged as to task the endurance of the men to the utmost, the infantry halted for the night. Gen. Terry, however, with the cavalry and the battery pushed on 14 miles further in hopes of opening communication with Custer, and camped at midnight near the mouth of the Little Big Horn.

Scouts sent out from Terry's camp early on the morning of the 26th discovered three Indians, who proved to be Crows who had accompanied Custer's regiment. They reported that a battle had been fought and that the Indians were killing white men in great numbers. Their story was not fully credited, as it was not expected that a conflict would occur so soon, or believed that serious disaster could have overtaken so large a force.

The infantry, which had broken camp very early, now came up, and the whole column crossed the Little Big Horn and moved up its western valley. It was soon reported that a dense heavy smoke was resting over the southern horizon far ahead, and in a short time it became visible to all. This was hailed as a sign that Custer had met the Indians, defeated them, and burned their village. The weary foot soldiers were elated and freshened by the sight, and pressed on with increased spirit and speed.

Custer's position was believed to be not far ahead, and efforts were repeatedly made during the afternoon to open communication with him; but the scouts who attempted to go through were met and driven back by hostile Indians who were hovering in the front. As evening came on, their numbers increased and large parties could be seen on the bluffs hurrying from place to place and watching every movement of the advancing soldiers.

At 8:40 in the evening the infantry had marched that day about 30 miles. The forks of the Big Horn, the place where Terry had requested Custer to report to him, were many miles behind and the expected messenger from Custer had not arrived. Daylight was fading, the men were fatigued, and the column was therefore halted for the night. The animals were picketed, guards were set, and the weary men, wrapped in their blankets and with their weapons beside them, were soon asleep on the ground.

Early on the morning of the 27th the march up the Little Big Horn was resumed. The smoke cloud was still visible and apparently but a short distance ahead. Soon a dense grove of trees was reached and passed through cautiously, and then the head of the column entered a beautiful level meadow about a mile in width, extending along the west side of the stream and overshadowed east and west by high bluffs. It soon became apparent that this meadow had recently been the site of an immense Indian village, and the great number of temporary brushwood and willow huts indicated that many Indians beside the usual inhabitants had rendezvoused there. It was also evident that it had been hastily deserted. Hundreds of lodge-poles, with finely-dressed buffalo-robes and other hides, dried meat, stores, axes, utensils, and Indian trinkets were left behind; and in two tepees or lodges still standing, were the bodies of nine Indians who had gone to the "happy hunting-grounds."

Every step of the march now revealed some evidence that a conflict had taken place not far away. The dead bodies of Indian horses were seen, and cavalry equipments and weapons, bullet-pierced clothing, and blood-stained gloves were picked up; and at last the bodies of soldiers

and their horses gave positive proof that a disastrous battle had taken place. The Crow Indians had told the truth.

The head of the column was now met by a breathless
scout, who came running up with the intelligence that
Major Reno with a body of troops was intrenched on a
bluff further on, awaiting relief. The soldiers pushed
ahead in the direction pointed out, and soon came in
sight of men and horses intrenched on top of a hill on
the opposite or east side of the river. Terry and Gibbon
immediately forded the stream and rode toward the
group. As they approached the top of the hill, they were
welcomed by hearty cheers from a swarm of soldiers
who came out of their intrenchments to meet their
deliverers. The scene was a touching one. Stout-hearted
soldiers who had kept bravely up during the hours of
conflict and danger now cried like children, and the
pale faces of the wounded lighted up as hope revived
within them.

The story of the relieved men briefly told was as follows:—After separating from Custer about noon, June
25th, (as related in the last chapter) Reno proceeded to
the river, forded it, and charged down its west bank
toward the village, meeting at first with but little resistance. Soon however he was attacked by such numbers as
to be obliged to dismount his men, shelter his horses in
a strip of woods, and fight on foot. Finding that they
would soon be surrounded and defeated, he again
mounted his men, and charging upon such of the
enemy as obstructed his way, retreated across the river,
and reached the top of a bluff followed closely by Indians. Just then Benteen, returning from his detour southward, discovered Reno's perilous position, drove back

the Indians, and joined him on the hill. Shortly afterward, the company which was escorting the mule train also joined Reno. The seven companies thus brought together had been subsequently assailed by Indians; many of the men had been killed and wounded, and it was only by obstinate resistance that they had been enabled to defend themselves in an entrenched position. The enemy had retired on the evening of the 26th.

After congratulations to Reno and his brave men for their successful defence enquiries were made respecting Custer, but no one could tell where he was. Neither he or any of his men had been seen since the fight commenced, and the musketry heard from the direction he took had ceased on the afternoon of the 25th. It was supposed by Reno and Benteen that he had been repulsed, and retreated northerly towards Terry's troops.

A search for Custer and his men was immediately began, and it revealed a scene calculated to appal the stoutest heart. Although neither Custer or any of that part of his regiment which he led to combat were found alive to tell the tale, an examination of their trail and the scene of conflict enabled their comrades to form some idea of the engagement in which they perished.

★   ★   ★

General Custer's trail, from the place where he left Reno's and turned northward, passed along and in the rear of the crest of hills on the east bank of the stream for nearly three miles, and then led, through an opening in the bluff, down to the river. Here Custer had evidently attempted to cross over to attack the village. The trail then turned back on itself, as if Custer had been repulsed and obliged to retreat, and branched to the northward, as if he had been prevented from returning southerly by the way he came, or had determined to retreat in the direction from which Terry's troops were advancing.

Several theories as to the subsequent movements of the troops have been entertained by persons who visited the grounds. One is, that the soldiers in retreating took advantage of two ravines; that two companies under Capt. T. W. Custer and Lieut. A. E. Smith, were led by Gen. Custer up the ravine nearest the river, while the upper ravine furnished a line of retreat for the three companies of Capt. G. W. Yates, Capt. M. W. Keogh, and Lieut. James Calhoun. At the head of this upper ravine, a mile from the river, a stand had been made by Calhoun's company; the skirmish lines were marked by rows of the slain with heaps of empty cartridge shells before them, and Lieuts. Calhoun and Crittenden lay dead just behind the files. Further on, Capt. Keogh had fallen surrounded by his men; and still further on, upon a hill, Capt. Yates' company took its final stand. Here, according to this theory, Yates was joined by what remained of the other two companies, who had been furiously assailed in the lower ravine; and here Gen. Custer and the last survivors of the five companies met their death, fighting bravely to the end.

Another theory of the engagement is, that Custer attempted to retreat up the lower ravine in columns of companies; that the companies of Custer and Smith being first in the advance and last in the retreat, fell first in the slaughter which followed the retrograde movement; that Yates' company took the position on the hill, and perished there with Custer and other officers; and that the two other companies, Keogh's and Calhoun's, perished while fighting their way back towards Reno—a few reaching the place where Custer first struck the high banks of the river.

Still another theory is, that the main line of retreat was by the upper ravine; that Calhoun's company was thrown across to check the Indians, and was the first annihilated. That the two companies of Capt. Custer and Lieut. Smith retreated from the place where Gen. Custer was killed into the lower ravine, and were the last survivors of the conflict.

Near the highest point of the hill lay the body of General Custer, and near by were those of his brother Captain Custer, Lieut. Smith, Capt. Yates, Lieut. W. V. Riley of Yates' company, and Lieut. W. W. Cooke. Some distance away, close together, were found another brother of Gen. Custer—Boston Custer, a civilian, who had accompanied the expedition as forage master of the 7th Cavalry—and his nephew Armstrong Reed, a youth of nineteen, who was visiting the General at the time the expedition started, and accompanied it as a driver of the herd of cattle taken along. The wife of Lieut. Calhoun was a sister of the Custers and she here lost her husband, three brothers, and a nephew.

Other officers of Custer's battalion killed but not already mentioned, were Asst. Surgeon L. W. Lord, and Lieuts. H. M. Harrington, J. E. Porter, and J. G. Sturgis. The last named was a West Point graduate of 1875, and a son of General S. D. Sturgis, the Colonel of the 7th Cavalry, who had been detained by other duties when his regiment started on this expedition. The bodies of the slain were rifled of valuables and all were mutilated excepting Gen. Custer, and Mark Kellogg—a correspondent of the *New York Herald*. Gen. Custer was clad in a buckskin suit; and Canadian—Mr. Macdonald—was subsequently informed by Indians who were in the fight, that for this reason he was not mangled, as they took him to be some brave hunter accidentally with the troops. Others believe that Custer was passed by from respect for the heroism of one whom the Indians had learned to fear and admire.

The dead were buried June 28th, where they fell, Major Reno and the survivors of his regiment performing the last sad rites over their comrades.

A retreat to the mouth of Big Horn River was now ordered and successfully effected, the wounded being comfortably transported on mule litters to the mouth of the Little Big Horn, where they were placed on a steamboat and taken to Fort Lincoln. Gibbon's Cavalry followed the Indians for about ten miles, and ascertained that they had moved to the south and west by several trails. A good deal of property had been thrown away by them to lighten their march, and was found scattered about. Many of their dead were also discovered secreted in ravines a long distance from the battle field.

At the boat was found one of Custer's scouts, who had been in the fight—a Crow named Curley; his story was as follows:—

"Custer kept down the river on the north bank four miles, after Reno had crossed to the south side above. He thought Reno would drive down the valley, to attack the village at the upper end, while he (Custer) would go in at the lower end. Custer had to go further down the river and further away from Reno than he wished on account of the steep bank along the north side; but at last he found a ford and dashed for it. The Indians met him and poured in a heavy fire from across the narrow river. Custer dismounted to fight on foot, but could not get his skirmishers over the stream. Meantime hundreds of Indians, on foot and on ponies, poured over the river, which was only about three feet deep, and filled the ravine on each side of Custer's men. Custer then fell back to some high ground behind him and seized the ravines in his immediate vicinity. The Indians completely surrounded Custer and poured in a terrible fire on all sides. They charged Custer on foot in vast numbers, but were again and again driven back.

"The fight began about 2 o'clock, and lasted almost until the sun went down over the hills. The men fought desperately, and after the ammunition in their belts was exhausted went to their saddlebags, got more and continued the fight. Custer lived until nearly all of his men had been killed or wounded, and went about encouraging his soldiers to fight on. He got a shot in the left side and sat down, with his pistol in his hand. Another shot struck Custer in the breast, and he fell over. The last officer killed was a man who rode a white horse—believed to be Lieut. Cooke, as Cooke and Calhoun were the only officers who rode white horses.

"When he saw Custer hopelessly surrounded he watched his opportunity, got a Sioux blanket, put it on, and worked up a ravine, and when the Sioux charged, he got among them and they did not know him from one of their own men. There were some mounted Sioux, and seeing one fall, he ran to him, mounted his pony, and galloped down as if going towards the white men, but went up a ravine and got away. As he rode off he saw, when nearly a mile from the battle field, a dozen or more soldiers in a ravine, fighting with Sioux all around them. He thinks all were killed, as they were outnumbered five to one, and apparently dismounted. The battle was desperate in the extreme, and more Indians than white men must have been killed."

The following extract is from a letter written to Gen. Sheridan by Gen. Terry at his camp on the Big Horn, July 2d:—

"We calculated it would take Gibbon's command until the 26th to reach the mouth of the Little Big Horn, and that the wide sweep I had proposed Custer should make would require so much time that Gibbon would be able to co-operate with him in attacking any Indians that might be found on the stream. I asked Custer how long his marches would be. He said they would be at the rate of about 30 miles a day. Measurements were made and calculations based on that rate of progress. I talked with him about his strength, and at one time suggested that perhaps it would be well for me to take Gibbon's cavalry and go with him. To the latter suggestion he replied:—that, without reference to the command, he would prefer his own regiment alone. As a homogeneous body, as much could be done with it as with the two combined. He expressed the utmost confidence that he had all the force that he could need, and I shared his confidence. The plan adopted was the only one which promised to bring the infantry into action, and I desired to make sure of things by getting up every available man. I offered Custer the battery of Gatling guns, but he declined it, saying that it might embarrass him, and that he was strong enough without it. The movements proposed by General Gibbon's column were carried out to the letter, and had the attack been deferred until it was up, I cannot doubt that we should have been successful."

★   ★   ★

As the foregoing biography of Gen. Custer has been confined chiefly to his military career, it may be well in conclusion to give some account of his personal characteristics; and this can be best done in s the language of those who knew him well. A gentleman who accompanied Gen. Custer on the Yellowstone and Black Hills expeditions, contributed to the *New York Tribune* the following:—

"Gen. Custer was a born cavalryman. He was never more in his element than when mounted on Dandy, his favorite horse, and riding at the head of his regiment. He once said to me, 'I would rather be a private in the cavalry than a line officer in the infantry.' He was the personification of bravery and dash. If he had only added discretion to his valor he would have been a perfect soldier. His impetuosity very often ran away with his judgment. He was impatient of control. He liked to act independently of others, and take all the risk and all the glory to himself. He frequently got himself into trouble by assuming more authority than really belonged to his rank. It was on the Yellowstone expedition where he came into collision with Gen. Stanley, his superior officer, and was placed under arrest and compelled to ride at the rear of his column for two or three days, until Gen. Rosser, who fought against Custer in the Shenandoah Valley during the war but was then acting as engineer of the Northern Pacific Railroad, succeeded in effecting a reconciliation. Custer and Stanley afterward got on very well, and perhaps the quarrel would never have occurred if the two generals had been left alone to themselves without the intervention of camp gossips, who sought to foster the traditional jealousy between infantry and cavalry. For Stanley was the soul of generosity, and Custer did not really mean to be arrogant; but from the time when he entered West Point to the day when he fell on the Big Horn, he was accustomed to take just as much liberty as he was entitled to.

"For this reason, Custer worked most easily and effectively when under general orders, when not hampered by special instructions, or his success made dependent on anybody else. Gen. Terry understood his man when, in the order directing him to march up the Rosebud, he very liberally said: 'The Department Commander places too much confidence in your zeal, energy, and ability to wish to impose upon you precise orders which might hamper your action when nearly in contact with the enemy.' But Gen. Terry did not understand Custer if he thought he would wait for Gibbon's support before attacking an Indian camp. Undoubtedly he ought to have done this; but with his native impetuosity, his reckless daring, his confidence in his own regiment, which had never failed him, and his love of public approval, Custer could no more help charging this Indian camp, than he could help charging just so many buffaloes. He had never learned to spell the word 'defeat;' he knew nothing but success, and if he had met the Indians on the open plains, success would undoubtedly have been his; for no body of Indians could stand the charge of the

7th Cavalry when it swept over the Plains like a whirl-wind. But in the Mauvaises Terres and the narrow valley of the Big Horn he did it at a fearful risk.

"With all his bravery and self-reliance, his love of inde-pendent action, Custer was more dependent than most men on the kind approval of his fellow. He was even vain; he loved display in dress and in action. He would pay $40 for a pair of troop boots to wear on parade, and have everything else in keeping. On the Yellowstone expedi-tion he wore a bright red shirt, which made him the best mark for a rifle of any man in the regiment. I remon-strated with him for this reckless exposure, but found an appeal to his wife more effectual, and on the next cam-paign he wore a buckskin suit. He formerly wore his hair very long, letting it fall in a heavy mass upon his shoul-ders, but cut it off before going out on the Black Hills, producing quite a change in his appearance. But if vain and ambitious, Custer had none of those great vices which are so common and so distressing in the army. He never touched liquor in any form; he did not smoke, or chew, or gamble. He could outride almost any man in his regiment, I believe, if it were put to a test. When he set out to reach a certain point at a certain time, you could be sure that he would be there if he killed every horse in the command. He was sometimes too severe in forcing marches, but he never seemed to get tired himself, and he never expected his men to be so. In cutting our way through the forest of the Black Hills, I have often seen him take an ax and work as hard as any of the pioneers. He was never idle when he had a pretext for doing any-thing, whatever he did he did thoroughly. He would over-shoot the mark, but never fall short. He fretted in garrison sometimes, because it was too inactive; but he found an outlet here for his energies in writing articles for the press.

"He had a remarkable memory. He could recall in its proper order every detail of any action, no matter how remote, of which he was participant. He was rather verbose in writing, and had no gifts as a speaker; but his writings interested the masses from their close attention to details, and from his facility with the pen as with the sword in bringing a thing to a climax. As he was apt to overdo in action, so he was apt to exaggerate in statement, not from any willful disregard of the truth, but because he saw things bigger than they really were. He did not distort the truth; he magnified it. He was a natural optimist. He took rose-colored views of everything, even of the miserable lands of the Northern Pacific Railroad. He had a historical memory, but not a historical mind. He was no philosopher; he could reel off facts from his mind better than he could analyze or mass them. He was not a student, or a deep thinker. He loved to take part in events rather than to brood over them. He was fond of fun, genial and pleasant in his manner; a loving and devoted husband. It was my privilege to spend two weeks in his family at one time, and I know how happy he was in his social relations."

The following rambling remarks are accredited to a general, who name is not given:—

"The truth about Custer is, that he was a pet soldier, who had risen not above his merit, but higher than men of equal merit. He fought with Phil Sheridan, and through the patronage of Sheridan he rose; but while Sheridan liked his valor and dash he never trusted his judgment. He was to Sheridan what Murat was to Napoleon. While Sheridan is always cool, Custer was always aflame. Rising to high command early in life, he lost the reposed necessary to success in high command. . . . Then Custer must rush into politics, and went swinging around the circle with Johnson. He wanted to be a statesman, and but for Sheridan's influence with Grant, the republicans would have thrown him; but you see we all liked Custer, and did not mind his little freaks in that way any more than we would have minded temper in a woman. Sheridan, to keep Custer in his place, kept him out on the Plains at work. He gave him a fine command—one of the best cavalry regiments in the service. The colonel, Sturgis, was allowed to bask in the sunshine in a large city, while Custer was the real commander. In this service Custer did well, and vindicated the partiality of Sheridan as well as the kind feelings of his friends. . . . The old spirit which sent Custer swinging around the circle revived in him. He came East and took a prominent part in reforming the army. This made feeling, and drew upon Custer the anger of the inside forces of the administration.

"Then he must write his war memoirs. Well, in these memoirs he began to write recklessly about the army. He took to praising McClellan as the greatest man of the war, and, coming as it did when the democrats began to look lively, it annoyed the administration. Grant grew so much annoyed that even Sheridan could do no good, and Custer was disgraced. Technically it was not a disgrace. All that Grant did was to put Terry, a general, over Custer, a lieutenant-colonel, who had his regiment all the same; but all things considered, it was a disgrace."

The following is from an article by Gen. A. B. Nettleton, published in the *Philadelphia Times:*—

"It must be remembered that in fighting with cavalry, which was Custer's forte, instantaneous quickness of eye—that is the lightning-like formation and execution of successive correct judgments on a rapidly-shifting situation—is the first thing, and the second is the power of inspiring the troopers with that impetuous yet intelligent ardor with which a mounted brigade becomes a thunderbolt, and without which it remains a useless mass of horses and riders. These qualities Gen. Custer seemed to me to manifest, throughout the hard fighting of the last year of the war, to a degree that was simply astounding, and in a manner that marked him as one of the few really great cavalry commanders developed by the wars of the present century. Of fear, in the sense of dread of death or of bodily harm, he was absolutely destitute, yet his love of life and family and home was keen and constant, leaving no room in his nature for desperation, recklessness, or conscious rashness. In handling his division under Sheridan's general oversight, he seemed to act always on the belief that in campaigning with cavalry, when a certain work must be done, audacity is the truest caution. In action, when all was going well and success was only a question of time or of steady 'pounding,' Gen. Custer did not unnecessarily expose himself, but until the tide of battle had been turned in the right direction, and especially when disaster threatened, the foremost point in our division's line was almost invariably marked by the presence of Custer, his waving division tri-color and his plucky staff.

"A major-general of wide and splendid fame at twenty-five, and now slain at thirty-six, the gallant Custer had already lived long if life be measured by illustrious deeds."

The following is from a sketch of Gen. Custer published in the *Army and Navy Journal:*—

"Custer was passionately addicted to active and exciting sports as the turf and hunting. He was a splendid horseman and a lover of the horse; he attended many American race-meetings and ran his own horses several times in the West. His greyhounds and staghounds went with him at the head of his regiment, to be let slip at antelope or buffalo. With rifle or shotgun he was equally expert, and had killed his grizzly bear in the most approved fashion. . . . Bold to rashness; feverish in camp, but cool in action; with the personal vanity of a carpet knight, and the endurance and insensibility to fatigue of the hardiest and boldest rough rider a prince of scouts; a chief of guides, threading a trackless prairie with unerring eye of a native and the precision of the needle to the star; by no means a martinet, his men were led by the golden chain of love, admiration and confidence. He had the proverbial assurance of a hussar, but his personal appearance varied with occasion. During the war he was 'Custer of the golden locks, his broad sombrero turned up from his hard-bronzed face, the ends of his crimson cravat floating over his shoulder, gold galore spangling his jacket sleeves, a pistol in his boot, jangling spurs on his heels, and a ponderous claymore swinging at his side.' And long after, when he roamed a great Indian fighter on the Plains, the portrait was only slightly changed. The cavalry jacket was exchanged for the full suit of buckskin, beautifully embroidered by Indian maidens; across his saddle rested a modern sporting rifle, and at his horse's feet demurely walked hounds of unmixed breed. Again, within a few months, he appears in private society as an honored guest; scrupulously avoiding anything like display, but in a quiet conventional suit of blue, with the 'golden locks' closely shorn, and the bronzed face pale from recent indisposition, he moves almost unnoticed in the throng."

The faithful correspondent who perished with Gen. Custer on the Little Big Horn portrayed him thus:—

"A man of strong impulses, of great hearted friendships and bitter enmities; of quick, nervous temperament, undaunted courage, will, and determination; a man possessing electric mental capacity, and of iron frame and constitution; a brave, faithful, gallant soldier, who has warm friends and bitter enemies; the hardest rider, the greatest pusher; with the most untiring vigilance overcoming seeming impossibilities, and with an ambition to succeed in all things he undertakes; a man to do right, as he construes right, in every case; one respected and beloved by his followers, who would freely follow him into the 'jaws of hell.'"

Gen. Custer's last battle "will stand in history as one of the most heroic engagements ever fought, and his name will be respected so long as chivalry is applauded and civilization battles against barbarism."

Sitting Bull

[CHARLES A. EASTMAN]

It is not easy to characterize Sitting Bull, of all Sioux chiefs most generally known to the American people. There are few to whom his name is not familiar, and still fewer who have learned to connect it with anything more than the conventional notion of a blood-thirsty savage. The man was an enigma at best. He was not impulsive, nor was he phlegmatic. He was most serious when he seemed to be jocose. He was gifted with the power of sarcasm, and few have used it more artfully than he.

His father was one of the best-known members of the Unkpapa band of Sioux. The manner of this man's death was characteristic. One day, when the Unkpapas were attacked by a large war party of Crows, he fell upon the enemy's war leader with his knife. In a hand-to-hand combat of this sort, we count the victor as entitled to a war bonnet of trailing plumes. It means certain death to one or both. In this case, both men dealt a mortal stroke, and Jumping Buffalo, the father of Sitting

Bull, fell from his saddle and died in a few minutes. The other died later from the effects of the wound.

Sitting Bull's boyhood must have been a happy one. It was long after the day of the dog-travaux, and his father owned many ponies of variegated colors. It was said of him in a joking way that his legs were bowed like the ribs of the ponies that he rode constantly from childhood. He had also a common nickname that was much to the point. It was "Hunkeshnee", which means "Slow", referring to his inability to run fast, or more probably to the fact that he seldom appeared on foot. In their boyish games he was wont to take the part of the "old man", but this does not mean that he was not active and brave. It is told that after a buffalo hunt the boys were enjoying a mimic hunt with the calves that had been left behind. A large calf turned viciously on Sitting Bull, whose pony had thrown him, but the alert youth got hold of both ears and struggled until the calf was pushed back into a buffalo wallow in a sitting posture. The boys shouted: "He has subdued the buffalo calf! He made it sit down!" And from this incident was derived his familiar name of Sitting Bull.

It is a mistake to suppose that Sitting Bull, or any other Indian warrior, was of a murderous disposition. It is true that savage warfare had grown more and more harsh and cruel since the coming of white traders among them, bringing guns, knives, and whisky. Yet it was still regarded largely as a sort of game, undertaken in order to develop the manly qualities of their youth. It was the degree of risk which brought honor, rather than the number slain, and a brave must mourn thirty days, with blackened face and loosened hair, for the enemy whose life he had taken. While the spoils of war were allowed, this did not extend to territorial aggrandizement, nor was there any wish to overthrow another nation and enslave its people. It was a point of honor in the old days to treat a captive with kindness. The common impression that the Indian is naturally cruel and revengeful is entirely opposed to his philosophy and training. The revengeful tendency of the Indian was aroused by the white man. It is not the natural Indian who is mean and tricky; not Massasoit but King Philip; not Attackullakulla but Weatherford; not Wabashaw but Little Crow; not Jumping Buffalo but Sitting Bull! These men lifted their hands against the white man, while their fathers held theirs out to him with gifts.

Remember that there were councils which gave their decisions in accordance with the highest ideal of human justice before there were any cities on this continent; before there were bridges to span the Mississippi; before this network of railroads was dreamed of! There were primitive communities upon the very spot where Chicago or New York City now stands, where men were as children, innocent of all the crimes now committed there daily and nightly. True morality is more easily maintained in connection with the simple life. You must accept the truth that you demoralize any race whom you have subjugated.

From this point of view we shall consider Sitting Bull's career. We say he is an untutored man: that is true so far as learning of a literary type is concerned; but he was not an untutored man when you view him from the standpoint of his nation. To be sure, he did not learn his lessons from books. This is second-hand information at best. All that he learned he verified for himself and put into daily practice. In personal appearance he was rather commonplace and made no immediate impression, but as he talked he seemed to take hold of his hearers more and more. He was bull-headed; quick to grasp a situation, and not readily induced to change his mind. He was not suspicious until he was forced to be so. All his meaner traits were inevitably developed by the events of his later career.

Sitting Bull's history has been written many times by newspaper men and army officers, but I find no account of him which is entirely correct. I met him personally in 1884, and since his death I have gone thoroughly into the details of his life with his relatives and contemporaries. It has often been said that he was a physical coward and not a warrior. Judge of this for yourselves from the deed which first gave him fame in his own tribe, when he was about twenty-eight years old.

In an attack upon a band of Crow Indians, one of the enemy took his stand, after the rest had fled, in a deep ditch from which it seemed impossible to dislodge him. The situation had already cost the lives of several warriors, but they could not let him go to repeat such a boast over the Sioux!

"Follow me!" said Sitting Bull, and charged. He raced his horse to the brim of the ditch and struck at the enemy with his coup-staff, thus compelling him to expose himself to the fire of the others while shooting his assailant. But the Crow merely poked his empty gun into his face and dodged back under cover. Then Sitting Bull stopped; he saw that no one had followed him, and he also perceived that the enemy had no more ammunition left. He rode deliberately up to the barrier and threw his loaded gun over it; then he went back to his party and told them what he thought of them.

"Now," said he, "I have armed him, for I will not see a brave man killed unarmed. I will strike him again with my coup-staff to count the first feather; who will count the second?"

Again he led the charge, and this time they all followed him. Sitting Bull was severely wounded by his own gun in the hands of the enemy, who was killed by those that came after him. This is a record that so far as I know was never made by any other warrior.

The second incident that made him well known was his taking of a boy captive in battle with the Assiniboines. He saved this boy's life and adopted him as his brother. Hohay, as he was called, was devoted to Sitting Bull and helped much in later years to spread his fame. Sitting Bull was a born diplomat, a ready speaker, and in middle life he ceased to go upon the warpath, to become the councilor of his people. From this time on, this man represented him in all important battles, and upon every brave deed done was wont to exclaim aloud:

"I, Sitting Bull's boy, do this in his name!"

He had a nephew, now living, who resembles him strongly, and who also represented him personally upon the field; and so far as there is any remnant left of his immediate band, they look upon this man One Bull as their chief.

When Sitting Bull was a boy, there was no thought of trouble with the whites. He was acquainted with many of the early traders, Picotte, Choteau, Primeau, Larpenteur, and others, and liked them, as did most of his people in those days. All the early records show this friendly attitude of the Sioux, and the great fur companies for a century and a half depended upon them for the bulk of their trade. It was not until the middle of the last century that they woke up all of a sudden to the danger threatening their very existence. Yet at that time many of the old chiefs had been already depraved by the whisky and other vices of the whites, and in the vicinity of the forts and trading posts at Sioux City, Saint Paul, and Cheyenne, there was general demoralization. The drunkards and hangers-on were ready to sell almost anything they had for the favor of the trader. The better and stronger element held aloof. They would not have anything of the white man except his hatchet, gun, and knife. They utterly refused to cede their lands; and as for the rest, they were willing to let him alone as long as he did not interfere with their life and customs, which was not long.

It was not, however, the Unkpapa band of Sioux, Sitting Bull's band, which first took up arms against the whites; and this was not because they had come less in contact with them, for they dwelt on the Missouri River, the natural highway of trade. As early as 1854, the Ogallalas and Brules had trouble with the soldiers near Fort Laramie; and again in 1857 Inkpaduta massacred several families of settlers at Spirit Lake, Iowa. Finally, in 1869, the Minnesota Sioux, goaded by many wrongs, arose and murdered many of the settlers, afterward fleeing into the country of the Unkpapas and appealing to them for help, urging that all Indians should make common cause against the invader. This brought Sitting Bull face to face with a question which was not yet fully matured in his own mind; but having satisfied himself of the justice of their cause, he joined forces with the renegades during the summer of 1863, and from this time on he was an acknowledged leader.

In 1865 and 1866 he met the Canadian half-breed, Louis Riel, instigator of two rebellions, who had come across the line for safety; and in fact at this time he harbored a number of outlaws and fugitives from justice. His conversations with these, especially with the French mixed-bloods, who inflamed his prejudices against the Americans, all had their influence in making of the wily Sioux a determined enemy to the white man. While among his own people he was always affable and genial, he became boastful and domineering in his dealings with the hated race. He once remarked that "if we wish to make any impression upon the pale-face, it is necessary to put on his mask."

Sitting Bull joined in the attack on Fort Phil Kearny and in the subsequent hostilities; but he accepted in good faith the treaty of 1868, and soon after it was signed he visited Washington with Red Cloud and Spotted Tail, on which occasion the three distinguished chiefs attracted much attention and were entertained at dinner by President Grant and other notables. He considered that the life of the white man as he saw it was no life for his people, but hoped by close adherence to the terms of this treaty to preserve the Big Horn and Black Hills country for a permanent hunting ground. When gold was discovered and the irrepressible gold seekers made their historic dash across the plains into this forbidden paradise, then his faith in the white man's honor was gone forever, and he took his final and most persistent stand in defense of his nation and home. His bitter and at the same time well-grounded and philosophical dislike of the conquering race is well expressed in a speech made before the purely Indian council before referred to, upon the Powder

River. I will give it in brief as it has been several times repeated to me by men who were present.

"Behold, my friends, the spring is come; the earth has gladly received the embraces of the sun, and we shall soon see the results of their love! Every seed is awakened, and all animal life. It is through this mysterious power that we too have our being, and we therefore yield to our neighbors, even to our animal neighbors, the same right as ourselves to inhabit this vast land.

"Yet hear me, friends! we have now to deal with another people, small and feeble when our forefathers first met with them, but now great and overbearing. Strangely enough, they have a mind to till the soil, and the love of possessions is a disease in them. These people have made many rules that the rich may break, but the poor may not! They have a religion in which the poor worship, but the rich will not! They even take tithes of the poor and weak to support the rich and those who rule. They claim this mother of ours, the Earth, for their own use, and fence their neighbors away from her, and deface her with their buildings and their refuse. They compel her to produce out of season, and when sterile she is made to take medicine in order to produce again. All this is sacrilege.

"This nation is like a spring freshet; it overruns its banks and destroys all who are in its path. We cannot dwell side by side. Only seven years ago we made a treaty by which we were assured that the buffalo country should be left to us forever. Now they threaten to take that from us also. My brothers, shall we submit? or shall we say to them: 'First kill me, before you can take possession of my fatherland!'"

As Sitting Bull spoke, so he felt, and he had the courage to stand by his words. Crazy Horse led his forces in the field; as for him, he applied his energies to state affairs, and by his strong and aggressive personality contributed much to holding the hostiles together.

It may be said without fear of contradiction that Sitting Bull never killed any women or children. He was a fair fighter, and while not prominent in battle after his young manhood, he was the brains of the Sioux resistance. He has been called a "medicine man" and a "dreamer." Strictly speaking, he was neither of these, and the white historians are prone to confuse the two. A medicine man is a doctor or healer; a dreamer is an active war prophet who leads his war party according to his dream or prophecy. What is called by whites "making medicine" in war time is again a wrong conception. Every warrior carries a bag of sacred or lucky charms, supposed to protect the wearer alone, but it has nothing to do with the success or safety of the party as a whole. No one can make any "medicine" to affect the result of a battle, although it has been said that Sitting Bull did this at the battle of the Little Big Horn.

When Custer and Reno attacked the camp at both ends, the chief was caught napping. The village was in danger of surprise, and the women and children must be placed in safety. Like other men of his age, Sitting Bull got his family together for flight, and then joined the warriors on the Reno side of the attack. Thus he was not in the famous charge against Custer; nevertheless, his voice was heard exhorting the warriors throughout that day.

During the autumn of 1876, after the fall of Custer, Sitting Bull was hunted all through the Yellowstone region by the military. The following characteristic letter, doubtless written at his dictation by a half-breed interpreter, was sent to Colonel Otis immediately after a daring attack upon his wagon train.

"I want to know what you are doing, traveling on this road. You scare all the buffalo away. I want to hunt in this place. I want you to turn back from here. If you don't, I will fight you again. I want you to leave what you have got here and turn back from here.

I am your friend
Sitting Bull.

I mean all the rations you have got and some powder. Wish you would write me as soon as you can."

Otis, however, kept on and joined Colonel Miles, who followed Sitting Bull with about four hundred soldiers. He overtook him at last on Cedar Creek, near the Yellowstone, and the two met midway between the lines for a parley. The army report says: "Sitting Bull wanted peace in his own way." The truth was that he wanted nothing more than had been guaranteed to them by the treaty of 1868—the exclusive possession of their last hunting ground. This the government was not now prepared to grant, as it had been decided to place all the Indians under military control upon the various reservations.

Since it was impossible to reconcile two such conflicting demands, the hostiles were driven about from pillar to post for several more years, and finally took refuge across the line in Canada, where Sitting Bull had placed his last hope of justice and freedom for his race. Here he was joined from time to time by parties of malcontents from the reservation, driven largely by starvation and ill-treatment to seek another home. Here, too, they were followed by United States commissioners, headed by General Terry, who endeavored to persuade him to return, promising abundance of food and fair treatment, despite the fact that the exiles were well aware of the miserable condition of the "good Indians" upon the reservations. He first refused to meet them at all, and only did so when advised to that effect by Major Walsh of the Canadian mounted police. This was his characteristic remark: "If you have one honest man in Washington, send him here and I will talk to him."

Sitting Bull was not moved by fair words; but when he found that if they had liberty on that side, they had little else, that the Canadian government would give them protection but no food; that the buffalo had been all but exterminated and his starving people were already beginning to desert him, he was compelled at last, in 1881, to report at Fort Buford, North Dakota, with his band of hungry, homeless, and discouraged refugees. It was, after all, to hunger and not to the strong arm of the military that he surrendered in the end.

In spite of the invitation that had been extended to him in the name of the "Great Father" at Washington, he was immediately thrown into a military prison, and afterward handed over to Colonel Cody ("Buffalo Bill") as an advertisement for his "Wild West Show." After traveling about for several years with the famous showman, thus increasing his knowledge of the weaknesses as well as the strength of the white man, the deposed and humiliated chief settled down quietly with his people upon the Standing Rock agency in North Dakota, where his immediate band occupied the Grand River district and set to raising cattle and horses. They made good progress; much better, in fact, than that of the "coffee-coolers" or "loafer" Indians, received the missionaries kindly and were soon a church-going people.

When the Commissions of 1888 and 1889 came to treat with the Sioux for a further cession of land and a reduction of their reservations, nearly all were opposed to consent on any terms. Nevertheless, by hook or by crook, enough signatures were finally obtained to carry the measure through, although it is said that many were those of women and the so-called "squaw-men", who had no rights in the land. At the same time, rations were cut down, and there was general hardship and dissatisfaction. Crazy Horse was long since dead; Spotted Tail had fallen at the hands of one of his own tribe; Red Cloud had become a feeble old man, and the disaffected among the Sioux began once more to look to Sitting Bull for leadership.

At this crisis a strange thing happened. A half-breed Indian in Nevada promulgated the news that the Messiah had appeared to him upon a peak in the Rockies, dressed in rabbit skins, and bringing a message to the red race. The message was to the effect that since his first coming had been in vain, since the white people had doubted and reviled him, had nailed him to the cross, and trampled upon his doctrines, he had come again in pity to save the Indian. He declared that he would cause the earth to shake and to overthrow the cities of the whites and destroy them, that the buffalo would return, and the land belong to the red race forever! These events were to come to pass within two years; and meanwhile they were to prepare for his coming by the ceremonies and dances which he commanded.

This curious story spread like wildfire and met with eager acceptance among the suffering and discontented people. The teachings of Christian missionaries had prepared them to believe in a Messiah, and the prescribed ceremonial was much more in accord with their traditions than the conventional worship of the churches. Chiefs of many tribes sent delegations to the Indian prophet; Short Bull, Kicking Bear, and others went from among the Sioux, and on their return all inaugurated the dances at once. There was an attempt at first to keep the matter secret, but it soon became generally known and seriously disconcerted the Indian agents and others, who were quick to suspect a hostile conspiracy under all this religious enthusiasm. As a matter of fact, there was no thought of an uprising; the dancing was innocent enough, and pathetic enough their despairing hope in a pitiful Saviour who should overwhelm their oppressors and bring back their golden age.

When the Indians refused to give up the "Ghost Dance" at the bidding of the authorities, the growing suspicion and alarm focused upon Sitting Bull, who in spirit had never been any too submissive, and it was determined to order his arrest. At the special request of Major McLaughlin, agent at Standing Rock, forty of his Indian police were sent out to Sitting Bull's home on Grand River to secure his person (followed at some little distance by a body of United States troops for reinforcement, in case of trouble). These police are enlisted from among the tribesmen at each agency, and have proved uniformly brave and faithful. They entered the cabin at daybreak, aroused the chief from a sound slumber, helped him to dress, and led him unresisting from the house; but when he came out in the gray dawn of that December morning in 1890, to find his cabin surrounded by armed men and himself led away to he knew not what fate, he cried out loudly:

"They have taken me: what say you to it?"

Men poured out of the neighboring houses, and in a few minutes the police were themselves surrounded with an excited and rapidly increasing throng. They harangued the crowd in vain; Sitting Bull's blood was up, and he again appealed to his men. His adopted brother, the Assiniboine captive whose life he had saved so many years before, was the first to fire. His shot killed Lieutenant Bull Head, who held Sitting Bull by the arm. Then there was a short but sharp conflict, in which Sitting Bull and six of his defenders and six of the Indian police were slain, with many more wounded. The chief's young son, Crow Foot, and his devoted "brother" died with him. When all was over, and the terrified people had fled precipitately across the river, the soldiers appeared upon the brow of the long hill and fired their Hotchkiss guns into the deserted camp.

Thus ended the life of a natural strategist of no mean courage and ability. The great chief was buried without honors outside the cemetery at the post, and for some years the grave was marked by a mere board at its head. Recently some women have built a cairn of rocks there in token of respect and remembrance.

Buffalo Bill

[WILLIAM F. CODY]

The scouts at Fort Larned, when I arrived there, were commanded by Dick Curtis—an old guide, frontiersman and Indian interpreter. There were some three hundred lodges of Kiowa and Comanche Indians camped near the fort. These Indians had not as yet gone upon the warpath, but were restless and discontented, and their leading chiefs, Satanta, Lone Wolf, Kicking Bird, Satank, Sittamore, and other noted warriors, were rather saucy. The post at the time was garrisoned by only two companies of infantry and one of cavalry.

General Hazen, who was at the post, was endeavoring to pacify the Indians and keep them from going on the warpath. I was appointed as his special scout, and one morning he notified me that he was going to Fort Harker, and wished me to accompany him as far as Fort Zarah, thirty miles distant. The General usually traveled in an ambulance, but this trip he was to make in a six-mule wagon, under the escort of a squad of twenty infantrymen. So, early one morning in August, we started; arriving safely at Fort Zarah at twelve o'clock. General Hazen thought it unnecessary that we should go farther, and he proceeded on his way to Fort Harker without an escort, leaving instructions that we should return to Fort Larned the next day.

After the General had gone I went to the sergeant in command of the squad, and told him that I was going back that very afternoon, instead of waiting till the next morning; and I accordingly saddled up my mule and set out for Fort Larned. I proceeded uninterrupt-edly until I got about half-way between the two posts, when at Pawnee Rock I was suddenly "jumped" by about forty Indians, who came dashing up to me, extending their hands and saying, "How! How!" They were some of the same Indians who had been hanging around Fort Larned in the morning. I saw that they had on their war-paint, and were evidently now out on the war-path.

My first impulse was to shake hands with them, as they seemed so desirous of it. I accordingly reached out my hand to one of them, who grasped it with a tight grip, and jerked me violently forward; another pulled my mule by the bridle, and in a moment I was com-pletely surrounded. Before I could do anything at all, they had seized my revolvers from the holsters, and I received a blow on the head from a tomahawk which nearly rendered me senseless. My gun, which was lying across the saddle, was snatched from its place, and finally the Indian, who had hold of the bridle, started off towards the Arkansas River, leading the mule, which was being lashed by the other Indians who were following.

The savages were all singing, yelling, and whooping, as only Indians can do, when they are having their little game all their own way. While looking towards the river I saw, on the opposite side, an immense village moving down along the bank, and then I became convinced that the Indians had left the post and were now starting out on the war-path. My captors crossed the stream with me, and as we waded through the shallow water they continued to lash the mule and myself. Finally they brought me before an important looking body of Indians, who proved to be the chiefs and principal warriors. I soon recognized old Satanta among them, as well as others whom I knew, and I supposed it was all over with me.

The Indians were jabbering away so rapidly among themselves that I could not understand what they were saying. Satanta at last asked me where I had been; and, as good luck would have it, a happy thought struck me. I told him I had been after a herd of cattle or "whoa-haws," as they called them. It so happened that the Indians had been out of meat for several weeks, as the large herd of cattle which had been promised them had not yet arrived, although expected by them.

The moment that I mentioned that I had been searching for the "whoa-haws," old Satanta began questioning me in a very eager manner. He asked me where the cattle were, and I replied that they were back only a few miles, and that I had been sent by General Hazen to inform him that the cattle were coming, and that they were intended for his people. This seemed to please the old rascal, who also wanted to know if there were any soldiers with the herd, and my reply was that there were. Thereupon the chiefs held a consultation, and presently Satanta asked me if General Hazen had really said that they should have the cattle. I replied in the affirmative, and added that I had been directed to bring the cattle to them. I followed this up with a very dignified inquiry, asking why his young men had treated me so. The old wretch intimated that it was only "a freak of the boys"; that the young men had wanted to see if I was brave; in fact, they had only meant to test my bravery, and that the whole thing was a joke.

The veteran liar was now beating me at my own game of lying; but I was very glad of it, as it was in my favor. I did not let him suspect that I doubted his veracity, but I remarked that is a rough way to treat friends. He immediately ordered his young men to give me back my arms, and scolded them for what they had done. Of course, the sly old dog was now playing it very fine, as he was anxious to get possession of the cattle, with which he believed "there was a heap of soldiers coming." He had concluded it was not best to fight the soldiers if he could get the cattle peaceably.

Another council was held by the chiefs, and in a few minutes old Satanta came and asked me if I would go over and bring the cattle down to the opposite side of the river, so that they could get them. I replied, "Of course; that's my instruction from General Hazen."

Satanta said I must not feel angry at his young men, for they had only been acting in fun. He then inquired if I wished any of his men to accompany me to the cattle herd. I replied that it would be better for me to go alone, and then the soldiers could keep right on to Fort Larned, while I could drive the herd down on the bottom. So, wheeling my mule around, I was soon re-crossing the river, leaving old Satanta in the firm belief that I had told him a straight story, and was going for the cattle, which only existed in my imagination.

I hardly knew what to do, but thought that if I could get the river between the Indians and myself I would have a good three-quarters of a mile the start of them, and could then make a run for Fort Larned, as my mule was a good one.

Thus far my cattle story had panned out all right; but just as I reached the opposite bank of the river, I looked behind and saw that ten or fifteen Indians who had begun to suspect something crooked, were following me. The moment that my mule secured a good foothold on the bank, I urged him into a gentle lope towards the place where, according to my statement, the cattle were to be brought. Upon reaching a little ridge, and riding down the other side out of view, I turned my mule and headed him westward for Fort Larned. I let him out for all that he was worth, and when I came out on a little rise of ground, I looked back, and saw the Indian village in plain sight. My pursuers were now on the ridge which I had passed over, and were looking for me in every direction.

Presently they spied me, and seeing that I was running away, they struck out in swift pursuit, and in a few minutes it became painfully evident that they were gaining on me. They kept up the chase as far as Ash Creek, six miles from Fort Larned. I still led them half a mile, as their horses had not gained much during the last half of the race. My mule seemed to have gotten his second wind, and as I was on the old road I had played the whip and spurs on him without much cessation. The Indians likewise had urged their steeds to the utmost.

Finally, upon reaching the dividing ridge between Ash Creek and Pawnee Fork, I saw Fort Larned only four miles away. It was now sundown, and I heard the evening gun at the fort. The troops of the garrison little dreamed that there was a man flying for his life from the Indians and trying to reach the post. The Indians were once more gaining on me, and when I crossed the Pawnee Fork, two miles from the post, two or three of them were only a quarter of a mile behind me. Just as I had gained the opposite bank of the stream I was overjoyed to see some soldiers in a government wagon, only a short distance off. I yelled at the top of my voice, and riding up to them, told them that the Indians were after me.

Denver Jim, a well-known scout, asked how many there were, and upon my informing him that there were about a dozen, he said: "Let's drive the wagon into the trees, and we'll lay for 'em." The team was hurriedly driven in among the trees and low box-elder bushes, and there secreted.

We did not have to wait long for the Indians, who came dashing up, lashing their horses, which were panting and blowing. We let two of them pass by, but we opened a lively fire on the next three or four, killing two at the first crack. The others following, discovered that they had run into an ambush, and whirling off into the brush they turned and ran back in the directions whence they had come. The two who had passed heard the firing and made their escape. We scalped the two that we had killed, and appropriated their arms and equipments; and then catching their horses, we made our way into the post. The soldiers had heard us firing, and as we were approaching the fort the drums were being beaten, and the buglers were sounding the call to fall in. The officers had thought that Satanta and his Indians were coming in to capture the fort.

It seems that on the morning of that day, two hours after General Hazen had taken his departure, old Satanta drove into the post in an ambulance, which he had received some months before as a present from the government. He appeared to be angry and bent on mischief. In an interview with Captain Parker, the commanding officer, he asked why General Hazen had left the post without supplying the beef cattle which had been promised to him. The Captain told him that the cattle were surely on the road, but he could not explain why they were detained.

The interview proved to be a stormy one, and Satanta made numerous threats, saying that if he wished, he could capture the whole post with his warriors. Captain Parker, who was a brave man, gave Satanta to understand that he was reckoning beyond his powers, and would find it a more difficult undertaking than he had any idea of, as they were prepared for him at any moment. The interview finally terminated, and Satanta angrily left the officer's presence. Going over to the sutler's store he sold his ambulance to Mr. Tappan the past trader, and with a portion of the proceeds he secretly managed to secure some whisky from some bad men around the fort. There are always to be found around every frontier post some men who will sell whisky to the Indians at any time and under any circumstances, notwithstanding it is a flagrant violation of both civil and military regulations.

Satanta mounted his horse, and taking the whisky with him, he rode rapidly away and proceeded straight to his village. He had not been gone over an hour, when he returned to the vicinity of the post accompanied by his warriors who came in from every direction, to the number of seven or eight hundred. It was evident that the irate old rascal was "on his ear," so to speak, and it looked as if he intended to carry out his threat of capturing the fort. The garrison at once turned out and prepared to receive the red-skins, who, when within half a mile, circled around the fort and fired numerous shots into it, instead of trying to take it by assault.

While this circular movement was going on, it was observed that the Indian village in the distance was packing up, preparatory to leaving, and it was soon under way. The mounted warriors remained behind some little time, to give their families an opportunity to get away, as they feared that the troops might possibly in some manner intercept them. Finally, they encircled the post several times, fired some farewell rounds, and then galloped away over the prairie to overtake their fast departing village. On their way thither, they surprised and killed a party of woodchoppers down on the Pawnee Fork, as well as some herders who were guarding beef cattle; some seven or eight men in all, were killed, and it was evident that the Indians meant business.

The soldiers with the wagon—whom I had met at the crossing of the Pawnee Fork—had been out for the bodies of the men. Under the circumstances it was no wonder that the garrison, upon hearing the reports of our guns when we fired upon the party whom we ambushed, should have thought the Indians were coming back to give them another "turn."

We found that all was excitement at the post; double guards had been put on duty, and Captain Parker had all the scouts at his headquarters. He was endeavoring to get some one to take some important dispatches to General Sheridan at Fort Hays. I reported to him at once, and stated where I had met the Indians and how I had escaped from them.

"You was very fortunate, Cody, in thinking of that cattle story; but for that little game your hair would now be an ornament to a Kiowa's lodge," said he.

Just then Dick Curtis spoke up and said: "Cody, the Captain is anxious to send some dispatches to General Sheridan, at Fort Hays, and none of the scouts here seem to be very willing to undertake the trip. They say they are not well enough acquainted with the country to find the way at night."

As a storm was coming up it was quite dark, and the scouts feared that they would lose the way; besides it was a dangerous ride, as a large party of Indians were known to be camped on Walnut Creek, on the direct road to Fort Hays. It was evident that Curtis was trying to induce me to volunteer. I made some evasive answer to Curtis, for I did not care to volunteer after my long day's ride. But Curtis did not let the matter drop. Said he:

"I wish, Bill, that you were not so tired by your chase of to-day, for you know the country better than the rest of the boys, and I am certain that you could go through."

"As far as the ride to Fort Hays is concerned, that alone would matter but little to me," I said, "but it is a risky piece of work just now, as the country is full of hostile Indians; still if no other scout is willing to volunteer, I will chance it. I'll go, provided I am furnished with a good horse. I am tired of being chased on a government mule by Indians." At this Captain Nolan, who had been listening to our conversation, said:

"Bill, you may have the best horse in my company. You can take your choice if you will carry these dispatches. Although it is against regulations to dismount an enlisted man, I have no hesitancy in such a case of urgent necessity as this is, in telling you that you may have any horse you may wish."

"Captain, your first sergeant has a splendid horse, and that's the one I want. If he'll let me ride that horse, I'll be ready to start in one hour, storm or no storm," said I.

"Good enough, Bill; you shall have the horse; but are you sure you can find your way on such a dark night as this?"

"I have hunted on nearly every acre of ground between here and Fort Hays, and I can almost keep my route by the bones of the dead buffaloes," I confidently replied.

"Never fear, Captain, about Cody not finding the way; he is as good in the dark as he is in the daylight," said Curtis.

An orderly was sent for the horse, and the animal was soon brought up, although the sergeant "kicked" a little against letting him go. After eating a lunch and filling a canteen with brandy, I went to headquarters and put my own saddle and bridle on the horse I was to ride. I then got the dispatches, and by ten o'clock was on the road to Fort Hays, which was sixty-five miles distant across the country. The scouts had all bidden me a hearty good-bye, and wished me success, not knowing when, if ever, they would again gaze upon "my warlike form," as the poet would say.

It was dark as pitch, but this I rather liked, as there was little probability of any of the red-skins seeing me unless I stumbled upon them accidentally. My greatest danger was that my horse might run into a hole and fall down, and in this way get away from me. To avoid any such accident, I tied one end of my rawhide lariat to the bridle and the other end to my belt. I didn't propose to be left on foot, alone out on the prairie.

It was, indeed, a wise precaution that I had taken, for within the next three miles the horse, sure enough, stepped into a prairie-dog's hole, and down he went, throwing me clear over his head. Springing to his feet, before I could catch hold of the bridle, he galloped away into the darkness; but when he reached the full length of the lariat, he found that he was picketed to Bison William. I brought him up standing, and after finding my gun, which had dropped to the ground, I went up to him and in a moment was in the saddle again, and went on my way rejoicing keeping straight on my course until I came to the ravines leading into Walnut Creek, twenty-five miles from Fort Larned, where the country became rougher, requiring me to travel slower and more carefully, as I feared the horse might fall over the bank, it being difficult to see anything five feet ahead. As a good horse is not very apt to jump over a bank, if left to guide himself, I let mine pick his own way. I was now proceeding as quietly as possible, for I was in the vicinity of a band of Indians who had recently camped in that locality. I thought that I had passed somewhat above the spot, having made a little circuit to the west with that intention; but as bad luck would have it this time, when I came up near the creek I suddenly rode in among a herd of horses. The animals became frightened and ran off in every direction.

I knew at once that I was among Indian horses, and had walked into the wrong pew; so without waiting to apologize, I backed out as quickly as possible. At this moment a dog, not fifty yards away, set up a howl, and then I heard some Indians engaged in conversation;—they were guarding the horses and had been sleeping. Hearing my horse's retreating footsteps toward the hills, and thus becoming aware that there had been an enemy in their camp, they mounted their steeds and started for me.

I urged my horse to his full speed, taking the chances of his falling into holes, and guided him up the creek bottom. The Indians followed me as fast as they could by the noise I made, but I soon distanced them; and then crossed the creek.

When I had traveled several miles in a straight course, as I supposed, I took out my compass and by the light of a match saw that I was bearing two points to the east of north. At once changing my course to the direct route, I pushed rapidly on through the darkness towards Smoky Hill River. At about three o'clock in the morning I began traveling more cautiously, as I was afraid of running into another band of Indians. Occasionally I scared up a herd of buffaloes, or antelopes, or coyotes, or deer, which would frighten my horse for a moment, but with the exception of these slight alarms I got along all right.

After crossing Smoky Hill River, I felt comparatively safe as this was the last stream I had to cross. Riding on to the northward I struck the old Santa Fe trail, ten miles from Fort Hays, just at break of day.

My horse did not seem much fatigued, and being anxious to make good time and get as near the post as possible before it was fairly daylight as there might be bands of Indians camped along Big Creek, I urged him forward as fast as he could go. As I had not "lost" any Indians, I was not now anxious to make their acquaintance, and shortly after *reveille* rode into the post. I proceeded directly to General Sheridan's headquarters, and was met at the door, by Colonel Moore, *aid-de-camp* on General Sheridan's staff who asked me on what business I had come.

"I have dispatches for General Sheridan, and my instructions from Captain Parker, commanding Fort Larned, are that they shall be delivered to the General as soon as possible," said I.

Colonel Moore invited me into one of the offices, and said he would hand the dispatches to the General as soon as he got up.

"I prefer to give these dispatches to General Sheridan myself, and at once," was my reply.

The General, who was sleeping in the same building, hearing our voices, called out, "Send the man in with the dispatches." I was ushered into the General's presence, and as we had met before he recognized me and said:

"Hello, Cody, is that you?"

"Yes, sir; I have some dispatches here for you, from Captain Parker," said I, as I handed the package over to him.

He hurriedly read them, and said they were important; and then he asked me all about General Hazen and where he had gone, and about the breaking out of the Kiowas and Comanches. I gave him all the information that I possessed, and related the events and adventures of the previous day and night.

"Bill," said he, "you must have had a pretty lively ride. You certainly had a close call when you ran into the Indians on Walnut Creek. That was a good joke that you played on old Satanta. I suppose you're pretty tired after your long journey?"

"I am rather weary, General, that's a fact, as I have been in the saddle since yesterday morning;" was my reply, "but my horse is more tired than I am, and needs attention full as much if not more," I added. Thereupon the General called an orderly and gave instructions to have my animal well taken care of, and then he said, "Cody, come in and have some breakfast with me."

"No, thank you, General," said I, "Hays City is only a mile from here, and I prefer riding over there, as I know about every one in the town, and want to see some of my friends."

"Very well; do as you please, and come to the post afterwards as I want to see you," said he.

"Bidding him good-morning, and telling him that I would return in a few hours, I rode over to Hays City, and at the Perry House I met many of my old friends who were of course all glad to see me. I took some refreshments and a two hours nap, and afterward returned to Fort Hays, as I was requested.

As I rode up to the headquarters I noticed several scouts in a little group, evidently engaged in conversation on some important matter. Upon inquiry I learned that General Sheridan had informed them that he was desirous of sending a dispatch to Fort Dodge, a distance of ninety-five miles.

The Indians had recently killed two or three men while they were carrying dispatches between Fort Hays and Fort Dodge, and on this account none of the scouts seemed at all anxious to volunteer, although a reward of several hundred dollars was offered to any one who would carry the dispatches. They had learned of my experiences of the previous day, and asked me if I did not think it would be a dangerous trip. I gave it as my opinion that a man might possibly go through without seeing an Indian, but that the changes were ten to one that he would have an exceedingly lively run and a hard time before he reached his destination, if he ever got there at all.

Leaving the scouts to decide among themselves as to who was to go, I reported to General Sheridan, who also informed me that he wished some one to carry dispatches to Fort Dodge. While we were talking, his chief of scouts Dick Parr, entered and stated that none of the scouts had yet volunteered. Upon hearing that I got my "brave" up a little, and said:

"General, if there is no one ready to volunteer, I'll carry your dispatches myself."

"I had not thought of asking you to do this duty, Cody, as you are already pretty hard worked. But it is really important that these dispatches should go through," said the General.

"Well, if you don't get a courier by four o'clock this afternoon, I'll be ready for business at that time. All I want is a fresh horse," said I; "meantime I'll take a little more rest."

It was not much of a rest, however, that I got, for I went over to Hays City again and had "a time with the boys." I came back to the post at the appointed hour, and finding that no one had volunteered, I reported to General

Sheridan. He had selected an excellent horse for me, and on handing me the dispatches he said:

"You can start as soon as you wish—the sooner the better; and good luck go with you, my boy."

In about an hour afterwards I was on the road, and just before dark I crossed Smoky Hill River. I had not yet urged my horse much, as I was saving his strength for the latter end of the route, and for any run that I might have to make in the case the "wild-boys" should "jump" me. So far I had not seen a sign of Indians, and as evening came on I felt comparatively safe.

I had no adventures worth relating during the night, and just before daylight I found myself approaching Saw-log Crossing, on the Pawnee Fork, having then ridden about seventy miles.

A company of colored cavalry, commanded by Major Cox, was stationed at this point, and I approached their camp cautiously, for fear that the pickets might fire upon me—as the darkey soldiers were liable to shoot first and cry "halt" afterwards. When within hearing distance I yelled out at the top of my voice, and was answered by one of the pickets. I told him not to shoot, as I was a scout from Fort Hays; and then, calling the sergeant of the guard, I went up to the vidette of the post, who readily recognized me. I entered the camp and proceeded to the tent of Major Cox, to whom I handed a letter from General Sheridan requesting him to give me a fresh horse. He at once complied with the request.

After I had slept an hour and had eaten a lunch, I again jumped into the saddle, and before sunrise I was once more on the road. It was twenty-five miles to Fort

Dodge, and I arrived there between nine and ten o'clock, without having seen a single Indian.

After delivering the dispatches to the commanding officer, I met Johnny Austin, chief of scouts at this post, who was an old friend of mine. Upon his invitation I took a nap at his house, and when I awoke, fresh for business once more, he informed me that the Indians had been all around the post for the past two or three days, running off cattle and horses, and occasionally killing a stray man. It was a wonder to him that I had met with none of the red-skins on the way there. The Indians, he said, were also very thick on the Arkansas River, between Fort Dodge and Fort Larned, and making considerable trouble. Fort Dodge was located sixty-five miles west of Fort Larned, the latter post being on the Pawnee Fork, about five miles from its junction with the Arkansas River.

The commanding officer at Fort Dodge was anxious to send some dispatches to Fort Larned, but the scouts, like those at Fort Hays, were rather backward about volunteering, as it was considered a very dangerous undertaking to make the trip. As Fort Larned was my post, and as I wanted to go there anyhow, I said to Austin that I would carry dispatches, and if any of the boys wished to go along, I would like to have them for company's sake. Austin reported my offer to the commanding officer, who sent for me and said he would be happy to have me take his dispatches, if I could stand the trip on top of all that I had already done.

"All I want is a good fresh horse, sir," said I.

"I am sorry to say that we haven't a decent horse here, but we have a reliable and honest government mule, if that will do you," said the officer.

"Trot out your mule," said I, "that's good enough for me. I am ready at any time, sir."

The mule was forthcoming, and at dark I pulled out for Fort Larned, and proceeded uninterruptedly to Coon Creek, thirty miles out from Dodge. I had left the main wagon road some distance to the south, and had traveled parallel with it, thinking this to be a safer course, as the Indians might be lying in wait on the main road for dispatch bearers and scouts.

At Coon Creek I dismounted and led the mule by the bridle down to the water, where I took a drink, using my hat for a dipper. While I was engaged in getting the water, the mule jerked loose and struck out down the creek. I followed him in hopes that he would catch his foot in the bridle rein and stop, but this he seemed to have no idea of doing. He was making straight for the wagon road, and I did not know what minute he might run into a band of Indians. He finally got on the road, but instead of going back toward Fort Dodge, as I naturally expected he would do, he turned eastward toward Fort Larned, and kept up a little jog trot just ahead of me, but would not let me come up to him, although I tried it again and again. I had my gun in my hand, and several times I was strongly tempted to shoot him, and would probably have done so had it not been for fear of bringing Indians down upon me, and besides he was carrying the saddle for me. So I trudged on after the obstinate "critter," and if there ever was a government mule that deserved and received a good round cursing it was that one. I had neglected the precaution of tying one end of my lariat to his bit and the other to my belt, as I had done a few nights before, and I blamed myself for this gross piece of negligence.

Mile after mile I kept on after that mule, and every once in a while I indulged in strong language respecting the whole mule fraternity. From Coon Creek to Fort Larned it was thirty-five miles, and I finally concluded that my prospects were good for "hoofing" the whole distance. We—that is to say, the confounded mule and myself—were making pretty good time. There was nothing to hold the mule, and I was all the time trying to catch him—which urged him on. I made every step count, for I wanted to reach Fort Larned before daylight, in order to avoid if possible the Indians, to whom it would have been "pie" to have caught me there on foot.

The mule stuck to the road and kept on for Larned, and I did the same thing. Just as day was beginning to break, we—that is the mule and myself—found ourselves on a hill looking down into the valley of the Pawnee Fork, in which Fort Larned was located, only four miles away; and when the morning gun belched forth we were within half a mile of the post.

"Now," said I, "Mr. Mule, it is my turn," and raising my gun to my shoulder, in "dead earnest" this time, I blazed away, hitting the animal in the hip. Throwing a second cartridge into the gun, I let him have another shot, and I continued to pour the lead into him until I had him completely laid out. Like the great majority of government mules, he was a tough one to kill, and he clung to life with all the tenaciousness of his obstinate nature. He was, without doubt, the toughest and meanest mule I ever saw, and he died hard.

The troops, hearing the reports of the gun, came rushing out to see what was the matter. They found that the mule had passed in his chips, and when they learned the cause they all agreed that I had served him just right. Taking the saddle and bridle from the dead body, I proceeded into the post and delivered the dispatches to Captain Parker. I then went over to Dick Curtis' house, which was headquarters for the scouts, and there put in several hours of solid sleep.

During the day General Hazen returned from Fort Harker, and he also had some important dispatches to send to General Sheridan. I was feeling quite elated over my big ride; and seeing that I was getting the best of the other scouts in regard to making a record, I volunteered to carry General Hazen's dispatches to Fort Hays. The General accepted my services, although he thought it was unnecessary for me to kill myself. I told him that I had business at Fort Hays, and wished to go there anyway, and it would make no difference to the other scouts, for none of them appeared willing to undertake the trip.

Accordingly, that night I left Fort Larned on an excellent horse, and next morning at daylight found myself once more in General Sheridan's headquarters at Fort Hays. The General was surprised to see me, and still more so when I told him of the time I had made in riding to Fort Dodge, and that I had taken dispatches from Fort Dodge to Fort Larned; and when, in addition to this, I mentioned my journey of the night previous, General Sheridan thought my ride from post to post, taken as a whole, was a remarkable one, and he said that he did not know of its equal. I can safely say that I have never heard of its being beaten in a country infested with hostile Indians.

To recapitulate: I had ridden from Fort Larned to Fort Zarah (a distance of sixty-five miles) and back in twelve hours, including the time when I was taken across the Arkansas by the Indians. In the succeeding twelve hours I had gone from Fort Larned to Fort Hays, a distance of sixty-five miles. In the next twenty-four hours I had gone from Fort Hays to Fort Dodge, a distance of ninety-five miles. The following night I had traveled from Fort Dodge thirty miles on muleback and thirty-five miles on foot to Fort Larned; and the next night sixty-five miles more to Fort Hays. Altogether I had ridden (and walked) 355 miles in fifty-eight riding hours, or an average of over six miles an hour. Of course, this may not be regarded as very fast riding, but taking into consideration the fact that it was mostly done in the night and over a wild country, with no roads to follow, and that I had to be continually on the look out for Indians, it was thought at the time to be a big ride, as well as a most dangerous one.

Eddie Rickenbacker

[EDDIE RICKENBACKER]

O n September 15th the weather was ideal for flying. I left the aerodrome at 8:30 in the morning on a voluntary patrol, taking the nearest air route to the lines.

I had reached an altitude of 16,000 feet by the time I had reached the trenches. The visibility was unusually good. I could see for miles and miles in every direction. I was flying alone, with no idea as to whether other planes of our own were cruising about the sector or not. But barely had I reached a position over No Man's Land when I noticed a formation of six enemy Fokkers at about my altitude coming towards me from the direction of Conflans.

I turned and began the usual tactics of climbing into the sun. I noticed the Fokkers alter their direction and still climbing move eastward towards the Moselle. I did not see how they could help seeing me, as scarcely half a mile separated us. However, they did not attack nor did they indicate that they suspected my presence beyond continuing steadily their climb for elevation. Three complete circles they made on their side of the lines. I did the same on my side.

Just at this moment I discovered four Spad machines far below the enemy planes and some three miles inside the German lines. I decided at once they must belong to the American Second Fighting Group, at that time occupying the aerodrome at Souilly. They appeared to be engaged in bombing the roads and strafing enemy infantry from a low altitude. The Spads of the Second Pursuit Group had but recently been equipped with bomb racks for carrying small bombs.

The leader of the Fokker Formation saw the Spads at about the same moment I did. I saw him dip his wings and stick down his nose. Immediately the six Fokkers began a headlong pique directly down at the Spads. Almost like one of the formation I followed suit.

Inside the first thousand feet I found I was rapidly overtaking the enemy machines. By the time we had reached 5,000 feet I was in a position to open fire upon the rear man. Not once had any of them looked around. Either they had forgotten me in their anxiety to get at their prey or else had considered I would not attempt to take them all on single-handed. At all events I was given ample time to get my man dead into my sights before firing.

I fired one long burst. I saw my tracer bullets go straight home into the pilot's seat. There came a sudden burst of fire from his fuel tank and the Fokker continued onwards in its mad flight—now a fiery furnace. He crashed a mile inside his own lines.

His five companions did not stay to offer battle. I still held the upper hand and even got in a few bursts at the next nearest machine before he threw himself into a vrille and escaped me. The sight of one of their members falling in flames evidently quite discouraged them. Abandoning all their designs on the unsuspecting Spads below they dived away for Germany and left me the field.

I returned to my field, secured a car and drove immediately up to the lines to our Balloon Section. I wanted to get my victories confirmed—both this one of to-day and the Fokker that I had brought down yesterday in the same sector. For no matter how many pilots may have witnessed the bringing down of an enemy plane, official confirmation of their testimony must be obtained from outside witnesses on the ground. Often these are quite impossible to get. In such a case the victory is not credited to the pilot.

Upon the tragic death of Major Lufbery, who at that time was the leading American Ace, with 18 victories, the title of American Ace of Aces fell to Lieutenant Paul Frank Baer of Fort Wayne, Ind., a member of the Lafayette Escadrille 103. Baer then had 9 victories and had never been wounded.

Baer is a particularly modest and lovable boy, and curiously enough he is one of the few fighting pilots I have met who felt a real repugnance in his task of shooting down enemy aviators.

When Lufbery fell, Baer's Commanding Officer, Major William Thaw, called him into the office and talked seriously with him regarding the opportunity before him as America's leading Ace. He advised Baer to be cautious and he would go far. Two days later Baer was shot down and slightly wounded behind the German lines!

Thereafter, Lieutenant Frank Bayliss of New Bedford, Mass., a member of the crack French Escadrille of the Cigognes, Spad 3, held the American title until he was killed in action on June 12th, 1918. Bayliss had 13 victories to his credit.

Then David Putnam, another Massachusetts boy, took the lead with 12 victories over enemy aeroplanes. Putnam, as I have said, was, like Lufbery, shot down in flames but a day or two before my last victory.

Lieutenant Tobin of San Antonio, Texas, and a member of the third Pursuit Group (of which Major William Thaw was the Commanding Officer), now had six official victories. He led the list. I for my part had five victories confirmed. But upon receiving confirmation for the two Fokkers I had vanquished yesterday and to-day, I would have my seven and would lead Tobin by one. So it was with some little interest and impatience that I set off to try to find ground witnesses of my last two battles about St. Mihiel.

Mingled with this natural desire to become the leading fighting Ace of America was a haunting superstition that did not leave my mind until the very end of the war. It was that the very possession of this title—Ace of Aces— brought with it the unavoidable doom that had overtaken all its previous holders. I wanted it and yet I feared to learn that it was mine! In later days I began to feel that his superstition was almost the heaviest burden that I carried with me into the air. Perhaps it served to redouble my caution and sharpened my fighting senses. But never was I able to forget that the life of a title-holder is short.

Eating my sandwiches in the car that day I soon ran though St. Mihiel and made my way on the main road east to Apremont and then north to Thiaucourt. I knew that there had been a balloon up near there both days and felt certain that their observers must have seen my two combats overhead.

Unfortunately the road from Apremont to Thiaucourt was closed, owing to the great number of shell-holes and trenches which criss-crossed it. After being lost for two hours in the forest which lies between St. Mihiel and Vigneulles, I was finally able to extricate myself and found I had emerged just south of Vigneulles. I was about one mile south of our trenches. And standing there with map in hand wondering where to go next to find our balloons, I got an unexpected clue.

A sudden flare of flames struck my sight off to the right. Running around the trees I caught a view of one of our balloons between me and Thiaucourt completely immersed in flames! Half-way down was a graceful little parachute, beneath which swung the observer as he settled slowly to Mother Earth!

And as I gazed I saw a second balloon two or three miles further east towards Pont-à-Mousson perform the same maneuver. Another of our observers was making the same perilous jump! A sly Heinie had slipped across our lines and had made a successful attack upon the two balloons and had made a clean getaway. I saw him climbing up away from the furious gale of anti-aircraft fire which our gunners were speeding after him. I am afraid my sympathies were almost entirely with the airman as I watched the murderous bursting of Archy all around his machine. At any rate I realized exactly how he was feeling, with his mixture of satisfaction over the success of his undertaking and of panic over the deadly mess of shrapnel about him.

In half an hour I arrived at the balloon site and found them already preparing to go aloft with a second balloon. And at my first question they smiled and told me they had seen my Fokker of this morning's combat crash in flames. They readily signed the necessary papers to this effect, thus constituting the required confirmation for my last victory. But for the victory of yesterday that I claimed they told me none of the officers were present who had been there on duty at that time. I must go to the 3rd Balloon Company just north of Pont-à-Mousson and there I would find the men I wanted to see.

After watching the new balloon get safely launched with a fresh observer in the basket, a process which consumed some ten or fifteen minutes, I retraced my steps and made my way back to my motor. The observer whom I had seen descending under his parachute had in the meantime made his return to his company headquarters. He was unhurt and quite enthusiastic over the splendid landing he had made in the trees. Incidentally I learned that but two or three such forced descents by parachute from a flaming balloon are permitted any one observer. These jumps are not always so simple and frequently very serious if not fatal injuries are received in the parachute jump. Seldom does one officer care to risk himself in a balloon basket after his third jump. And this fear for his own safety limits very naturally his service and bravery in that trying business. The American record in this perilous profession is held, I believe, by Lieutenant Phelps of New York, who made five successive jumps from a flaming balloon.

On my way to the 3rd Balloon Company I stopped to enquire the road from a group of infantry officers whom I met just north of Pont-à-Mousson. As soon as I stated my business, they unanimously exclaimed that they had all seen my flight above them yesterday and had seen my victim crash near them. After getting them to describe the exact time and place and some of the incidents of the fight I found that it was indeed my combat they had witnessed. This was a piece of real luck for me. It ended my researches on the spot. As they were very kindly signing their confirmation I was thinking to myself, "Eddie! You are the American Ace of Aces!" And so I was for the minute.

Returning home, I lost no time in putting in my reports. Reed Chambers came up to me and hit me a thump on the back.

"Well, Rick!" he said, "how does it feel?"

"Very fine for the moment, Reed," I replied seriously, "but any other fellow can have the title any time he wants it, so far as I am concerned."

I really meant what I was saying. A fortnight later when Frank Luke began his marvelous balloon strafing he passed my score in a single jump. Luke, as I have said, was on the same aerodrome with me, being a member of 27 Squadron. His rapid success even brought 27 Squadron ahead of 95 Squadron for a few days.

The following day I witnessed a typical expedition of Luke's from our own aerodrome. Just about dusk on September 16th Luke left the Major's headquarters and walked over to his machine. As he came out of the door he pointed out the two German observation balloons to the east of our field, both of which could be plainly seen with the naked eye. They were suspended in the sky about two miles back of the Boche lines and were perhaps four miles apart.

"Keep you eyes on these two balloons," said Frank as he passed us. "You will see that first one there go up in flames exactly at 7:15 and the other will do likewise at 7:19."

We had little idea he would really get either of them, but we all gathered together out in the open as the time grew near and kept our eyes glued to the distant specks in the sky. Suddenly Major Hartney exclaimed, "There goes the first one!" It was true! A tremendous flare of flame lighted up the horizon. We all glanced at our watches. It was exactly on the dot!

The intensity of our gaze towards the location of the second Hun balloon may be imagined. It had grown too dusk to distinguish the balloon itself, but we well knew the exact point in the horizon where it hung. Not a word was spoken as we alternately glanced at the second-hands of our watches and then at the eastern skyline. Almost upon the second our watching group yelled simultaneously. A small blaze first lit up the point at which we were gazing. Almost instantaneously another gigantic burst of flames announced to us that the second balloon had been destroyed! It was a most spectacular exhibition.

We all stood by on the aerodrome in front of Luke's hangar until fifteen minutes later we heard through the darkness the hum of his returning motor. His mechanics were shooting up red Very lights with their pistols to indicate to him the location of our field. With one short circle above the aerodrome he shut off his motor and made a perfect landing just in front of our group. Laughing and hugely pleased with his success, Luke jumped out and came running over to us to receive our heartiest congratulations. Within a half hour's absence from the field Frank Luke had destroyed a hundred thousand dollars' worth of enemy property! He had returned absolutely unscratched.

A most extraordinary incident had happened just before Luke had left the ground. Lieutenant Jeffers of my Squadron had been out on patrol with the others during the afternoon and did not return with them. I was becoming somewhat anxious about him when I saw a homing aeroplane coming from the lines towards our field. It was soon revealed as a Spad and was evidently intending to land at our field, but its course appeared to be very peculiar. I watched it gliding steeply down with engine cut off. Instead of making for the field, the pilot, whoever he was, seemed bent upon investigating the valley to the north of us before coming in. If this was Jeff he was taking a foolish chance, since he had already been out longer than the usual fuel supply could last him.

Straight down at the north hillside the Spad continued its way. I ran out to see what Jeff was trying to do. I had a premonition that everything was not right with him.

Just as his machine reached the skyline I saw him make a sudden effort to redress the plane. It was too late. He slid off a little on his right wing, causing his nose to turn back towards the field—and then he crashed in the fringe of bushes below the edge of the hill. I hurried over to him.

Imagine my surprise when I met him walking towards me, no bones broken, but wearing a most sheepish expression on his face. I asked him what in the world was the matter.

"Well," he replied, "I might as well admit the truth! I went to sleep coming home, and didn't wake up until I was about ten feet above the ground. I didn't have time to switch on my engine or even flatten out! I'm afraid I finished the little 'bus!"

Extraordinary as this tale seemed, it was nevertheless true. Jeffers had set his course for home at a high elevation over the lines and cutting off his engine had drifted smoothly along. The soft air and monotonous luxury of motion had lulled him to sleep. Subconsciously his hand controlled the joystick or else the splendid equilibrium of the Spad had kept it upon an even keel without control. Like the true old coach-horse it was, it kept the stable door in sight and made directly for it. Jeff's awakening might have been in another world, however, if he had not miraculously opened his eyes in the very nick of time!

The next day, September 18th, our group suffered a loss that made us feel much vindictiveness as well as sorrow. Lieutenant Heinrichs and Lieutenant John Mitchell, both of 95 Squadron, were out together on patrol when they encountered six Fokker machines. They immediately began an attack.

Mitchell fired one burst from each gun and then found them both hopelessly jammed. He signaled to Heinrichs that he was out of the battle and started for home. But at the same moment Heinrichs received a bullet through his engine which suddenly put it out of action. He was surrounded by enemy planes and some miles back of the German lines. He broke through the enemy line and began his slow descent. Although it was evident he could not possibly reach our lines, the furious Huns continued swooping upon him, firing again and again as he coasted down.

Ten different bullets struck his body in five different attacks. He was perfectly defenseless against any of them. He did not lose consciousness, although one bullet shattered his jawbone and bespattered his goggles so that he could not see through the blood. Just before he reached the ground he managed to push up his goggles with his unwounded arm. The other was hanging limp and worthless by his side.

He saw he was fairly into a piece of woodland and some distance within the German lines. He swung away and landed between the trees, turning his machine over as he crashed, but escaping further injury himself. Within an hour or two he was picked up and taken to a hospital in Metz.

After the signing of the Armistice we saw Heinrichs again at the Toul Hospital. He was a mere shell of himself. Scarcely recognizable even by his old comrades, a first glance at his shrunken form indicated that he had been horribly neglected by his captors. His story quickly confirmed this suspicion.

For the several weeks that he had lain in the Metz hospital he told us that the Germans had not reset either his jaw or his broken arm. In fact he had received no medical attention whatsoever. The food given him was bad and infrequent. It was a marvel that he had survived this frightful suffering!

In all fairness to the Hun I think it is his due to say that such an experience as Heinrichs suffered rarely came to my attention. In the large hospital in which he was confined there were but six nurses and two doctors. They had to care for several scores of wounded. Their natural inclination was to care first for their own people. But how any people calling themselves human could have permitted Heinrichs' suffering to go uncared for during all those weeks passes all understanding. Stories of this kind which occasionally came to our ears served to steel our hearts against any mercy towards the enemy pilots in our vicinity.

And thus does chivalry give way before the horrors of war—even in aviation!

CAPTAIN OF THE HAT-IN-THE-RING SQUADRON

The Three-Fingered Lake is a body of water well known to the American pilots who have flown over the St. Mihiel front. It lies four or five miles directly north of Vigneulles and is quite the largest body of water to be seen in this region. The Germans have held it well within their lines ever since the beginning of the war.

At the conclusion of the American drive around St. Mihiel, which terminated victoriously twenty-two hours after it began, the lines were pushed north of Vigneulles until they actually touched the southern arm of Three-Fingered Lake. Our resistless doughboys pushing in from both directions, met each other in the outskirts of Vigneulles at two o'clock in the morning. Some fifteen thousand Boches and scores of guns were captured within the territory that had thus been pinched out.

With this lake barrier on the very edge of their lines, the Huns had adroitly selected two vantage points on their end of the water from which to hoist their observation balloons. From this position their observers had a splendid view of our lines and noted every movement in our rear. They made themselves a tremendous nuisance to the operations of our Staff Officers.

Frank Luke, the star Balloon Strafer of our group, was, as I have said, a member of the 27th Squadron. On the evening of September 18th he announced that he was going up to get those two balloons that swung above the Three-Fingered Lake. His pal, Lieutenant Wehrner, of the same squadron accompanied Luke as usual.

There was a curious friendship between Luke and Wehrner. Luke was an excitable, highstrung boy, and his impetuous courage was always getting him into trouble. He was extremely daring and perfectly blind and indifferent to the enormous risks he ran. His superior officers and his friends would plead with him to be more cautious, but he was deaf to their entreaties. He attacked like a whirlwind, with absolute coolness but with never a thought of his own safety. We all predicted that Frank Luke would be the greatest air-fighter in the world if he would only learn to save himself unwise risks. Luke came from Phoenix, Arizona.

Wehrner's nature, on the other hand, was quite different. He had just one passion, and that was his love for Luke. He followed him about the aerodrome constantly. When Luke went up, Wehrner usually managed to go along with him. On these trips Wehrner acted as an escort or guard, despite Luke's objections. On several occasions he had saved Luke's life. Luke would come back to the aerodrome and excitedly tell every one about it, but no word would Wehrner say on the subject. In fact Wehrner never spoke except in monosyllables on any subject. After a successful combat he would put in the briefest possible report and sign his name. None of us ever heard him describe how he brought the enemy machine down.

Wehrner hovered in the air above Luke while the latter went in for the balloon. If hostile aeroplanes came up, Wehrner intercepted them and warded off the attack until Luke had finished his operations. These two pilots made an admirable pair for this work and over a score of victories were chalked up for 27 Squadron through the activities of this team.

On the evening of the 18th, Luke and Wehrner set off at five o'clock. It was just getting dark. They flew together at a medium level until they reached the lake. There they separated, Luke diving straight at the balloon which lay to the west, Wehrner staying aloft to guard the sky against a surprise attack from Hun aeroplanes.

Luke's balloon rose out of the swampy land that borders the upper western edge of Three-Fingered Lake. The enemy defenses saw his approach and began a murderous fire through which Luke calmly dived as usual. Three separate times he dived and fired, dived and fired. Constantly surrounded with a hail of bullets and shrapnel, flaming onions and incendiary bullets, Luke returned to the attack the third time and finally completed his errand of destruction. The huge gas-bag burst into flames. Luke zoomed up over the balloon and looked about for his friend. He was not in view at the moment, but another sight struck Luke's searching eyes. A formation of six Fokkers was bearing down upon him from out of Germany. Perhaps Wehrner had fired the red signal light which had been the warning agreed upon, and he had failed to see it in the midst of all that Archy fire. At any rate he was in for it now.

The German Fokkers were to the west of him. The second balloon was to the east. With characteristic fool-hardiness Luke determined to withdraw by way of the other balloon and take one burst at it before the Huns reached him. He accordingly continued straight on east, thus permitting the pursuing formation of Fokkers to cut him off at the south.

With his first dive Luke shot down the second balloon. It burst into towering flames, which were seen for miles around. Again he passed through a living stream of missiles fired at him from the ground, and escaped unhurt!

As he began his flight towards home he discovered that he was completely cut off by the six Fokkers. He must shoot his way through single-handed. To make it worse, three more Fokkers were rapidly coming upon him from the north. And then Luke saw his pal, Wehrner.

Wehrner had all this time been patrolling the line to the north of Luke's balloons. He had seen the six Fokkers, but had supposed that Luke would keep ahead of them and abandon his attempt at the second enemy balloon. He therefore fired his signal light, which was observed by our balloon observers but not by Luke, and immediately set off to patrol a parallel course between the enemy planes and Luke's road home. When he saw Luke dart off to the second balloon, Wehrner realized at once that Luke had not seen his signal and was unaware of the second flight of Fokkers coming directly upon him. He quickly sheered off and went forward to meet them.

What Luke saw was the aeroplane of his devoted pal receiving a direct fire from all three of the approaching Fokker pilots. The next instant it fell over in the air and slowly began to fall. Even as it hesitated in its flight, a burst of flames issued from the Spad's tank. Wehrner was shot down in flames while trying to save his comrade! It was a deliberate sacrifice of himself for his friend!

Completely consumed with fury, Luke, instead of seeking safety in flight, turned back and hurled himself upon the three Fokkers. He was at a distinct disadvantage, for they had the superiority both in altitude and position, not to mention numbers. But regardless as ever of what the chances were, Luke climbed upwards at them, firing as he advanced.

Picking out the pilot on the left, Luke kept doggedly on his track firing at him until he suddenly saw him burst into flame. The other two machines were in the meantime on Luke's tail and their tracer bullets were flashing unnoticed by his head. But as soon as he saw the end of his first enemy he made a quick renversement on number two and, firing as he came about, he shot down the second enemy machine with the first burst. The third piqued for Germany and Luke had to let him go.

All this fighting had consumed less time than it takes to tell it. The two Fokkers had fallen in flames within ten seconds of each other. With rage still in his heart Luke looked about him to discover where the six enemy machines had gone. They had apparently been satisfied to leave him with their three comrades, for they were now disappearing back towards the east. And just ahead of them Luke discerned fleecy white clouds of Archy smoke breaking north of Verdun. This indicated that our batteries were firing at enemy aeroplanes in that sector.

As he approached Verdun Luke found that five French Spads were hurrying up to attack an L. V. G. machine of the Huns, the same target at which our Archy had been firing. The six Fokkers had seen them coming and had gone to intercept them. Like a rocket Luke set his own Spad down at the L. V. G. It was a two-seater machine and was evidently taking photographs at a low altitude.

Our Archy ceased firing as Luke drew near. He hurled himself directly down at the German observer, firing both guns as he dove. The enemy machine fell into a vrille and crashed just a few hundred yards from our old Verdun aerodrome. In less than twenty minutes Lieutenant Luke had shot down two balloons, two fighting Fokkers and one enemy photographing machine—a feat that is almost unequaled in the history of this war!

Luke's first question when he arrived at our field was, "Has Wehrner come back?"

He knew the answer before he asked the question, but he was hoping against hope that he might find himself mistaken. But Wehrner had indeed been killed. The joy of Luke over his marvelous victories vanished instantly. He was told that with these five victories he had a total of eleven, thus passing me and making Luke the American Ace of Aces. But this fact did not interest him. He said he would like to go up to the front in a car and see if anything had been heard from Wehrner.

The following morning Major Hartney, Commanding Officer of our Group, took Luke and myself up to Verdun to make inquiries. Shortly after lunch the officer in charge of confirmations came to us and told Lieutenant Luke that not only had his five victories of yesterday been officially confirmed, but that three old victories had likewise been that morning confirmed, making Luke's total fourteen instead of eleven. And these fourteen victories had been gained by Frank Luke in *eight days!* The history of war aviation, I believe, has not a similar record. Not even the famous Guynemer, Fonck, Ball, Bishop or the noted German Ace of Aces, Baron von Richthofen, ever won fourteen victories in a single fortnight at the front. Any air-craft, whether balloon or aeroplane, counts as one victory, and only one, with all the armies.

In my estimation there has never during the four years of war been an aviator at the front who possessed the confidence, ability and courage that Frank Luke had shown during that remarkable two weeks.

In order to do this boy honor and show him that every officer in the Group appreciated his wonderful work, he was given a complimentary dinner that night by the Squadrons. Many interesting speeches were made. When it came Luke's turn to respond he got up laughing, said he was having a bully time—and sat down! Major Hartney came over to him and presented him with a seven days' leave in Paris—which at that time was about the highest gift at the disposal of commanding officers at the front.

Among all the delightful entertainers who came over to the front from the United States to help cheer up the fighting men, none except our own Elsie Janis, who is an honorary member of our Squadron, were quite so highly appreciated by our fellows as the Margaret Mayo' Y. M. C. A. troup, which gave us an entertainment just a night or two after this. The players included such well known talent as Elizabeth Brice, Lois Meredith, Bill Morrisey, Tommy Gray and Mr. Walker—all of New York. After a hurried preparation, we cleaned up one of the hangars, prepared a stage and made a dressing room by hanging a curtain over a truck and trailer. After a merry dinner in 94's mess hall everybody crowded into the "theater," and the way the boys laughed and shouted there, during the performance, must have sounded hysterical to the actors; but to my mind this hysteria was only an outlet for the pent-up emotion and an indication of the tension and strain under which we had so long been living. At any rate it was the best show I have ever seen at the front, barring always the one evening Miss Janis appeared on our aerodrome for an entertainment.

The night of September 24th, Major Marr returned from Paris and announced that he had received orders to return to America. Shortly afterward Major Hartney handed me an order promoting me to the Command of the 94 Squadron!

My pride and pleasure at receiving this great honor I cannot put into words. I had been with 94 since its first day at the front. I was a member of this, the very first organization to go over the lines. I had seen my old friends disappear and be replaced by other pilots whom I had learned to admire and respect. And many of these had in turn disappeared!

Now but three members of the original organization were left—Reed Chambers, Thorn Taylor and myself. And I had been given the honor of leading this distinguished Squadron! It had had Lufbery, Jimmy Hall and Dave Peterson as members. And it led all the rest in number of victories over the Huns.

But did it? I walked over to the Operations Office and took a look at the records. I had a suspicion that Frank Luke's wonderful run of the past few days had put 27 Squadron ahead of us.

My suspicions were quite correct. The sober fact was that this presumptuous young 27 had suddenly taken a spurt, thanks to their brilliant Luke, and now led the Hat-in-the-Ring Squadron by six victories! I hurried over to 94 quarters and called together all my pilots.

The half hour we had together that evening firmly fixed a resolve in the aspirations of 94's members. No other American Squadron at the front would ever again be permitted to approach so near our margin of supremacy. From that hour every man in 94 Squadron, I believe, felt that the honor of his Squadron was at stake in this matter of bringing down Huns. At all events, within a week my pilots had overtaken 27's lead and never again did any American Squadron even threaten to overtop our lead.

After a talk that night with the pilots, I went over and called the mechanics to a caucus. We had half an hour's talk together and I outlined to them just what our pilots proposed to do with their help. And they understood that it was only by their wholesouled help that their Squadron's success would be possible. How nobly these boys responded to our appeal was well proved in the weeks that followed. Rarely indeed was a dud motor found in 94 Squadron henceforward. Never did a squadron of pilots receive more faithful attendance from their helpers in the hangar than was given us by these enthusiastic air mechanics of the Hat-in-the-Ring Squadron. I honestly believe that they felt the disgrace of being second more keenly than did we pilots.

Finally, I had a long and serious conference with myself that night. After I had gone to bed I lay awake for several hours, thinking over the situation. I was compelled to believe that I had been chosen Squadron Commander because, first, I had been more successful than the other pilots in bringing down enemy aeroplanes; and second, because I had the power to make a good leader over other pilots. That last proposition caused me infinite thought. Just how and wherein could I do the best by my followers?

I suppose every squadron leader has this same problem to decide, and I cannot help but believe that on his decision as to how he shall lead his pilots depends in a great measure the extent of his success—and his popularity.

To my mind there was but one procedure. I should never ask any pilot under me to go on a mission that I myself would not undertake. I would lead them by example as well as precept. I would accompany the new pilots and watch their errors and help them to feel more confidence by sharing their dangers. Above all, I would work harder than ever I did as mere pilot. There was no question about that. My days of loafing were over!

To avoid the red-tape business at the aerodrome—the making out of reports, ordering materials and seeing that they came in on time, looking after details of the mess, the hangars and the comfort of the enlisted men— all this work must be put under competent men, if I expected to stay in the air and lead patrols. Accordingly I gave this important matter my attention early next morning. And the success of my appointments was such that from that day to this I have never spent more than thirty minutes a day upon the ground business connected with 94's operations.

Full of this early enthusiasm I went up on a lone patrol the very first morning of my new responsibility, to see how much I had changed for the better or the worse.

Within half an hour I returned to the aerodrome with two more victories to my credit—the first double-header I had so far won!

AN EVENTFUL "D" DAY

September 25th, 1918, was my first day as Captain of the 94 Squadron. Early that forenoon I started for the lines alone, flew over Verdun and Fort Douaumont, then turned east towards Etain. Almost immediately I picked up a pair of L. V. G. two-seater machines below me. They were coming out of Germany and were certainly bent upon a expedition over our lines. Five Fokker machines were above them and somewhat behind, acting as protection for the photographers until the lines were reached.

Climbing for the sun for all I was worth, I soon had the satisfaction of realizing that I had escaped their notice and was now well in their rear. I shut down my motor, put down my head and made a bee line for the nearest Fokker.

I was not observed by the enemy until it was too late for him to escape. I had him exactly in my sights when I pulled both triggers for a long burst. He made a sudden attempt to pull away, but my bullets were already ripping through his fusilage and he must have been killed instantly. His machine fell wildly away and crashed just south of Etain.

It had been my intention to zoom violently upwards and protect myself against the expected attack from the four remaining Fokkers as soon as I had finished the first man. But when I saw the effect of my attack upon the four dumbfounded Boches I instantly changed my tactics and plunged straight on through their formation to attack the photographing L. V. G.'s ahead. For the Heinies were so surprised by finding a Spad in their midst and seeing one of their number suddenly drop that the remaining three viraged to right and left. Their one idea was to escape and save their own skins. Though they did not actually pique for home, they cleared a space large enough for me to slip through and continue my dive upon the two-seaters before they could recover their formation.

The two-seaters had seen my attack and had already put down their heads to escape. I plunged along after them, getting the rear machine in my sights as I drew nearer to him. A glance back over my shoulder showed me that the four Fokkers had not yet reformed their line and were even now circling about with the purpose of again solidifying their formation. I had a few seconds yet before they could begin their attack.

The two L. V. G. machines began to draw apart. Both observers in the rear seats were firing at me, although the range was still too long for accurate shooting. I dove more steeply, passed out of the gunner's view under the nearest machine and zoomed quickly up at him from below. But the victory was not to be an easy one. The pilot suddenly kicked his tail around, giving the gunner another good aim at me. I had to postpone shooting until I had more time for my own aiming. And in the meantime the second photographing machine had stolen up behind me and I saw tracer bullets go whizzing and streaking past my face. I zoomed up diagonally out of range, made a renversement and came directly back at my first target.

Several times we repeated these maneuvers, the four Fokkers still wrangling among themselves about their formation. And all the time we were getting farther and farther back into Germany. I decided upon one bold attack and if this failed I would get back to my own lines before it was too late.

Watching my two adversaries closely, I suddenly found an opening between them. They were flying parallel to each other and not fifty yards apart. Dropping down in a sideslip until I had one machine between me and the other I straightened out smartly, leveled my Spad and began firing.

The nearest Boche passed directly through my line of fire and just as I ceased firing I had the infinite satisfaction of seeing him gush forth flames. Turning over and over as he fell the L. V. G. started a blazing path to earth just as the Fokker escort came tearing up to the rescue. I put on the gas and piqued for my own lines.

Pleased as I was over this double-header, the effect it might have upon my pilots was far more gratifying to me.

Arriving at the aerodrome at 9:30 I immediately jumped into a motorcar, called to Lieutenant Chambers to come with me and we set off at once to get official confirmation for this double victory. We took the main road to Verdun, passed through the town and gained the hills beyond the Meuse, towards Etain. Taking the road up to Fort de Tavannes we passed over that bloody battle-field of 1916 where so many thousand German troops fell before French fire in the memorable Battle for Verdun. At the very crest of the hill we were halted by a French poilu, who told us the rest of the road was in full view of the Germans and that we must go no farther.

We asked him as to whether he had seen my combat overhead this morning. He replied in the affirmative and added that the officers in the adjacent fort too had witnessed the whole fight through their field glasses. We thanked him and leaving our car under his care took our way on foot to the Fort.

Two or three hundred yards of shell-holes sprinkled the ground between us and the Fort. We made our way through them, gained admittance to the interior of the Fort and in our best Pidgin French stated our errand to M. le Commandant. He immediately wrote out full particulars of the combat I had had with the L. V. G., signed it and congratulated me upon my victory with a warm shake of the hand. Having no further business at this place, we made our adieus and hastened back to our car.

Plunging through the shallowest shell-holes we had traversed about half the distance to our car, which stood boldly out on the top of the road, when a shrill whining noise made us pause and listen. The next instant a heavy explosion announced that a shell had landed about fifty yards short of us. Simultaneously with the shower of gravel and dirt which headed our way we dropped unceremoniously on our faces in the bottom of the deepest shell-hole in our vicinity.

The Huns had spotted our car and were actually trying to get its range!

Two or three times we crawled out of our hole, only to duck back at the signal of the next coming shell. After six or eight shots the Boche gunners evidently considered their target too small, for they ceased firing long enough for us to make a bolt across the intervening holes and throw ourselves into the waiting automobile. I most fervently wished that I had turned the car around before leaving it, and I shall never forget the frightful length of time it took me to get our car backed around and headed in the right direction. We lost no time in getting down that hill.

Next day was to be an important one for us and for the whole American Army. Officially it was designated as

"D" day and the "Zero hour," by the same code, was set for four o'clock in the morning. At that moment the artillery barrage would begin and forty thousand dough-boys who were posted along the front line trenches from the Meuse to the Argonne Forest would go over the top. It was the 26th day of September, 1918.

Precisely at four o'clock I was awakened by my orderly who informed me that the weather was good. Hastily get-ting out of doors, I looked over the dark sky, wondering as I did so how many of our boys it would claim before this day's work was done! For we had an important part to play in this day's operations. Headquarters had sent us orders to attack all the enemy observation balloons along that entire front this morning and to continue the attacks until the infantry's operations were completed. Accord-ingly every fighting squadron had been assigned certain of these balloons for attack and it was our duty to see that they were destroyed. The safety of thousands of our attacking soldiers depended upon our success in eliminat-ing these all-watching eyes of the enemy. Incidentally, it was the first balloon strafing party that 94 Squadron had been given since I had been made its leader and I desired to make a good showing on this first expedition.

Just here it may be well to point out the difficulties of balloon strafing, which make this undertaking so unat-tractive to the new pilot.

German "Archy" is terrifying at first acquaintance. Pilots affect a scorn for it, and indeed at high altitudes the probabilities of a hit are small. But when attacking a bal-loon which hangs only 1,500 feet above the guns (and this altitude is of course known precisely to the anti-air-craft gunner) Archy becomes far more dangerous.

So when a pilot begins his first balloon attacking expeditions, he knows that he runs a gauntlet of fire that may be very deadly. His natural impulse is to make a nervous plunge into the zone of danger, fire his bullets, and get away. Few victories are won with this method of attack.

The experienced balloon strafers, particularly such daring airmen as Coolidge and Luke, do not consider the risks or terrors about them. They proceed in the attack as calmly as though they were sailing through a stormless sky. Regardless of flaming missiles from the ground, they pass through the defensive barrage of fire, and often return again and again, to attack the target, until it finally bursts into flame from their incendiary bullets.

The office charts informed me that day would break this morning at six o'clock. Consequently we must be ready to leave the ground in our machines at 5:20, permitting us thirty minutes in which to reach our objectives, and ten minutes in which to locate our individual balloons. For it is essential to strike at these well defended targets just at the edge of dawn. Then the balloons are just starting aloft, and our attacking aeroplanes are but scantily visible from below. Moreover enemy aeroplanes are not apt to be about so early in the morning, unless the enemy has some inkling of what is going on.

I routed out five of my best pilots, Lieutenants Cook, Chambers, Taylor, Coolidge and Palmer; and as we gathered together for an early breakfast, we went over again all the details of our pre-arranged plans. We had two balloons assigned to our Squadron, and three of us were delegated to each balloon. Both lay along the Meuse between Brabant and Dun. Every one of us had noted down the exact location of his target on the evening before. It would be difficult perhaps to find them before daylight if they were still in their nests, but we were to hang about the vicinity until we did find them, if it took all day. With every man fully posted on his course and objective, we put on our coats and walked over to the hangars.

I was the last to leave the field, getting off the ground at exactly 5:20. It was still dark and we had to have the searchlights turned onto the field for a moment to see the ground while we took off. As soon as we lifted into the darkness the lights were extinguished. And then I saw the most marvelous sight that my eyes have ever seen.

A terrific barrage of artillery fire was going on ahead of me. Through the darkness the whole western horizon was illumined with one mass of sudden flashes. The big guns were belching out their shells with such rapidity that there appeared to be millions of them shooting at the same time. Looking back I saw the same scene in my rear. From Luneville on the east to Rheims on the west there was not one spot of darkness along the whole front. The French were attacking along both our flanks at the same time with us in order to help demoralize the weakening Boche. The picture made me think of a giant switchboard which emitted thousands of electric flashes as invisible hands manipulated the plugs.

So fascinated did I become over this extraordinary fireworks display that I was startled upon peering over the side of my machine to discover the city of Verdun below my aeroplane's wings. Fastening my course above the dim outline of the Meuse River I followed its windings down stream, occasionally cutting across little peninsulas which I recognized along the way. Every inch of this route was as familiar to me as was the path around the corner of my old home. I knew exactly the point in the Meuse Valley where I would leave the river and turn left to strike the spot where my balloon lay last night. I did not know what course the other pilots had taken. Perhaps they had already—

Just as these thoughts were going through my mind I saw directly ahead of me the long snaky flashes of enemy tracer bullets from the ground piercing the sky. There was the location of my balloon and either Cook or Chambers was already attacking it. The enemy had discovered them and were putting up the usual hail of flaming projectiles around the balloon site. But even as the flaming bullets continued streaming upwards I saw a gigantic flame burst out in their midst! One of the boys had destroyed his gas-bag!

Even before the glare of the first had died I saw our second enemy balloon go up in flames. My pilots had succeeded beyond my fondest expectations. Undoubtedly the enemy would soon be swinging new balloons up in their places, but we must wait awhile for that. I resolved to divert my course and fly further to the north where I knew of the nest of another German observation balloon near Damvillers.

Dawn was just breaking as I headed more to the east and tried to pick out the location of Damvillers. I was piercing the gloom with my eyes when again—straight in front of my revolving propeller I saw another gush of flame which announced the doom of another enemy balloon—the very one I had determined to attack. While I was still jubilating over the extraordinary good luck that had attended us in this morning's expedition, I glanced off to my right and was almost startled out of my senses to discover that a

German Fokker was flying alongside me not a hundred yards away! Not expecting any of the enemy aeroplanes to be abroad at this early hour, I was naturally upset for the moment. The next instant I saw that he had headed for me and was coming straight at my machine. We both began firing at the same time. It was still so dark that our four streams of flaming bullets cut brilliant lines of fire through the air. For a moment it looked as though our two machines were tied together with four ropes of fire. All my ammunition was of the incendiary variety for use against gas-bags. The Hun's ammunition was part tracer, part incendiary and part regular chunks of lead.

As we drew nearer and nearer I began to wonder whether this was to be a collision or whether he would get out of my way. He settled the question by tipping down his head to dive under me. I instantly made a renversement which put me close behind him and in a most favorable position for careful aim. Training my sights into the center of his fusilage I pulled both triggers. With one long burst the fight was over. The Fokker fell over onto one wing and dropped aimlessly to earth. It was too dark to see the crash, and moreover I had all thoughts of my victory dissipated by a sudden ugly jerk to my motor which immediately developed into a violent vibration. As I turned back towards Verdun, which was the nearest point to our liens, I had recurring visions of crashing down into Germany to find myself a prisoner. This would be a nice ending to our glorious balloon expedition!

Throttling down to reduce the pounding I was able just to maintain headway. If my motor failed completely I was most certainly doomed, for I was less than a thousand feet above ground and could glide but a few hundred yards without power. Providence was again with me, for I cleared the lines and made our Verdun aerodrome where one flight of the 27th Squadron was housed. I landed without damage and hastily climbed out of my machine to investigate the cause of my trouble.

Imagine my surprise when I discovered that one blade of my propeller had been shot in two by my late adversary! He had evidently put several holes through it when he made his head-on-attack. And utterly unconscious of the damage I had received, I had reversed my direction and shot him down before the weakened blade gave way! The heavy jolting of my engine was now clear to me— only half of the propeller caught the air.

Lieutenant Jerry Vasconceles of Denver, Colorado, was in charge of the Verdun field on which I had landed. He soon came out and joined me as I was staring at my broken propeller. And then I learned that he had just landed himself from a balloon expedition. A few questions followed and then we shook hands spontaneously. He had shot down the Damvillers balloon himself—the same one for which I had been headed. And as he was returning he had seen me shoot down my Fokker! This was extremely lucky for both of us, for we were able each to verify the other's victory for him, although of course corroboration from ground witnesses was necessary to make these victories official.

His mechanics placed a new propeller on my Spad, and none the worse for its recent rough usage the little 'bus took me rapidly home. I landed at 8:30 on my own field. And there I heard great news. Our Group had that morning shot down ten German balloons! My victory over the

Fokker made it eleven victories to be credited us for this hour's work. And we had not lost a single pilot!

As the jubilant and famished pilots crowded into the mess hall one could not hear a word through all the excited chatter. Each one had some strange and fearful adventure to relate about his morning's experiences. But the tale which aroused howls of laughter was the droll story told by Lieutenant White of the 147th Squadron.

White had searched long and earnestly for the balloon that he desired to attack. He thought himself hopelessly lost in the darkness, when off to one side he distinguished the dark outline of what he thought was his balloon. Immediately redressing his machine he tipped downwards and began plugging furious streams of flaming bullets into his target. He made a miscalculation in his distance and before he could swerve away from the dark mass ahead of him his machine had plunged straight through it!

And then he discovered that he had been piquing upon a round puff of black smoke that had just been made by a German Archy!

FRANK LUKE STRAFES
HIS LAST BALLOON

Neither side could afford to leave its lines undefended by observation balloons for a longer period than was necessary for replacements. Our onslaught of the early morning had destroyed so many of the Huns' Drachen, however, that it was quite impossible for them to get new balloons up at once, along their entire sector.

That same afternoon I flew along their lines to see what progress they were making in replacements of their observation posts. The only balloon I could discover in our sector was one which lifted its head just behind the town of Sivry-sur-Meuse. I made a note of its position and decided to try to bring in down early next morning.

Accordingly I was up again at the same hour the following day and again found the sky promised clear weather. Leaving the field at 5:30, I again took a course over Verdun in order to pick up the Meuse River there and follow it as a guide.

On this occasion I caught a grand view of No Man's Land as seen from the air by night. It was not yet daylight when I reached the lines and there I caught a longitudinal view of the span of ground that separated the two opposing armies. For upon both sides of this span of ground a horizontal line of flashes could be seen issuing from the mouth of rival guns. The German batteries were drawn up along their front scarcely a mile back of their line. And on our side a vastly more crowded line of flashes indicated the overwhelming superiority in numbers of guns that the American artillerymen were using to belabor the already vanquished Huns. So far as my eye could reach, this dark space lay outlined between the two lines of living fire. It was a most spectacular sight. I followed down its course for a few miles, then turned again to the north and tried to find the Meuse River.

After ten minutes' flight into Germany, I realized I had crossed the river before I began to turn north and that I must be some distance inside the enemy's lines. I dropped down still lower as I saw the outlines of a town in front of me and circling above it I discovered that I had penetrated some 25 miles inside Hunland and was now over the village of Stenay. I had overshot Sivry by about twenty miles.

I lost no time in heading about towards France. Opening up the throttle, I first struck west and followed this course until I had the Meuse River again under my nose. Then turning up the river, I flew just above the road which follows along its banks. It was now getting light enough to distinguish objects on the ground below.

This Muese River highway is a lovely drive to take in the daytime, for it passes through a fertile and picturesque country. The little city of Dun-sur-Meuse stands out on a small cliff which juts into a bend of the river, making a most charming picture of what a medieval town should look like. I passed directly down Main Street over Dun-sur-Meuse and again picked up the broad highway that clung to the bank of the river. Occasional vehicles were now abroad below me. Day had broken and the Huns were up and ready for work.

It occurred to me that I might as well fly a bit lower and entertain the passing Huns with a little bullet-dodging as we met each other. My morning's work was spoiled anyway. It was becoming too late to take on a balloon now. Perhaps I might meet a general in his automobile and it would be fun to see him jump for the ditch and throw himself down on his face at the bottom. If I was fortunate enough to get him that would surely be helping along the war!

Ahead of me I saw a truck moving slowly in the same direction I was going. "Here goes for the first one!" I said to myself. I tipped down the nose of my machine and reached for my triggers.

As my nose went down something appeared over my top wing which took away my breath for an instant. There directly in my path was a huge enemy observation balloon! It was swaying in the breeze and the cable which held it to earth ran straight down until it reached the moving truck ahead of me. Then it became clear as daylight to me. The Huns were towing a new balloon up the road to its position for observation! They had just received a replacement from the supply station of Dun-sur-Meuse, and after filling it with gas were now getting it forward as rapidly as possible. It was just the target I had been searching for!

Forgetting the truck and crew, I flattened out instantly and began firing at the swaying monster in the air. So close to it had I come before I saw it that I had only time to fire a burst of fifty shots when I was forced to make a vertical virage, to avoid crashing through it. I was then but four or five hundred feet above ground.

Just as I began the virage I heard the rat-tat-tat-tat of a machine-gun fire from the truck on the road beneath me. And mingled with this drum fire I heard the sound of an explosion in the fusilage just behind my ear! One of their explosive bullets had come very close to my head and had exploded against a longeron or wire in the tail of the aeroplane! There was nothing I could do about that how-ever, except to fly along as steadily as possible until I reached a place of safety and could make an investigation of the damage received. I cleared the side of the gas-bag and then as I passed I turned and looked behind me.

The enemy balloon was just at the point of exploding and the observer had already leaped from his basket and was still dropping through air with his parachute not yet opened. It was a very short distance to Mother Earth, and sometimes a parachute needs two or three hundred feet fall in which to fully open and check the swiftness of the falling body. I wondered whether this poor chap had any chance for his life in that short distance and just what bones he was likely to break when he landed. And then came a great burst of fire, as the whole interior of the big balloon became suddenly ignited. I couldn't resist one shout of exultation at the magnificent display of fireworks I had thus set off, hoping in the meantime that its dull glare would reach the eyes of some of our own balloon observers across the lines who would thus be in a position to give me the confirmation of my eleventh victory.

Again I decided to pay a call at Jerry Vasconcelle's field at Verdun and there get out and ascertain the extent of the damage in the tail of my Spad. Jerry welcomed me with some amusement and wanted to know whether this dropping in on him was to be a daily occurrence. Yesterday it had been a broken prop and to-day a broken tail. Before answering him I got out, and together we made a minute examination of my machine.

A neat row of bullet holes ran back down the tail of my machine. They were as nicely spaced as if they had been put in by careful measurement. The first hole was about four inches back of the pad on which my head rests when I am in the seat. The others were directly back of it at regular intervals. One, the explosive bullet, had struck the longeron that runs the length of the fusilage, and this had made the sharp explosion that I had heard at the time. The gunners on the truck had done an excellent bit of shooting!

None of the holes were in a vital part of the machine. I took off the field after a short inspection and soon covered the fifteen or sixteen miles that lay between the Verdun field and our own.

Upon landing I found very bad news awaiting me.

On the previous afternoon Lieutenant Sherry and Lieutenant Nutt, both of 94 Squadron, had gone out on patrol and had failed to come in. Long after dark their mechanics remained on the field pooping up Very lights, in the hope that they might still be searching about, trying to find their way. At last we abandoned all hope ourselves and waited for the morning's news from outside sources.

Now it had arrived and to my great joy it was in the form of a telephone call from old "Madam" Sherry himself. But his next message informed us that Nutt had been killed in combat! And Sherry himself had been through an experience that might easily have turned one's hair gray. Just before lunch time Sherry came in by automobile and told us the story of his experiences.

He and Nutt had attacked an overwhelming formation of eight Fokker machines. They had stolen up on the Heinies and counted upon getting one or two victims before the others were aware of their presence. But the attack failed and suddenly both American pilots were having the fight of their lives. The Hun pilots were not only skilful and experienced, but they worked together with such nicety that Sherry and Nutt were unable either to hold their own or to escape.

Soon each was fighting a separate battle against four enemy machines. Sherry saw Nutt go crashing down and later learned that he had been shot through the heart and killed in air. A moment later Sherry's machine received several bullets in the motor which put it immediately out of commission. Dropping swiftly to earth, Sherry saw that the Hun pilots were not taking any chances but were determined to kill him as he fell.

He was two miles and more in the air when he began his forced descent. All the way down the enemy pilots pursued him, firing through his machine continuously as it glided smoothly towards earth. Only by miracles a dozen times repeated did he escape death from their bullets. He saw the lines below him and made desperate efforts to glide his machine to our side of the fence despite the furious attempts of the Boches to prevent this escape. At last he crashed in one of the million shell-holes that covered No Man's Land of last week. His machine turned over and broke into a score of fragments, Sherry being thrown some yards away where he landed unhurt at the bottom of another shell-hole.

While he was still pinching himself to make sure he was actually unhurt he discovered his implacable enemies piquing upon him with their Fokkers and firing long bursts of bullets into his shell-hole with their machine-guns!

Sherry clung as closely to the sides of his hole as he could and watched the dirt fly up all around him as the Fokkers made dive after dive at him. It must have been like watching a file of executioners leveling their guns at one and firing dozens of rounds without hitting one. Except that in Sherry's case, it was machine-guns that were doing the firing!

Finally the Fokkers made off for Germany. Crawling out of his hole, Sherry discovered that a formation of Spads had come to his rescue and had chased the Germans homewards. And then he began to wonder on which side of the trenches he had fallen. For he had been too busy dodging Fokkers to know where his crippled machine was taking him.

One can imagine Sherry's joy when he heard a dough-boy in perfectly good United States yell from a neighboring shell-hole:—

"Hey guy! Where the h—'s your gas-mask?"

Madam didn't care for the moment whether he had a gas-mask or not, so glad was he to learn that he had fallen among friends and was still in the land of the living.

He quickly tumbled into the next shell-hole, where he found his new friend. The latter informed him that he was still in No Man's Land, that the German infantry were but a hundred yards away and that gas shells had been coming across that space all the afternoon. He even gave Madam his own gas-mask and his pistol, saying he guessed he was more used to gas than an aviator would be! He advised Sherry to lay low where he was until nightfall, when he would see him back into our lines. And thus Lieutenant Sherry spent the next few hours reviewing the strange episodes that flavor the career of an aviator.

Sherry finished his story with a grim recital of what had occurred when they went out next morning to recover Nutt's body. It too had fallen in No Man's Land, but the Americans had advanced a few hundred yards during the night and now covered the spot where Nutt's body lay. Sherry accompanied a squad of doughboys out to the spot where Nutt's smashed machine had lain during the night. They found poor Nutt, as I have said, with several bullets through the heart.

They extricated the body from the wreckage and were beginning to dig a grave when a shot from a hidden Hun sniper struck one of the burial party in the foot. The others jumped to their guns and disappeared through the trees. They soon returned with a look of savage satisfaction on their faces, although Sherry had not heard a shot fired. While they continued their work he strolled off in the direction from which they had returned.

Behind a trench dugout he found the German sniper who had had the yellowness to fire upon a burial party. The man's head was crushed flat with the butts of the doughboys' guns!

★   ★   ★

"Frank Luke, the marvelous balloon strafer of the 27th, did not return last night!"

So reads the last entry in my flight diary of September 29, 1918. Re-reading that line brings back to me the common anxiety of the whole Group over the extraordinary and prolonged absence of their most popular member. For Luke's very mischievousness and irresponsibility made every one of us feel that he must be cared for and nursed back into a more disciplined way of fighting— and flying—and living. His escapades were the talk of the camp and the despair of his superior officers. Fully a month after his disappearance his commanding officer, Alfred Grant, Captain of the 27th Squadron, told me that if Luke ever did come back he would court-martial him first and then recommend him for the Legion of Honor!

In a word, Luke mingled with his disdain for bullets a very similar distaste for the orders of his superior officers. When imperative orders were given him to come immediately home after a patrol Luke would unconcernedly land at some French aerodrome miles away, spend the night there and arrive home after dark the next night. But as he almost invariably landed with one or two more enemy balloons to his credit, which he had destroyed on the way home, he was usually let off with a reprimand and a caution not to repeat the offense.

As blandly indifferent to reprimands as to orders, Luke failed to return again the following night. This studied disobedience to orders could not be ignored, and thus Captain Grant had stated that if Luke ever did return he must be disciplined for his insubordination. The night of September 27th Luke spent the night with the French Cigognes on the Toul aerodrome.

The last we had heard from Luke was that at six o'clock on the night of September 28th he left the French field where he had spent the night, and flying low over one of the American Balloon Headquarters he circled over their heads until he had attracted the attention of the officers, then dropped them a brief note which he had written in his aeroplane. As may well be imagined, Luke was a prime favorite with our Balloon Staff. All the officers of that organization worshiped the boy for his daring and his wonderful successes against the balloon department of their foes. They appreciated the value of balloon observation to the enemy and knew the difficulties and dangers in attacking these well-defended posts.

Running out and picking up the streamer and sheet of paper which fell near their office they unfolded the latter and read:

"Look out for enemy balloon at D-2 and D-4 positions.—Luke."

Already Luke's machine was disappearing in the direction of the first balloon which lay just beyond the Meuse. It was too dark to make out its dim outline at this distance, but as they all gathered about the front of their "office" they glued their eyes to the spot where they knew it hung. For Luke had notified them several times previously as to his intended victims and every time they had been rewarded for their watching.

Two minutes later a great read glow lit up the north-western horizon and before the last of it died away the second German balloon had likewise burst into flames! Their intrepid hero had again fulfilled his promise! They hastened into their headquarters and called up our operations officer and announced Frank Luke's last two victories. Then we waited for Luke to make his dramatic appearance.

But Luke never came! That night and the next day we rather maligned him for his continued absence, supposing naturally enough that he had returned to his French friends for the night. But when no news of him came to us, when repeated inquiries elicited no information as to his movements after he had brought down his last balloon, every man in the Group became aware that we had lost the greatest airman in our army. From that day to this not one word of reliable information has reached us concerning Luke's disappearance. Not a single clue to his death and burial was ever obtained from the Germans! Like Guynemer, the miraculous airman of France, Frank Luke was swallowed by the skies and no mortal traces of him remain!

Crazy Horse

[CHARLES A. EASTMAN]

Crazy Horse was born on the Republican River about 1845. He was killed at Fort Robinson, Nebraska, in 1877, so that he lived barely thirty-three years.

He was an uncommonly handsome man. While not the equal of Gall in magnificence and imposing stature, he was physically perfect, an Apollo in symmetry. Furthermore he was a true type of Indian refinement and grace. He was modest and courteous as Chief Joseph; the difference is that he was a born warrior, while Joseph was not. However, he was a gentle warrior, a true brave, who stood for the highest ideal of the Sioux. Notwithstanding all that biased historians have said of him, it is only fair to judge a man by the estimate of his own people rather than that of his enemies.

The boyhood of Crazy Horse was passed in the days when the western Sioux saw a white man but seldom, and then it was usually a trader or a soldier. He was carefully brought up according to the tribal customs. At that period the Sioux prided themselves on the training and development of their sons and daughters, and not a step in that development was overlooked as an excuse to bring the child before the public by giving a feast in its honor. At such times the parents often gave so generously to the needy that they almost impoverished themselves, thus setting an example to the child of self-denial for the general good. His first step alone, the first word spoken, first game killed, the attainment of manhood or womanhood, each was the occasion of a feast and dance in his honor, at which the poor always benefited to the full extent of the parents' ability.

Big-heartedness, generosity, courage, and self-denial are the qualifications of a public servant, and the average Indian was keen to follow this ideal. As every one knows, these characteristic traits become a weakness when he enters a life founded upon commerce and gain. Under such conditions the life of Crazy Horse began. His mother, like other mothers, tender and watchful of her boy, would never once place an obstacle in the way of his father's severe physical training. They laid the spiritual and patriotic foundations of his education in such a way that he early became conscious of the demands of public service.

He was perhaps four or five years old when the band was snowed in one severe winter. They were very short of food, but his father was a tireless hunter. The buffalo, their main dependence, were not to be found, but he was out in the storm and cold every day and finally brought in two antelopes. The little boy got on his pet pony and rode through the camp, telling the old folks to come to his mother's teepee for meat. It turned out that neither his father nor mother had authorized him to do this. Before they knew it, old men and women were lined up before the teepee home, ready to receive the meat, in answer to his invitation. As a result, the mother had to distribute nearly all of it, keeping only enough for two meals.

On the following day the child asked for food. His mother told him that the old folks had taken it all, and added: "Remember, my son, they went home singing praises in your name, not my name or your father's. You must be brave. You must live up to your reputation."

Crazy Horse loved horses, and his father gave him a pony of his own when he was very young. He became a fine horseman and accompanied his father on buffalo hunts, holding the pack horses while the men chased the buffalo and thus gradually learning the art. In those days the Sioux had but few guns, and the hunting was mostly done with bow and arrows.

Another story told of his boyhood is that when he was about twelve he went to look for the ponies with his little brother, whom he loved much, and took a great deal of pains to teach what he had already learned. They came to some wild cherry trees full of ripe fruit, and while they were enjoying it, the brothers were startled by the growl and sudden rush of a bear. Young Crazy Horse pushed his brother up into the nearest tree and himself sprang upon the back of one of the horses, which was frightened and ran some distance before he could control him. As soon as he could, however, he turned him about and came back, yelling and swinging his lariat over his head. The bear at first showed fight but finally turned and ran. The old man who told me this story added that young as he was, he had some power, so that even a grizzly did not dare to tackle him. I believe it is a fact that a silver-tip will dare anything except a bell or a lasso line, so that accidentally the boy had hit upon the very thing which would drive him off.

It was usual for Sioux boys of his day to wait in the field after a buffalo hunt until sundown, when the young calves would come out in the open, hungrily seeking their mothers. Then these wild children would enjoy a mimic hunt, and lasso the calves or drive them into camp. Crazy Horse was found to be a determined little fellow, and it was settled one day among the larger boys that they would "stump" him to ride a good-sized bull calf. He rode the calf, and stayed on its back while it ran bawling over the hills, followed by the other boys on their ponies, until his strange mount stood trembling and exhausted.

At the age of sixteen he joined a war party against the Gros Ventres. He was well in the front of the charge, and at once established his bravery by following closely one of the foremost Sioux warriors, by the name of Hump, drawing the enemy's fire and circling around their advance guard. Suddenly Hump's horse was shot from under him, and there was a rush of warriors to kill or capture him while down. But amidst a shower of arrows the youth leaped from his pony, helped his friend into his own saddle, sprang up behind him, and carried him off in safety, although they were hotly pursued by the enemy. Thus he associated himself in his maiden battle with the wizard of Indian warfare, and Hump, who was then at the height of his own career, pronounced Crazy Horse the coming warrior of the Teton Sioux.

At this period of his life, as was customary with the best young men, he spent much time in prayer and solitude. Just what happened in these days of his fasting in the wilderness and upon the crown of bald buttes, no one will ever know; for these things may only be known when one has lived through the battles of life to an honored old age. He was much sought after by his youthful associates, but was noticeably reserved and modest; yet in the moment of danger he at once rose above them all—a natural leader! Crazy Horse was a typical Sioux brave, and from the point of view of our race an ideal hero, living at the height of the epical progress of the American Indian and maintaining in his own character all that was most subtle and ennobling of their spiritual life, and that has since been lost in the contact with a material civilization.

He loved Hump, that peerless warrior, and the two became close friends, in spite of the difference in age. Men called them "the grizzly and his cub." Again and again the pair saved the day for the Sioux in a skirmish with some neighboring tribe. But one day they undertook a losing battle against the Snakes. The Sioux were in full retreat and were fast being overwhelmed by superior numbers. The old warrior fell in a last desperate charge; but Crazy Horse and his younger brother, though dismounted, killed two of the enemy and thus made good their retreat.

It was observed of him that when he pursued the enemy into their stronghold, as he was wont to do, he often refrained from killing, and simply struck them with a switch, showing that he did not fear their weapons nor care to waste his upon them. In attempting this very feat, he lost this only brother of his, who emulated him closely. A party of young warriors, led by Crazy Horse, had dashed upon a frontier post, killed one of the sentinels, stampeded the horses, and pursued the herder to the very gate of the stockade, thus drawing upon themselves the fire of the garrison. The leader escaped without a scratch, but his young brother was brought down from his horse and killed.

While he was still under twenty, there was a great winter buffalo hunt, and he came back with ten buffaloes' tongues which he sent to the council lodge for the councilors' feast. He had in one winter day killed ten buffalo cows with his bow and arrows, and the unsuccessful hunters or those who had no swift ponies were made happy by his generosity. When the hunters returned, these came chanting songs of thanks. He knew that his father was an expert hunter and had a good horse, so he took no meat home, putting in practice the spirit of his early teaching.

He attained his majority at the crisis of the difficulties between the United States and the Sioux. Even before that time, Crazy Horse had already proved his worth to his people in Indian warfare. He had risked his life again and again, and in some instances it was considered almost a miracle that he had saved others as well as himself. He was no orator nor was he the son of a chief. His success and influence was purely a matter of personality. He had never fought the whites up to this time, and indeed no "coup" was counted for killing or scalping a white man.

Young Crazy Horse was twenty-one years old when all the Teton Sioux chiefs (the western or plains dwellers) met in council to determine upon their future policy toward the invader. Their former agreements had been by individual bands, each for itself, and every one was friendly. They reasoned that the country was wide, and that the white traders should be made welcome. Up to this time they had anticipated no conflict. They had permitted the Oregon Trail, but now to their astonishment forts were built and garrisoned in their territory.

Most of the chiefs advocated a strong resistance. There were a few influential men who desired still to live in peace, and who were willing to make another treaty. Among these were White Bull, Two Kettle, Four Bears, and Swift Bear. Even Spotted Tail, afterward the great peace chief, was at this time with the majority, who decided in the year 1866 to defend their rights and territory by force. Attacks were to be made upon the forts within their country and on every trespasser on the same.

Crazy Horse took no part in the discussion, but he and all the young warriors were in accord with the decision of the council. Although so young, he was already a leader among them. Other prominent young braves were Sword (brother of the man of that name who was long captain of police at Pine Ridge), the younger Hump, Charging Bear, Spotted Elk, Crow King, No Water, Big Road, He Dog, the nephew of Red Cloud, and Touch-the-Cloud, intimate friend of Crazy Horse.

The attack on Fort Phil Kearny was the first fruits of the new policy, and here Crazy Horse was chosen to lead the attack on the woodchoppers, designed to draw the soldiers out of the fort, while an army of six hundred lay in wait for them. The success of this stratagem was further enhanced by his masterful handling of his men. From this time on a general war was inaugurated; Sitting Bull looked to him as a principal war leader, and even the Cheyenne chiefs, allies of the Sioux, practically acknowledged his leadership. Yet during the following ten years of defensive war he was never known to make a speech, though his teepee was the rendezvous of the young men. He was depended upon to put into action the decisions of the council, and was frequently consulted by the older chiefs.

Like Osceola, he rose suddenly; like Tecumseh he was always impatient for battle; like Pontiac, he fought on while his allies were suing for peace, and like Grant, the silent soldier, he was a man of deeds and not of words. He won from Custer and Fetterman and Crook. He won every battle that he undertook, with the exception of one or two occasions when he was surprised in the midst of his women and children, and even then he managed to extricate himself in safety from a difficult position.

Early in the year 1876, his runners brought word from Sitting Bull that all the roving bands would converge upon the upper Tongue River in Montana for summer feasts and conferences. There was conflicting news from the reservation. It was rumored that the army would fight the Sioux to a finish; again, it was said that another commission would be sent out to treat with them.

The Indians came together early in June, and formed a series of encampments stretching out from three to four miles, each band keeping separate camp. On June 17, scouts came in and reported the advance of a large body of troops under General Crook. The council sent Crazy Horse with seven hundred men to meet and attack him. These were nearly all young men, many of them under twenty, the flower of the hostile Sioux. They set out at night so as to steal a march upon the enemy, but within three or four miles of his camp they came unexpectedly upon some of his Crow scouts. There was a hurried exchange of shots; the Crows fled back to Crook's camp, pursued by the Sioux. The soldiers had their warning, and it was impossible to enter the well-protected camp. Again and again Crazy Horse charged with his bravest men, in the attempt to bring the troops into the open, but he succeeded only in drawing their fire. Toward afternoon he withdrew, and returned to camp disappointed. His scouts remained to watch Crook's movements, and later brought word that he had retreated to Goose Creek and seemed to have no further disposition to disturb the Sioux. It is well known to us that it is Crook rather than Reno who is to be blamed for cowardice in connection with Custer's fate. The latter had no chance to do anything, he was lucky to save himself; but if Crook had kept on his way, as ordered, to meet Terry, with his one thousand regulars and two hundred Crow and Shoshone scouts, he would inevitably have intercepted Custer in his advance and saved the day for him, and war with the Sioux would have ended right there. Instead of this, he fell back upon Fort Meade, eating his horses on the way, in a country swarming with game, for fear of Crazy Horse and his braves!

The Indians now crossed the divide between the Tongue and the Little Big Horn, where they felt safe from immediate pursuit. Here, with all their precautions, they were caught unawares by General Custer, in the midst of their midday games and festivities, while many were out upon the daily hunt.

On this twenty-fifth of June, 1876, the great camp was scattered for three miles or more along the level river bottom, back of the thin line of cottonwoods— five circular rows of teepees, ranging from half a mile to a mile and a half in circumference. Here and there stood out a large, white, solitary teepee; these were the lodges or "clubs" of the young men. Crazy Horse was a member of the "Strong Hearts" and the "Tokala" or Fox lodge. He was watching a game of ring-toss when the warning came from the southern end of the camp of the approach of troops.

The Sioux and the Cheyennes were "minute men", and although taken by surprise, they instantly responded. Meanwhile, the women and children were thrown into confusion. Dogs were howling, ponies running hither and thither, pursued by their owners, while many of the old men were singing their lodge songs to encourage the warriors, or praising the "strong heart" of Crazy Horse.

That leader had quickly saddled his favorite war pony and was starting with his young men for the south end of the camp, when a fresh alarm came from the opposite direction, and looking up, he saw Custer's force upon the top of the bluff directly across the river. As quick as a flash, he took in the situation—the enemy had planned to attack the camp at both ends at once; and knowing that Custer could not ford the river at that point, he instantly led his men northward to the ford to cut him off. The Cheyennes followed closely. Custer must have seen that wonderful dash up the sage-bush plain, and one wonders whether he realized its meaning. In a very few minutes, this wild general of the plains had outwitted one of the most brilliant leaders of the Civil War and ended at once his military career and his life.

In this dashing charge, Crazy Horse snatched his most famous victory out of what seemed frightful peril, for the Sioux could not know how many were behind Custer. He was caught in his own trap. To the soldiers it must have seemed as if the Indians rose up from the earth to overwhelm them. They closed in from three sides and fought until not a white man was left alive. Then they went down to Reno's stand and found him so well intrenched in a deep gully that it was impossible to dislodge him. Gall and his men held him there until the approach of General Terry compelled the Sioux to break camp and scatter in different directions.

While Sitting Bull was pursued into Canada, Crazy Horse and the Cheyennes wandered about, comparatively undisturbed, during the rest of that year, until in the winter the army surprised the Cheyennes, but did not do them much harm, possibly because they knew that Crazy Horse was not far off. His name was held in wholesome respect. From time to time, delegations of friendly Indians were sent to him, to urge him to come in to the reservation, promising a full hearing and fair treatment.

For some time he held out, but the rapid disappearance of the buffalo, their only means of support, probably weighed with him more than any other influence. In July, 1877, he was finally prevailed upon to come in to Fort Robinson, Nebraska, with several thousand Indians, most of them Ogallala and Minneconwoju Sioux, on the distinct understanding that the government would hear and adjust their grievances.

At this juncture General Crook proclaimed Spotted Tail, who had rendered much valuable service to the army, head chief of the Sioux, which was resented by many. The attention paid Crazy Horse was offensive to Spotted Tail and the Indian scouts, who planned a conspiracy against him. They reported to General Crook that the young chief would murder him at the next council, and stampede the Sioux into another war. He was urged not to attend the council and did not, but sent another officer to represent him. Meanwhile the friends of Crazy Horse discovered the plot and told him of it. His reply was, "Only cowards are murderers."

His wife was critically ill at the time, and he decided to take her to her parents at Spotted Tail agency, whereupon his enemies circulated the story that he had fled, and a party of scouts was sent after him. They overtook him riding with his wife and one other but did not undertake to arrest him, and after he had left the sick woman with her people he went to call on Captain Lea, the agent for the Brules, accompanied by all the warriors of the Minneconwoju band. This volunteer escort made an imposing appearance on horseback, shouting and singing, and in the words of Captain Lea himself and the missionary, the Reverend Mr. Cleveland, the situation was extremely critical. Indeed, the scouts who had followed Crazy Horse from Red Cloud agency were advised not to show themselves, as some of the warriors had urged that they be taken out and horsewhipped publicly.

Under these circumstances Crazy Horse again showed his masterful spirit by holding these young men in check. He said to them in his quiet way: "It is well to be brave in the field of battle; it is cowardly to display bravery against one's own tribesmen. These scouts have been compelled to do what they did; they are no better than servants of the white officers. I came here on a peaceful errand."

The captain urged him to report at army headquarters to explain himself and correct false rumors, and on his giving consent, furnished him with a wagon and escort. It has been said that he went back under arrest, but this is untrue. Indians have boasted that they had a hand in bringing him in, but their stories are without foundation. He went of his own accord, either suspecting no treachery or determined to defy it.

When he reached the military camp, Little Big Man walked arm-in-arm with him, and his cousin and friend, Touch-the-Cloud, was just in advance. After they passed the sentinel, an officer approached them and walked on his other side. He was unarmed but for the knife which is carried for ordinary uses by women as well as men. Unsuspectingly he walked toward the guardhouse, when Touch-the-Cloud suddenly turned back exclaiming: "Cousin, they will put you in prison!"

"Another white man's trick! Let me go! Let me die fighting!" cried Crazy Horse. He stopped and tried to free himself and draw his knife, but both arms were held fast by Little Big Man and the officer. While he struggled thus, a soldier thrust him through with his bayonet from behind. The wound was mortal, and he died in the course of that night, his old father singing the death song over him and afterward carrying away the body, which they said must not be further polluted by the touch of a white man. They hid it somewhere in the Bad Lands, his resting place to this day.

Thus died one of the ablest and truest American Indians. His life was ideal; his record clean. He was never involved in any of the numerous massacres on the trail, but was a leader in practically every open fight. Such characters as those of Crazy Horse and Chief Joseph are not easily found among so-called civilized people. The reputation of great men is apt to be shadowed by questionable motives and policies, but here are two pure patriots, as worthy of honor as any who ever breathed God's air in the wide spaces of a new world.

Sources

"Pocahontas," from *The Story of Pocahontas* by Charles Dudley Warner (J. C. Weaver, 1897).

"Washington," from *The Life of George Washington* by M.L. Weems (King and Bird Printers, 1832).

"Paul Revere" from *Sons of Liberty* by Walter A. Dyer. (1920).

"Nathan Hale," from *Captain Nathan Hale, the Martyr-Spy* by James Parton (1866).

"David Crockett," from *David Crockett: His Life and Adventures* by John S. C. Abbott (Dodd & Mead, 1874).

"John Brown," from *Old John Brown* by Walter Hawkins (1913).

"Harriet Tubman," from *Harriet, the Moses of Her People* by Sarah H. Bradford (Geo. R. Lockwood & Son, 1886).

"General Custer," from *A History of the Sioux War* by Frances Fuller Victor (1881).

"Sitting Bull" from *Indian Heroes and Great Chieftains* by Charles A. Eastman (Little, Brown, 1918).

"Buffalo Bill," from *The Life of the Hon. William F. Cody* by William F. Cody (Frank E. Bliss, 1879).

"Eddie Rickenbacker" by Eddie Rickenbacker. From *Fighting the Flying Circus* by Eddie Rickenbacker. (Frederick A. Stokes, 1919).